DEATH IN A
TEXAS DESERT

DEATH IN A TEXAS DESERT

...And Other True Crime Stories from the *Dallas Observer*

Carlton Stowers

Republic of Texas Press

Dallas • Lanham • Boulder • New York • Toronto • Oxford

Published by Republic of Texas Press
An imprint of The Rowman & Littlefield Publishing Group, Inc.
4501 Forbes Boulevard, Suite 200
Lanham, MD 20706

Distributed by NATIONAL BOOK NETWORK

Library of Congress Cataloging-in-Publication Data
Stowers, Carlton.
   Death in a Texas Desert : and other true crime stores from the Dallas
Observer / Carlton Stowers ; introduction by Jim Schutze.
      p.   cm.
ISBN 1-55622-977-1 (alk. paper)
1. Crime—Case studies.   2. Criminals—Case studies.   I. Title.
HV6251 .S76 2003
364—dc21
                                                           2002151736

♾™ The paper used in this publication meets the minimum requirements of
American National Standard for Information Sciences—Permanence of Paper
for Printed Library Materials, ANSI/NISO Z39.48-1992.

Manufactured in the United States of America

For the staff . . .

CONTENTS

FOREWORD

There is a reason that Carlton Stowers is one the nation's most honored true-crime authors: he's not a true-crime writer. Stowers comes to the task from a broad background in journalism and writing. He brings with him an array of tools and talents that would make a good story shine in any other genre—and he has worked in most of them.

It so happens Stowers has been able to hone his skills to a particular acuity in writing narrative nonfiction crime stories—a happy event for those of us who love to read them. His sense of timing, a perfect pitch for voices, and a deep empathy for people in crisis give every story he writes a powerful universality.

And that's really what it's all about when we pick up a book to read for pleasure: the universals. We want to read good stories that delight our minds and move our hearts. We want to encounter characters with whom we can connect personally. We want to consider themes that run deep in life.

In the stories in this book, we always do: Gary Patterson, the hapless young draftsman who died because he was too easily flattered; Florence Brown, a girl in love whose murder went unsolved for almost a century; Billy F. Fowler, the dedicated cop who figured out that a legendary district attorney had sent the wrong man to prison for life. In every Stowers story there are people worth caring about who are caught up in a fascinating flow of events. It's a formula that worked for Homer, and it's one that still works for Stowers.

The true-crime genre, however, has suffered a bumpy ride. Although a staple of newspapers and magazines through the first half of the twentieth century, in-depth narrative crime writing slipped from front pages in the 1960s when the daily newspapers began striving for a more respectable, analytical profile. In the 1980s, the book-publishing industry brought true crime back in from the literary backstreets and found great success with well-written, well-edited nonfiction books about crime by serious writers and reporters. Of that era, Stowers was a prominent exemplar. His books, published by the best houses, were snapped up by Hollywood, and they twice earned him the "Edgar," an award that is "the Oscar of crime-writing."

In the book world and among writer–practitioners, there has been debate and angst about the decline of true crime as a crossover genre in the late 1990s. No one seems to know exactly what happened—why the genre retracted and why the shelf space went away—but everyone suspects that it had something to do with O. J. Simpson. It's possible that when the public got done buying all of the books published about Mr. Simpson's travails, there was no money left. Woe to those writers who had failed to get in at least one good O.J. book while it lasted.

Among the very few exceptions is Carlton Stowers, whose work continues to find success even among the younger readers whom publishers have been so unsuccessful at attracting with other fare. The reason he endures and continues to draw new readers to the genre is that he is not truly of the genre himself. He's a crack newsman and a fine writer who knows heartstrings when he hears them. The stories gathered here are the proof.

—Jim Schutze

DEATH IN A
TEXAS DESERT

DEATH
IN THE
DESERT

GARY PATTERSON FLEW TO EL PASO FOR A JOB INTERVIEW—AND NEVER RETURNED.
IT TOOK NEARLY TWO YEARS FOR THE TEXAS RANGERS AND WACO POLICE TO UNRAVEL
THE BIZARRE WEB OF LIES AND TREACHERY THAT LED TO HIS DISAPPEARANCE.

BY CARLTON STOWERS

"Commit a crime, and the earth
is made of glass. There is no such
thing as concealment."
—Ralph Waldo Emerson

PROLOGUE

The search had been under way
for three days in the early summer
blast furnace of the El Paso County
desert, and, finally, the young
female detective in charge was
experiencing the feelings of anticipation that homicide investigators
sometimes get. The victim's body,
she was certain, was somewhere
nearby. Today, after a year of frustration, false leads, and blind alleys,
they would finally find it.

There were dog teams, high-
tech equipment, and volunteers
from the military base and the
nearby prison on hand, along with
a veteran Texas Ranger. He had
been the first to discover what
appeared to be a human bone that
had been unearthed by foraging
animals. Then he had found a
weathered tennis shoe. Then
another bone.

They were getting close, and
the detective could feel an anxious
flood of continued on page 26

1

DEATH IN THE DESERT

Commit a crime, and the earth is made of glass. There is no such thing as concealment. . . .

—Ralph Waldo Emerson

The search had been underway for three days in the early summer blast furnace of the El Paso County desert, and, finally, the young female detective in charge was experiencing the feeling homicide investigators sometimes get: The victim's body, she was certain, was somewhere nearby. Today, after a year of frustration, false leads, and blind alleys, they would finally find it.

On hand were dog teams, high-tech equipment, and volunteers from the military base and nearby prison, along with representatives from the Border Patrol and a veteran Texas Ranger. They had been the first to discover what appeared to be a human bone that had been unearthed by foraging varmints . . . and then a weathered tennis shoe . . . and then another bone.

They were getting close, and the detective could feel an anxious flood of adrenaline fueling her optimism. Then suddenly, almost as if a midday mirage, they came upon a neatly formed pile of rocks. Beneath it were skeletal remains, and despite the grimness of the discovery everyone began to cheer and exchange high-fives. "I think," the detective proudly announced, "that we've finally found what we've been looking for."

Armed with photographs and dental records, she later accompanied the remains to the El Paso coroner's office to await confirmation that her case had finally been solved. While she sat, sipping from a cup of bitter coffee, a fellow officer wearing the badge of the local police department

1

walked past her without so much as a nod. Also carrying a folder of pictures and dental records, he huddled briefly with the coroner, then walked away with a broad smile.

The woman tried to stand but instead felt herself slowly wilting to the concrete floor, where she sat silently for several minutes, hoping the sudden wave of nausea would go away. Finally regaining her composure, she dialed the number of her partner who was anxiously waiting, hundreds of miles away.

"We finally found a body," the detective said. But then, after an unintentional pause, she added, "But it's not ours."

When the man calling himself Ned Wright first appeared in the offices of Waco's Brazos Environmental and Engineering Services in mid-April of 1997, talking of a hush-hush development his Florida-based Fortune 500 company had in mind, some thought it strange. Tanned and gray-haired, in his late forties, he offered few details of his company's plan, only to say it involved construction of a large modular home community and a great deal of money. He and his partner, he said, had heard good things about Brazos Environmental and were considering hiring members of the small Texas firm to do some of the groundwork on the project.

Though he would not divulge the name of his company or even provide a business card, Wright asked to review resumes of all Brazos Environmental employees. Sensing the possibility of a high-dollar contract, the firm's executives quickly extended their best Central Texas hospitality to the mysterious visitor. When he later suggested that he would like to personally meet everyone in the office—"I like to shake a man's hand and look him in the eye before I hire him," he explained—his hosts readily obliged.

Among those he met on his handshake tour of the offices was Gary Patterson, a thirty-three-year-old draftsman too far down the company pecking order to have a resume on file. For reasons neither Patterson nor his fellow employees quite understood, the Florida businessman took an immediate interest in him.

Before leaving Waco, Wright placed several calls to Patterson, explaining how impressed he'd been with him during their brief meeting. Would it be possible for him to get away for a few days to come to

Florida for a visit with his partner, the company's CEO, to discuss the possibility of coming to work for them? Patterson, struggling with a series of personal problems and more than a little weary of Waco at the time, was flattered by the attention and said he'd think it over.

The courtship, which both agreed was best kept secret, went on for three weeks. Ned Wright continued to phone Patterson regularly at his work number, sometimes giving a phony name, sometimes refusing to give a name at all. "Gary," the receptionist had begun to joke, "it's that strange guy from Florida who doesn't want me to know who he is." Finally, much to Wright's delight, Patterson agreed to fly to Florida for an interview. What the divorced draftsman would like to do, he suggested, was bring his new girlfriend along and tack a short sun-and-sand vacation onto the visit.

Suddenly Ned Wright's enthusiasm inexplicably cooled. Bringing a guest along, he advised Patterson, wasn't a good idea since what his company had in mind was only a quick down-and-back trip. Things had become so busy with the Florida company, in fact, that the time for even a brief visit was no longer right. Let him make new arrangements, Wright said, and get back with him.

Soon he was back in Waco with a new plan: Could Patterson fly to El Paso, where another development was underway, and meet with the company's CEO, who would be visiting the site there? The meeting would be little more than a formality, Wright assured. They had already discussed matters and were prepared to offer him not only a job with increased status, salary, and additional benefits but also a signing bonus of a new Chevrolet Suburban. Over lunch, Wright gave Patterson four one-hundred bills with which to purchase a plane ticket for the quick get-acquainted trip. If he took the job—"Which we're certainly hoping you will," Wright assured him—he could drive the Suburban back to Waco to give notice and begin putting his affairs in order. If not, they would fly him home in the corporate jet.

Excited by the seductive new opportunity but not wishing to jeopardize his job with Brazos Environmental, Patterson told only his girlfriend, his parents, and a few trusted friends at the office of the trip he would be taking on Saturday, May 3, 1997. On the morning of his scheduled departure, he left his young daughter, Crystal, with his parents and took a 7:30 American Eagle flight out of Waco. After reaching El Paso, he placed a brief call from the airport to his parents' home a few minutes before noon, Waco time, to let them know he had arrived.

Gary Patterson, lured into a world of bitter family hatred, international wrongdoing, and false identities, then vanished from the face of the earth.

During the next fifteen months, a bizarre and byzantine investigation—involving the Waco Police, Texas Rangers, FBI, a California private investigator, the U.S. marshals office, Secret Service, State Department, Border Patrol, the government of Honduras, and even the International Criminal Police Organization (Interpol)—sought to piece together a motive for the disappearance and determine what had happened to Patterson.

Yet it began as a routine missing person's case, filed the Monday morning after the young man's departure. A grim-faced D. C. Patterson appeared at the Waco police department and immediately made it clear that he was convinced his son had been the victim of foul play. In addition, he strongly suspected that a mean-spirited man named Sam Urick, Gary's former father-in-law, was somehow involved.

The harmony of the marriage of Gary Patterson and Lisa Urick had been short-lived, destined to dissolve into divorce and a bitter custody battle. Helping fuel the discontent was Lisa's father, a domineering, shadowy figure who liked to brag of his days as a CIA hit man, his money laundering escapades, and his association with a variety of well-known underworld figures. Whether such stories were true or not, young Patterson had no way of knowing, but he was convinced that his father-in-law was, at best, a shady character. He knew, for instance, of one occasion when Sam had appeared at a Waco bank with a suitcase bearing one hundred thousand dollars in cash. When bank officials demanded some kind of disclosure before allowing him to open an account, he angrily stormed out rather than say where the money had come from.

There was, however, a great deal about his father-in-law that Patterson did not know.

Though they lacked enough evidence for an arrest, the FBI had long suspected Urick's involvement in the 1986 bombing of a Berlin nightclub in which American military personnel were killed. According to a highly classified Bureau investigation called "Operation Circus," he was a known associate of rogue CIA agents Frank Terpil and Edmond

Wilson, both accused of selling stolen arms to terrorist countries. Urick not only was believed to have helped hide them out while they were federal fugitives, but he was also thought to be involved in the purchase and delivery of forty thousand pounds of plastic explosives to the Libyan terrorists who ultimately claimed credit for the German deaths.

All Patterson knew for certain about his wife's father was that he was a secretive wheeler-dealer who was routinely in and out of get-rich-quick ventures yet who publicly claimed to earn his living from a small trucking company called Southern Sales, which he owned and operated in Conroe, Texas. Urick had, in recent years, strong-armed his son-in-law into a variety of short-lived businesses in Waco—among them a storefront insurance agency and a marina—only to suddenly appear, raid the profits without explanation, and disappear for weeks, sometimes months, leaving Patterson to deal with irate customers and a parade of bill collectors.

On one occasion, two armed men had arrived at the insurance office, demanding to know where they could find Sam Urick. Lisa, working as the company bookkeeper, had been there with her infant daughter when the men arrived. Shortly after the unsettling encounter, Urick abruptly informed his son-in-law that he was closing the business.

Finally, Gary Patterson had had enough and told his wife that he would no longer enter into any kind of business arrangement with her father. He said that it was time that they make the break from her family. Distancing himself from Sam Urick, Patterson took the job with Brazos Environmental and Engineering as a draftsman. The idea did not sit well with Urick, who immediately began insisting to his daughter that she file for divorce. If she didn't, he threatened, he would take his granddaughter from her and see to it that she never saw the child again.

Thus, in October 1992, the couple's eight-year marriage ended, and Lisa Urick Patterson was awarded custody of the couple's two-year-old daughter. Father Gary, however, was granted liberal visitation. That part of the court's decision did not at all please the elder Urick.

By the fall of 1994, Lisa was on the run in an effort to prevent Patterson from seeing his child. Financed by her father, she and her daughter spent the next two years in hiding, moving from place to place—Nevada, California, even Alaska for a time—while Patterson and his family attempted to locate her. To some she met along the way, she explained that her husband was dead. To others she confided she was protecting her daughter from a father who had molested her. By the time a California-based private investigator found her living in Pilot Point, Oregon, Gary's father, D. C. Patterson, had paid him fourteen thousand dollars for his efforts. Gary, meanwhile, had returned to court where he was awarded custody of his daughter.

Lisa was arrested in August 1996 and returned to Waco where she was charged with interference with child custody and granted only limited and supervised visits with her daughter. Ironically, Lisa's sentencing hearing (at which she would receive probation) was held the day before the man calling himself Ned Wright showed up at the offices of Brazos Environmental and Engineering. Months would pass before the Pattersons had cause to reflect on a strange request they had earlier received from their estranged ex-daughter-in-law.

Lisa had phoned to ask them for a photograph of Gary. She wanted it, she said, for a locket she'd bought for her daughter.

Tales of a family divided and angry accusations aside, Waco police detectives Steve January and Kristina Woodruff agreed that their first order of business was to learn more about the man who had visited Gary Patterson.

As veteran officers, both had investigated countless domestic squabbles and heard a litany of wild and unfounded claims during their service in the Bible Belt city of one hundred thousand. Neither, however, had even the slightest hint that they were venturing into a dark maze of criminal activity that would occupy their lives for the next year and a half.

"One of the things we'd been told by people at Brazos Environmental," says Detective January, "was that he [Wright] had arrived and left by taxi. In Waco, that's pretty unusual." It provided a starting place for the investigation.

At the local Yellow Cab company, a driver recalled picking up a fare at the Fairfield Inn and taking him to Brazos Environmental. Later, he remembered, he'd received a call to drive the passenger back to the motel. Checking telephone records at the Fairfield, they found that several calls had been placed to Brazos Environmental from room 105. Registration records, however, indicated that the room had been occupied not by Ned Wright but by a man named Theodore Donald Young. In keeping with company policy, the motel had made a photocopy of the guest's driver's license when he'd checked in.

Returning to Patterson's workplace with a grainy black and white copy of the license photo, the detectives were quickly assured it was a picture of the Florida businessman who had earlier visited there. Ned Wright, it appeared, was actually Theodore Young, a man January and Woodruff would soon learn had been a federal fugitive since February 1995. Convicted in a $26 million fraud case in South Carolina and sentenced to serve fifty-one months in prison, Young had failed to surrender himself to prison authorities as ordered and had been at large since.

If the investigators had any doubts about the elder Patterson's claims that his son's father-in-law was somehow involved in the growing mystery, they were soon erased by the surreptitious efforts of the San Diego private investigator who had been hired to locate Lisa Patterson. Convinced that Lisa's father was financing her efforts to remain in hiding, Scott Settimo focused his efforts on tracking Urick, convinced that he would eventually lead him to his daughter. "He'd done a very thorough investigation," remembers January, "and was convinced Sam was a pretty shady character, involved in various kinds of business scams, frauds, and money laundering activities."

During a telephone conversation with the Waco detective, Settimo described trailing Urick during one of his frequent visits to the West Coast. At one point, he said, he'd approached Urick's parked Lincoln and seen what looked like a leather-bound day planner in the front seat. What it was, actually, was a book in which its owner kept addresses and phone numbers of friends and associates.

"Want me to send you a copy of it?" Settimo asked.

Opting not to press Settimo for details of how the phone book had made its way into his hands, January recited a Federal Express number and requested that he overnight it. What the detective would find among the numbers, foreign and domestic, that Urick had recorded were several with El Paso prefixes. One was listed beside the name Ted Young.

The detectives agreed that it was time to follow the same course Settimo had and focus their investigation on Sam Urick.

"I placed a call to him at his trucking company in Conroe in hopes of setting up an interview," January recalls. "I tried to persuade him to come to Waco to talk to us, but he insisted I come there. He made it clear he wanted me on his turf. And then, toward the end of the conversation, he began to say some really strange things. He started talking about my boys; even knew their names. 'I've had you checked out,' he said, 'and I know how much you love your kids.' And then he hung up."

Unnerved by the tone of Urick's voice, the detective quickly pushed the rewind button on the tape recorder attached to his phone, only to find that it had failed to record what he had perceived as a threat. Frustrated, Steve January kicked a trashcan across the room that housed the special crimes unit. The frustration would quickly be compounded. By the time January could schedule a visit to Conroe, Sam Urick had shut down the business and fled. The "trucking company" he'd left behind showed little evidence of being a legitimate business. In the yard was a single truck that had clearly seen better days. A computer check would reveal that Southern Sales had operated under a half-dozen previous names and company presidents. The only real evidence that any kind of business had been transacted out of the small office was long distance phone bills that often ran as high as two thousand dollars per month. Records showed a number of calls to various numbers in El Paso, and some to places as far away as Honduras.

The "missing person" case was quickly growing in scope and complications. "There were obviously a lot of things going on with the case," recalls Kristina Woodruff, "that were well beyond our jurisdiction. Steve and I were convinced that something bad had happened to Gary Patterson. But to find out what, we were going to need help."

The help they needed would come, and from two nearby sources— but not before unexpected obstacles were thrown into their path.

Texas Ranger Matt Cawthon knew nothing of the case until the wife of a friend working at Brazos Environmental mentioned Patterson's disappearance and made the offhand suggestion that he might in some way assist the Waco police. That same day he would visit the McLennan County sheriff's office, where a deputy aware of the basic facts of the investigation suggested it "just might be the biggest case we've had around here in some time."

Curious, Cawthon decided to stop into the Waco police department and introduce himself. Detectives January and Woodruff eagerly welcomed his interest and spent most of an afternoon outlining what they had learned during the two weeks they had been working the case. Their chief concern, they explained, was the jurisdictional problems they were facing. "What we had to determine," January says, "was how we were going to work a case where whatever might have happened took place hundreds of miles away. Basically, we were still working a missing person's case in Waco, and the guy we were looking for had disappeared in El Paso."

Cawthon suggested that a meeting of local, state, and federal agencies might help in mapping out some kind of strategy. They eventually decided to invite the McLennan County district attorney, assistant U.S. attorney for the Western District of Texas, and local representatives from the FBI and U.S. marshals office.

"What we did at the meeting," remembers Cawthon, "was go over everything Steve and Kristina had on the case. They detailed the Pattersons' divorce and custody battle, Urick's background, and the link they had made between him and Ted Young. They explained that they strongly felt that Young, the federal fugitive, was the key to determining what had happened to Gary Patterson."

When Young's background was being discussed, Cassie Roundtree, director of the local U.S. marshals office, excused herself from the table and went to a nearby phone. Only minutes later she returned, smiling. "We've got him," she announced. "We know all about him and where he is." Adding an impressive litany of details about the search and surveillance her office had been doing on Young, Roundtree said she'd just been given information that "Ted Young just crossed the border into Juárez, pulling a trailer."

Though she said nothing, Detective Woodruff found Roundtree's explanation troubling. She wondered why they had allowed Young to cross into Mexico rather than take him into custody, especially considering that he was a federal fugitive whose presence was known. "It just didn't make sense to me," the detective says.

For weeks, while being regularly assured by Roundtree that the search for Young was progressing and should be regarded as the sole jurisdiction of the U.S. marshals, the Ranger and police detectives waited. As patience grew thin, they began to wonder.

Finally, with the anniversary of Patterson's disappearance nearing the three-month mark, they opted to move ahead with their own investigation.

A welcomed addition to their efforts was Waco-based assistant U.S. attorney Bill Johnston. Though at the time heavily involved in the prosecution of members of the Branch Davidians in the aftermath of their infamous shoot-out with members of the ATF raid team at nearby Mount Carmel, he had made it clear that he was eager to support the Rangers and the police in any way possible.

"The first thing he did," recalls Cawthon, "was to help us solve the jurisdictional problem." The forty-one-year-old Johnston, a student of the law since his childhood days when his father had served as an assistant district attorney in Dallas, explained that the only way Patterson's disappearance could be viewed as a federal crime was if transportation across state lines was involved. "Finally, after doing some research, he came up with a statute referring to interstate flight that worked to our advantage. The commercial flight that Patterson had taken to El Paso had been scheduled to travel on to San Francisco that same day."

With that legal interpretation, the disappearance of Gary Patterson became a federal case, complete with the power to subpoena witnesses and seek cooperation of authorities in El Paso.

In El Paso, the FBI soon joined into the effort, agreeing to open a missing person's case.

For the next several months, Cawthon, January, and Woodruff blazed a steady trail from Waco to El Paso. Although Ted Young was not to be found, Urick's phone list provided them a road map into a netherworld of scam artists and con men, all somehow associated with and obligated to the man who had had their numbers.

There was Clark Paulson, who gave his occupation as "house sitter" for realtors who preferred that the high-dollar homes they were attempting to sell be occupied. On the side he bought and sold a few cars, without benefit of a license that made it legal for him to do so. Yes, he said, he knew both Urick and Young. Eventually, in fact, he would admit that Urick had contacted him several months earlier to say they he would be needing the use of his pickup. He'd delivered it to Young at the Red Roof Inn in El Paso and picked it up in the motel parking lot the following day.

William Brannon, another longtime Urick associate, owned six hundred isolated desert acres east of El Paso where his West Texas Minerals operation was located. Just a step ahead of an FBI investigation at the time, Brannon was scamming investors into believing that he was mining a rich new gold find. In truth, behind all his fast talk and snappy four-color brochures was one of the oldest cons on the book. Trucking in minute particles of real gold ore from nearby New Mexico, he and his employees liberally seeded the barren mine before each new sucker with deep pockets and get-rich dreams paid a visit.

Urick, he would finally admit, had been a regular visitor in his home, sometimes staying for weeks. Then there was an old buddy of Sam's who had left town before they had a chance to talk with him. He'd recently been indicted for defrauding the Royal Bank of Canada of almost $200 million.

On a hardscrabble road leading past a maze of plywood shacks and cardboard lean-tos was the home of a man named Ollie Martinez. Yes, he said, he knew Ted Young. Sam Urick, in fact, had come to his house looking for him on several occasions.

"We explained how important it was that we locate Ted," Cawthon says, "and he immediately volunteered to take us to where he was living."

"He's in Honduras," Martinez told them.

When the Waco investigators passed the information along to U.S. marshals in El Paso, they were quickly warned that Martinez was also a known hustler, most likely just looking for a free ride back home to Central America. What Cawthon and the police officers weren't told was that according to the Waco marshals office, Ted Young was now thought to be hiding out in either London or Honolulu.

Over weeks that grew into months, the case file had grown. If real progress was to be made, however, a dramatic breakthrough was badly needed. That event would be set in motion back in Waco in June 1998 when Lisa Urick Patterson, having failed to pay ordered court costs and fees in the aftermath of receiving her probated sentence, was arrested and placed in the McLennan County jail.

Before returning to try to talk with her, however, Cawthon wanted to play a hunch. For weeks he'd been reading accounts in the local papers of dozens of discarded bodies of young female factory workers found in the deserts outside nearby Juárez. What, he wondered, were the odds that Patterson had met the same fate? He decided that it was time to at least get a look at Brannon's ranch.

"When we arrived out there," he remembers, "this old Dodge Charger comes racing down a hill, spewing dust twenty feet into the air. The driver was head of security for West Texas Minerals, ex-military, and, it turns out, a real police buff. When we gave him a general idea of what we were up to, he said he was glad someone was looking at the place because he was pretty sure whatever was going on there wasn't legal. To my surprise, he agreed to meet with us when he got off work."

The following evening, as the man talked of the faux mining operation he was charged with guarding, Cawthon would subtly try to turn the conversation to the landscape of the ranch.

"I've walked every inch of that six hundred acres," the guard assured him.

"Ever find any bones out there?"

The guard nodded. "I've got some at home on the work bench in my garage," he said.

In short order they were at his house, collecting two bleached pieces of bone, explaining they would like to have a Baylor University anthropologist examine them. The guard shrugged. "Be my guest," he said.

Back in Waco, Dr. Susan Mackey-Wallace needed only a quick look at the first piece of bone Cawthon pulled from his briefcase to identify it as part of a human arm.

The time now seemed right to visit the county jail and talk with Lisa.

Lisa Urick Patterson made no secret of her instant dislike of Detective Woodruff. Rolling her eyes at the officer's shoulder-length blond hair, she immediately dubbed her "Barbie Doll" and refused to speak to her. Her attitude made it easy for January and Woodruff to quickly fall into their good cop–bad cop roles.

"At first," January says, "she wouldn't say anything. I explained to her that the window of opportunity was closing pretty fast and had, in the past day or so, gotten even tighter. I said, 'You're never going to believe what we found in the desert out in El Paso.' That seemed to finally get her attention."

A human bone, he told her. "She just leaned forward, the veins on her temples popping out. She was shaking, holding her stomach like she was cramping." Still, another twenty-four hours would pass before she began to talk.

Yes, she finally admitted, she had known that her father was planning to lure Gary to El Paso. "But only to beat him up," she insisted. "He knew Gary would come as soon as they offered the new Suburban. Gary loved new cars and toys like that." And, yes, it had been her father's idea that she lie to the Pattersons about the need for a photograph of her ex-husband. "The man who was going to approach Gary needed to know what he looked like," she deadpanned.

Slow moving and cautious to that point, U.S. attorney Johnston listened as the new evidence was outlined to him by the investigators. Almost exactly a year had passed since Gary Patterson had disappeared. It was time, he said, to get arrest warrants for Sam Urick and Ted Young and a search warrant for the ranch where the bones were found.

"But for every step forward," Cawthon reflects, "it seemed we took two back. We go out to the ranch, waving our warrant and looking like the Sugarland Express come to town, and start searching all over the desert for a body. John Aycock, one of the best Rangers around, went out to help us. And, sure enough, we find a body. But it isn't the one we were looking for."

Then, two months later, after following a paper trail and phone records they hoped were getting them close to the elusive Urick, word came out of the blue that he had been apprehended near Las Vegas. Unknown to the Rangers or the Waco police, the Department of Labor had teamed with the marshals to open an investigation into Urick's business-fraud activities. "They knew for three days prior to the arrest where he was," January remembers, "and never bothered to give us a call."

"It was time," Cawthon says, "for us to rethink making a visit to Honduras."

On the commercial flight from Miami in early August 1998 were Cawthon, fellow Ranger Clete Buckaloo, and agents of the Secret Service who agreed to run interference with the Honduran government and local police officials if necessary. In the capital city of Tegucigalpa, representatives from Interpol waited to help. For the Rangers, it was a venture into uncharted territory. At no time in history had the legendary

Texas law enforcement agency gone so far afield in an attempt to make an arrest. "We had hoped to take Ted into custody first," says Cawthon, "believing he would help us to make a stronger case against Sam. But when that idea fell apart, we felt we had to move quickly to Plan B."

Thus, while Cawthon was en route to Honduras, Waco detective January was making yet another trip to El Paso, this time to arrest Clark Paulson for his role in the Patterson disappearance.

Cawthon and Buckaloo barely settled into their hotel room to prepare for a briefing meeting with local state department officials when one of the Secret Service agents knocked at their door. "You guys know a U.S. marshal named Cassie Roundtree?" he asked. "She's apparently really blown a cork. She's calling Washington, going ballistic over the fact you guys are here. Just wanted you to know that if we suddenly get pulled off this thing and told to go home, it isn't our decision."

Cawthon immediately placed calls to Johnston and his superiors at the Rangers' headquarters. "Buy us some time," he pled.

For several days, while a battle was being waged from Waco to Washington over their right to be there, the Rangers began tracking Ted Young. Among the first things they learned was that there were computer records indicating the comings and goings of those entering or leaving Honduras. Ted Young, they found, was traveling on a passport issued to his twin brother Fred, who had helped him escape the country following his North Carolina conviction.

Among the travel dates were those matching the times Young had appeared in Waco, then El Paso.

Making a five-hour cross-country van ride to San Pedro Sula, they finally arrived at a ramshackled junkyard that locals said was run by "the gringo" in the photograph they were shown. "We sat up nearby and finally saw this gray-haired man emerge from the gate," says Cawthon. "I can't describe how I felt at the moment when I finally saw the man we'd been chasing after for fifteen months. I wanted to run across the road and hug him." Instead, Young was placed under arrest and taken to the local police station.

Only hours earlier, several thousand miles away, Detective January arrested Clark Paulson and was making arrangements to return with him to Waco.

Sitting in the solitary interview room of the crumbling San Pedro Sula jail, Young was certain he'd been arrested for his flight from the South Carolina fraud conviction. "I'm gonna tell you right now," he said, "the U.S. government has done nothing but fuck me over all my life. I didn't do a damn thing wrong and still they wanted to throw me in prison. It wasn't right. "

Cawthon quickly interrupted the harangue. "Ted," he said, "we're Texas Rangers. We're not here to talk to you about South Carolina or the U.S. government. That's all past business. We're here to talk to you about Gary Patterson."

Young's face suddenly paled and went blank. "I don't know anything about that." His voice fell to a whisper.

For the next half hour the Ranger methodically detailed the evidence he and the Waco police had gathered. "We know about you posing as Ned Wright," he said, ticking off details. "We know about the Fairfield Inn in Waco and the Red Roof Inn in El Paso. We know you were there with Clark Paulson and Sam Urick. We know, Ted. What you've got to decide is whether you want to cooperate with us or spend the rest of your life in the pen, protecting Sam."

Young silently stared at Cawthon for some time then released a deep sigh. "Okay," he said, "I'll give you what you want."

Finally, as the scared and defeated fugitive dictated his confession, Patterson's fate became known: Sam Urick phoned Young, asking him to come back to the United States and help with a problem he was having with his son-in-law. "I owed him some favors," Young said, "so I agreed." Urick, he said, had been shipping him old trucks to sell since he'd been hiding in Honduras. That was how he'd been earning his living. So, yes, he agreed to pose as Ned Wright and lure Patterson into Urick's presence.

Doing so, however, was harder than either expected. First, the Florida plan fell through when Patterson insisted on bringing his girlfriend. On another occasion, Young called Gary and asked that he meet him at the Waco airport one morning. He was to then drive Patterson to an area near China Springs where Urick was waiting to kill him and stuff his body into a waiting oil drum. "Something happened and Patterson didn't show up at the airport when I arrived," Young recalled.

Then they came up with the El Paso plan.

For much of that long-ago May day, Young said, he was forced to keep Patterson occupied, delaying the "meeting" until dark. They had lunch and visited several bars. By the time he finally announced it was time to go meet the CEO, in fact, Patterson was slightly tipsy. "I told him that on the way I had to drive out to this development site and pick up a soil sample," Young remembered. "As I drove Paulson's pickup out into the desert, Gary kept dozing off."

When they arrived at the prearranged location, Young pulled a .22 pistol from beneath the driver's seat and pointed it at Patterson. From the darkness, Sam Urick appeared at the passenger door. Pulling it open, he smiled and said, "I've got you now, motherfucker." With that he began wrapping duct tape around Patterson's arms and legs, then yanked him from the truck.

"Sam told me to go on back into town," Young said. "He said, 'Get out of here and don't come back until tomorrow. This is going to take all night.'" Young said he immediately returned to the Red Roof Inn and placed a call to a local escort service. "When I saw Sam the next morning, I asked where Gary was. He said, 'He's in the desert.'"

Cawthon pushed a notepad across the table. "Show me where," he demanded.

"The original plan," Young volunteered, "was to do it on an old ranch east of town. But they had these security people wandering around. So we decided on a spot adjacent to it."

Later that evening Steve January was packing to leave his El Paso hotel room when Cawthon reached him with the news of Young's arrest. "Get a search party together," the Ranger said. "I'm faxing you a map to where Gary Patterson's body is buried."

Coordinating activities from Bill Johnston's office, Kristina Woodruff reacted to the news with an ear-splitting scream of delight.

On August 3, 1998, digging at a spot located by one of the dogs borrowed from authorities in nearby Las Cruces, searchers needed only a few minutes to discover a body buried in a shallow grave. Halting the digging at the first sign of human remains, January ordered the area roped off. A helicopter was summoned to take aerial photographs and a video cameraman was lifted onto a hydralic "mule" to document the excavation. Dirt sifters and metal detectors were ordered to search for bullets or shell casings in the event the victim had been shot. The medical examiner was summoned.

A call to the El Paso assistant U.S. attorney's office became necessary. A lieutenant with the El Paso County sheriff's department, alerted to the plans for the search, angrily insisted that January was out of his jurisdiction and demanded that the case be turned over to local authorities. "I tried to explain to him that this was a federal investigation," the detective says, "but his response was that he didn't give a shit and was going to take over."

Alerted to the problem, the attorney offered a simple solution: Place an officer at the road leading into the area, she said. If the lieutenant shows up, arrest him.

"I knew the body was Gary Patterson," January says, "and all I wanted was to be absolutely certain we did everything as perfectly as possible. We'd come too far to take any chance of messing something up." The excavation would take from shortly after nine in the morning to midafternoon. The body that was finally unearthed and taken away to the medical examiner's office was still dressed in the white shirt, black jeans, and boots that investigators had been told Patterson wore on the morning of his ill-fated trip to El Paso.

Though it would not be until the following day that the coroner would rule that the body was, in fact, that of Gary Patterson, January had known. He was certain from the moment the grave was discovered that the lengthy search had finally ended. After fifteen months, everything came together in a lightning-like period of only ten days.

Calling the weary and sun-drained search crew together, he thanked them—for the Patterson family, for the Waco police department, and the Texas Rangers. He thought of saying more, but his voice began to break. With a silent nod he excused himself to the privacy of one of the SUV vehicles parked nearby.

And there, for the first time in his career as a law enforcement officer, he began to cry.

EPILOGUE

In a Waco courtroom late in September 1999, Sam Urick and Ted Young pled guilty to the murder of Gary Patterson. Urick, fifty-nine, received a life sentence, thereby heading off Bill Johnston's plan to seek the death penalty if the case went to trial. In the days following his arrest, he told of beating Patterson repeatedly with a pipe before burying him that night in the desert. He would not admit knowing, however, that he had likely buried his victim while he was still alive despite the coroner's findings that sand had been inhaled into the thorax. As he was led from the courtroom after sentencing, Urick turned briefly to glare in the direction of Patterson's father, who was sitting among the crowd.

Young, forty-nine, pled to being an accessory to murder-for-hire and carrying a firearm during a crime of violence and received a twenty-year sentence that would be added to the fifty-one months he still owed South Carolina authorities. Before entering into a plea, he told of Urick's driving him from El Paso to Corpus Christi then his taking $180 in cash that had been removed from Patterson's body. Young, still using his twin's passport, then crossed the border into Mexico and traveled back to Honduras.

Federal Judge Walter Smith Jr., after sentencing Urick and Young, noted from the bench that he was "troubled" by the lack of federal participation in the investigation. Though he made no specific mention of the U.S. marshals office, it was, to those on hand who knew the tangled history of the case, a clear rebuke.

Lisa Urick Patterson, having earlier pled guilty to a charge of misprision of a felony (knowing of plans to murder her ex-husband and not alerting authorities), received a three-year prison sentence that would be added to the two she was already serving for violation of terms of her parole. She has relinquished parental rights to her daughter, now nine, to her ex-husband's parents.

In El Paso, facing the same charges filed against Lisa, Craig Paulson, insisting he had no idea what the pickup he loaned Urick and Young would be used for, was acquitted.

In February, Bill Johnston resigned his position as assistant U.S. attorney after becoming the target of national controversy. Upon learning that Justice Department officials had not divulged critical evidence that the FBI had indeed fired pyrotechnic tear-gas grenades into the Davidian compound during the 1993 standoff, he wrote a letter to Attorney General Janet Reno alerting her to the matter. Soon thereafter, Johnston found himself persona non grata within his own Western District, stripped of responsibilities, and no longer even invited to staff meetings. Today he is a lawyer in private practice in Waco.

Though other cases now occupy the time of Detectives Woodruff and January, both stay in touch with Gary Patterson's family.

The .22 pistol that Ted Young had pointed at Gary Patterson that long-ago night in the desert was finally surrendered to the authorities by Sam Urick's wife. She said it had been a family heirloom. Today it sits on a shelf in the Texas Rangers headquarters office of Matt Cawthon.

No keepsake collector, he refers to it simply as "a reminder."

DALLAS Observer

ECHOES OF HATE

BOBBY FRANK CHERRY IS ONE OF THE MOST NOTORIOUS RACIST KILLERS IN AMERICAN HISTORY. TO TOM CHERRY, HE WAS JUST "DAD."

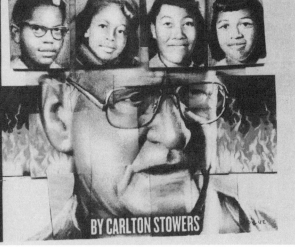

BY CARLTON STOWERS

June 20-26, 2002
FREE
Volume 22, Issue 25
dallasobserver.com

2

ECHOES OF HATE

The winding footpath that once connected the next-door homes of the two men is now overgrown, lost in a tangle of waist-high weeds and the shadows of the ancient oaks that green this quiet and serene Cedar Creek Lake area. Tom Cherry, wandering his backyard in the company of his dogs, points in the direction of the property he helped clear in preparation for the home where his aging and notorious father, Bobby Frank Cherry, used to live. As he does, he takes a long drag on one of the Kools he chain-smokes and shakes his head. The dogs rush to his side, playfully barking in concert, as if recognizing some hidden torment their master is feeling.

The old man's house is vacant now, sold a couple of years ago to help defray legal expenses. Tom's father—the man with whom he has endured a love–hate relationship for most of his forty-nine years; the man he once called his "hero"; the man whom he has not spoken to since an angry estrangement back in 1997—now sits in an Alabama prison, convicted last month of a horrendous crime he was accused of committing thirty-nine years ago.

Jurors agreed that Bobby Frank Cherry was one of four Ku Klux Klansmen who, at the height of the civil rights movement, bombed an all-black church in Birmingham in 1963, claiming the lives of four young girls and injuring twenty others.

Now, on this summer weekend of clear blue skies and the aroma of outdoor grilling underway somewhere down the road, the eldest of the seven Cherry children is alone, reflecting on the doubt and confusion that has haunted him and his family for decades.

"Dad and I always had a rocky, off-and-on relationship," the husky-voiced long-haul truck driver says. "If you agreed with him, you were his buddy. If you didn't, you weren't. There was never any in-between. It wasn't until I was a grown man that I finally figured out that he wasn't ever going to change."

Yet, he admits, it did not prevent his lifelong attempt to forge some kind of bond. That, he explains, is just what sons do, even if their father was mean and abusive, even if he abandoned his children to an orphanage soon after their mother died, even if he was a man who spewed racial slurs, wore his Klan robe proudly, and held to the belief that violence was the answer to the world's social ills. And so, after years of going his separate way, Tom Cherry followed his father to Texas and became his next-door neighbor.

"If I told you how I feel about my dad right now," he warns after a quick burst of laughter, "you'd think I'm crazy."

Then he becomes pensive as he continues: "There hasn't been an hour go by since the trial that I haven't thought about him sitting in jail, wondering what he's going through. It's an awful feeling, knowing there's nothing you can do about it. I feel so sorry for him.

"I love him. And I hate him. There's one part of me that wishes I'd killed him thirty years ago. There's another that feels all of what's happened to him is a result of the government plotting against him. And there's another that feels he got what he deserved."

What is difficult to determine is which Bobby Frank Cherry his conflicted son is remembering: The one who worked long, hard hours to provide for his family? The man he once wanted to grow up to be like? The one he says had a great sense of humor? Or the one who would fly into rages and physically abuse the mother who died when he was just fifteen?

"I never knew what it was that set him off," Tom says. "Actually, I don't think it was ever anything in particular." With that he recalls a long-ago Sunday morning in the Cherry family kitchen. "All my mother did was ask him to go to church with us," he says, "and Dad jumped up and cleared the breakfast table, throwing things and knocking stuff onto the floor. That's just the way he was."

Such temper tantrums motivated the nine-year-old Tom Cherry to run away from home. "I got to where I'd do it just about every time Momma and Dad would start fighting," he recalls. Watching as his father hit and slap his mother, Tom would pack his clothes and walk away. "I never got very far, though," he says.

On one occasion, he says, a friend of the family stopped him just a short distance from home and persuaded him to call his mother and tell her where he was. When he phoned, it was his father who angrily instructed him to stay where he was so he might come get him. "I was so nervous by the time he got there," Tom says, "that my stomach was hurting." When he told his father that, Bobby Frank Cherry doubled his fist and punched the youngster in the gut.

In retrospect, Tom Cherry can only guess at what fueled his dad's volatile anger and hatred for blacks. Likely, he suggests, it was a mind-set he inherited from his own father. That, Tom reasons, was simply the way of many Southern whites back in those days.

"There was this Christmas morning," he says, "when we were going over to my grandmother's house. We were in the area people called the Brick Garden—where the blacks lived—and Dad pulled up at this red light. The streets were pretty deserted, but all of a sudden, this black man appears and just lays across the hood of our car. He's cut and bleeding and asking for help."

Cherry remembers his father angrily backing up to force the man off the car, then just driving away. "I couldn't imagine why we didn't stop and help that fella," he says.

Nor did he understand why Bobby Frank Cherry rushed onto his front porch, brandishing a shotgun on a long-ago Halloween night when two small black children arrived to trick-or-treat. Or why, when he appeared at home one day with a ten-year-old black friend named Tyrone, his father ordered the visiting youngster out of the yard.

He tells of the time a black teenager stole a ball of twine Tom used to bind the newspapers he threw on his route. His dad immediately went in search of the youngster. "He asked him if he'd taken my cord, and the guy smarted off, said something like, 'Yeah, what are you gonna do about it?' Dad had a pistol hidden under a towel he'd wrapped around his hand. He stuck it in the guy's face and told him what would happen if he ever bothered me again."

He recalls the Klan gatherings he attended in the company of his father and how he viewed the burning crosses fashioned from old telephone poles and heard the impassioned speeches that warned of the disasters equality and integration promised. Cherry even recalls a small

"Clan church" hidden away in a rural area outside of town that he remembers attending with his father on a couple of occasions.

The relationship, however, would end when Tom was just fifteen. Rather than enter the orphanage with his siblings after his mother's death in 1968, he remained at home for a short time. "In about six months, though, Dad had remarried. And every time he went through a new wife he went through a new set of kids. So I decided it was time for me to leave."

In truth, he was leaving behind few good memories. "Dad could be charming as hell when he wanted to be, even affectionate at times. I'm not talking about hugging and kissing and telling his kids that he loved them. But just being nice."

Yet he has no recollection of ever sitting down with his father just to talk. "It seemed like he always had other things on his mind," Tom says. "Looking back, I think maybe we could have worked some things out if we'd just been able to talk to each other."

Instead, the pictures from the past are hardly pretty. On one occasion, he recalls, he actually pointed a shotgun at his father in an effort to make him stop beating his mother. He remembers times when he did not run away but, instead, was ordered from the house by the angered elder Cherry. "He'd get mad and run me off, then my mother would let things quiet down and come find me."

From the time he finally left home for good until he was an adult, he saw his father only occasionally. The parental influence, however, was never far from hand. Finding work in the shipyards of Pascagoula, Mississippi, he eventually followed his father's lead and joined the Klan himself. "It was back in the early seventies," he says, "and this fella I knew at the union hall talked me into it." Tom Cherry, however, didn't stay long. "They were stupid," he reflects, "always talking out of both sides of their mouth. You would hear them talking about how sorry the blacks were, then the next thing I knew I saw one of them parked in front of a black whorehouse.

"I've only got a seventh-grade education, but I know an idiot when I see one."

In short order, he put away the Klan robe he'd paid thirty-five dollars for and quit attending meetings.

A DIFFERENT TIME, DIFFERENT PLACE . . .

For almost four decades, the city of Birmingham, Alabama, has, like so much of the nation's Old South, slowly—and sometimes grudgingly—advanced beyond the ugly and evil reminders of a time when racial animosity was commonplace and condoned. Gone are the vows of a governor who once loudly promised segregation now and forever. Gone are the times when there was little hesitancy to spice the local language with the word *nigger*.

The angry and too often violent recollections of the sixties' civil rights movement are now relegated to the history books, remembered by an aging generation as the battleground whereon the foundation of a new social enlightenment was built. They still recall that it was in Birmingham where a single event so unimaginably cruel and evil-spirited occurred, forcing the city—and an entire nation—to wear its shame like a shroud. For all the new and shiny buildings, the equal opportunities, and revised thinking, that September Sunday morning of 1963 will forever be Birmingham's haunting moment, just as a tragic November day that same year indelibly marked the image of Dallas.

Back then the city's Sixteenth Street Baptist Church was more than a place of worship for members of the black community. Civil rights leaders regularly visited its pulpit to urge on the struggle for racial equality, and it was often the starting point for demonstrations that would sometimes end with marchers being dispersed by police wielding fire hoses and batons.

But on that day thirty-nine years ago, Reverend John Cross planned a traditional morning service that was to include a musical program performed by the youth choir. In preparation, four of its members—fourteen-year-olds Cynthia Wesley, Carole Robertson, and Addie Mae Collins, and eleven-year-old Denise McNair—had made a last-minute visit to the basement restroom. At 10:22 A.M., an explosion, triggered by a dozen sticks of dynamite placed outside the church, ripped a jagged hole in a corner of the old red brick building and claimed the lives of the four children who were still too young, too innocent to comprehend the social unrest that led to their deaths.

The aftermath of the blast was nightmarish. One of the youngsters was decapitated, another so badly ripped apart that she could only be identified by her clothing. A flying brick had lodged into the skull of another.

What possible motive could there have been for such evil? Just five days earlier Birmingham officials had reached a controversial decision to integrate the public schools.

"In many ways," says Mark Potok of the Southern Poverty Law Center, "the Sixteenth Street Church bombing was the most important moment in the history of the civil rights movement. What happened that day awoke the conscience of white America, a conscience that had been silently sleeping for a long time. The spectacle of these four little girls in their white dresses, blown to pieces, changed the political landscape of America." It was an event, historians agree, that also provided renewed determination to those leading the protests and hastened the writing of new civil rights law.

For all the public outrage, righteous political speeches demanding justice, and law enforcement's repeated vows the crime would be solved, there was legitimate concern, particularly in the black community, that justice would never be served. Despite the fact that investigators quickly focused on four suspects—local Klan members with long histories of violent acts—no arrests were made. Rumors abounded that potential witnesses feared for their lives if they were forced to testify, that prosecutors privately doubted a court in a state so determined to hold to the ideals of segregation would rule fairly, and that the local police lacked genuine motivation to thoroughly investigate.

By 1968, in fact, the FBI closed its investigation without filing any charges despite reports that a memorandum was submitted to director J. Edgar Hoover concluding that the bombing was plotted and carried out by four men: Robert Chambliss, Herman Cash, Thomas Blanton, and Bobby Frank Cherry. Years later a Justice Department report would determine that Hoover, wary of acquittal verdicts by all-white juries, had blocked all prosecution in the case. Meanwhile, the men suspected of committing the crime continued to freely walk the streets of Birmingham.

Tom Cherry was only eleven when the bombing occurred but was keenly aware of the interest the authorities immediately took in the activities of his father. "They began following him everywhere he went," he remembers. He says that even neighbors informed on him, telling the FBI anything they saw the elder Cherry doing. "They were even passing along the names of anybody who came in and out of our house."

Everything that occurred in and around the Cherry home came under suspicion. Tom remembers a time his mother rushed him to the hospital after he'd badly burned three fingers. Soon he was being asked by an FBI agent if the accident had resulted from his playing with one of his daddy's dynamite caps. No, he explained, it had been caused by matches.

"I never saw any dynamite in our home or anywhere else," Tom still insists.

It was not until 1977, after an aggressive Alabama attorney general named Bill Baxley reopened the case, that Chambliss, a man who reportedly delighted in his nickname of "Dynamite Bob," was finally tried, convicted, and received a life sentence. He died in prison eight years later at age eighty-one, still proclaiming his innocence despite the fact authorities presented evidence that he had purchased the dynamite used in the bombing and despite a yellowed FBI report stating that an eyewitness had seen him and three other men on the church grounds at around 2:00 A.M. on the date of the explosion.

Yet after Baxley left office, the case again became an afterthought despite the repeated outcries of local blacks that justice was not yet completed. Before any charges were ever brought against him, seventy-five-year-old Herman Cash died in 1994, leaving only the aging Blanton and Cherry as surviving suspects.

If punishment was to ever be dealt, time was running out.

There are conflicting reports about what breathed new life into yet another revival of interest in the case. Some say it was a series of secret meetings between new-thinking Birmingham civic leaders and the FBI; others point to the public awareness generated by the Oscar-nominated documentary *4 Little Girls*, directed by Spike Lee. Whatever the case, U.S. Attorney General Janet Reno ordered a reopening of the investigation in 1997, and a new generation of FBI agents went in search of Thomas

Blanton, the man long suspected of driving his associates to the bombing site, and Bobby Frank Cherry, who allegedly put the fatal bomb in place.

Their quest of the latter brought them to an isolated, tree-canopied road that winds around Cedar Creek Lake, just over an hour's drive south of Dallas.

THE OLD MAN IN TEXAS . . .

Most media accounts erroneously state that Bobby Frank Cherry's home was in the lakeside community of Mabank; however, Mabank is simply where Cherry and his fifth wife, Myrtle, received their mail. The closest town, in fact, is a little wide spot in the road called Payne Springs (population 683). Small businesses, fishing marinas, fruit stands, and flea markets throughout the maze of narrow, winding roads, serve the needs of those who have escaped the metropolitan pressures for the quiet life. In this part of the world hides a gothiclike sense of privacy, of secrets tightly guarded, and a palpable distrust of strangers.

This, remember, is the neighborhood where the infamous Betty Lou Beets once lived, killing off husbands and burying them in the yard. Not far away, John Joe Gray, self-professed militiaman, has barricaded himself on his property for the past couple of years rather than accept service of a warrant for his arrest. As former Henderson County sheriff Howard (Slick) Alfred once told the *Observer*, "There's all kinds of folks living over there [on the lake]. We've got people looking for nothing more than peace and quiet. And we've also got some who are running from something."

Few apparently knew that the grandfatherly Cherry, called "Cowboy" by those who knew him, was one of those on the run. A former marine, truck driver, and welder with an eighth-grade education, he'd moved from Birmingham in 1971, settling in Grand Prairie, where he opened a small carpet-cleaning business. Then in 1988, suffering a bad back, diabetes, and a heart condition that made a triple bypass necessary, Cherry retired and joined the caravan of Dallas-area residents headed for the bucolic isolation of Cedar Creek Lake.

He was living there when the FBI, which had interviewed him on numerous occasions in the immediate aftermath of the bombing, again came calling in the summer of 1997. Soon the community was abuzz with talk that the old man living on Hickory Street was a suspect in the long-ago Birmingham church bombing. For many, the suggestion generated responses like "impossible" and "inconceivable." "He's been a wonderful neighbor," a bike-riding young woman said. "Nice as he can be," added a local businessman. "Oh, there might have been an instance or two when it was pretty obvious that he didn't like blacks, but he never did anything but walk away. To the best of my knowledge he never hurt anybody."

"We never had a bit of trouble out of him," the retired Alfred says. "A few times the FBI would meet him at my office to talk, and he and I always got along just fine."

Angered by the renewed attention, Cherry quickly hired nearby Athens lawyer Gil Hargrave and demanded that he call a press conference. When members of the local media gathered, Cherry said, "I don't know anything about that bombing. I've never handled a stick of dynamite in my life, and I've never been on the grounds of that church. Still, they've been trying to arrest me for fifteen years."

On that day, his son Tom stood supportively at his side, labeling the renewal of the investigation nothing more than a "witch hunt."

It wasn't long after the Athens press conference, however, that the FBI visited Tom. "I spoke with them—what else could I do?—and answered their questions as best I could," he says, "then I called Dad over to the house so we could talk about it. I assured him that what I'd told them didn't amount to anything. But his reaction was pretty negative. The first thing he said to me was, 'You know they're going to try to drive a wedge between us.'"

It was a prophetic statement. Soon the elder Cherry received a call from a Henderson County law enforcement officer who confided that the reason his son was talking to the FBI was because he'd reached a deal with them. If Tom Cherry provided information that advanced their investigation, there was a good chance that the robbery sentence his own son was serving might be shortened.

"That," Tom says, "wasn't the case. It never happened. But Dad chose to take their word over mine." After that phone call, the father and son would never speak again.

For decades Bobby Frank Cherry steadfastly insisted that he had been nowhere near the Sixteenth Street Church on the night the bomb was put into place. He had, he repeatedly told authorities, been at home watching Saturday night wrestling on television and tending to his cancer-ridden wife, Virginia. It was an alibi that lost all credibility when investigators determined that (*a*) there had been no televised wrestling on the evening of September 14, 1963, and that (*b*) his wife's cancer had not been diagnosed until several years later.

Still, it would be another three years before an arrest was made. Members of Bobby Frank Cherry's own family were the ones who ultimately provided the information necessary for the long-delayed indictment. One by one, subpoenaed members of the Cherry clan told incriminating stories to investigators, a Birmingham grand jury, and the press.

In the summer of 1999, twenty-six-year-old Teresa Stacy, Tom Cherry's daughter who now lives near Fort Worth, was the first to point blame at her grandfather. After traveling to Birmingham to appear before the grand jury, the mother of two told reporters that her grandfather "said he helped bomb a church back in the sixties and killed a bunch of black folks." Cherry's involvement, in fact, had never been a big secret. At family gatherings, she said, her uncles would say things like "Grandpa helped blow up a bunch of niggers in Birmingham."

"When you're young," she told the press, "you don't know it's wrong. You look back now, and it's pretty sick."

It was, says fifty-year-old federal prosecutor Robert Posey, Stacy's willingness to get involved that set off a chain reaction that gave his case the "boost" it needed. "After seeing her grandfather's press conference on TV, she had called the FBI there in Texas to tell them what she'd heard as a youngster. When we contacted her, she agreed to appear before a grand jury. That took a great deal of courage."

After Stacy spoke out, her grandfather angrily retaliated, insisting to an Associated Press reporter that she was a "dope head and a prostitute."

"I can't forgive that," Tom Cherry says.

Soon, other former and current family members were coming forward. Willadean Brogdon, the third of Cherry's wives, arrived from Montana and also went public following her grand jury appearance. "He admitted it, he bragged about it," she told reporters. Her daughter, Gloria LaDow, by then living in Florida, also testified before the grand jury and later told media members that "[Cherry] bragged about lighting the fuse." Additionally, LaDow publicly accused her stepfather of sexually molesting her as a child.

Bobby Frank Cherry's dark past had returned to haunt him.

Finally, in May 2000, Cherry, then seventy, and Blanton, a sixty-one-year-old Wal-Mart cashier still living near Birmingham, were arrested and soon indicted on eight counts of murder. Four counts were for the deaths of the children with four additional counts added under the "universal malice" statute since the bomb was placed where it could have claimed the lives of others.

Cherry was also charged with the sexual assault of his stepdaughter three decades earlier. (Those charges were dismissed after Alabama officials were unsuccessful in efforts to locate complaining witness LaDow.)

Although Blanton was ultimately tried and convicted after a two-week trial—where secretly recorded FBI tapes of conversations in which he admitted his role in the bombing were played—it appeared for a time that the last of the remaining suspects might still escape prosecution. To the amazement of legal experts, none of the four ex-Klansmen ever offered information that might implicate the others.

Following a hearing in late 2001, at which his attorney argued that his client was suffering from severe dementia, Jefferson County circuit judge James Garrett ruled that Cherry was incompetent to stand trial and ordered him placed in a Tuscaloosa mental facility for treatment and further testing. During the hearing, which was a two-day exchange of mental health experts, a doctor who testified for the prosecution argued that Cherry was only faking and was in fact fully capable of assisting his lawyer and understanding the procedures of a trial.

In January, following additional evaluation, the judge reversed his earlier ruling and declared Cherry competent.

AT LONG LAST, THE TRIAL . . .

When the trial got underway at Birmingham's Criminal Justice Center, a jury of nine whites and three blacks listened as U.S. assistant district attorney Posey and special prosecutor Doug Jones methodically re-created the tension-filled times during which the historic church-bombing occurred. Posey, in his opening statement, set an aggressive tone: "He [Cherry] wore this crime on his chest like a badge of honor, like a Klan medal. He said his only regret was that he didn't kill more people."

Jurors, aging relatives of the victims, and members of the media from throughout the nation saw old black-and-white photographs of the damage the dynamite had done, viewed smiling pictures of the young victims, and heard painful recollections from several who had survived the blast.

They viewed grainy 1957 home-movie footage of a white mob attacking Reverend Fred Shuttlesworth, a local black civil-rights leader, as he attempted to enroll his daughter in an all-white Birmingham school. It offered, the prosecutors noted, a graphic example of the racial hatred and violence that had roamed their city's streets in those days.

Afterward, Bobby Birdwell, once a boyhood friend of Tom Cherry, was called to the stand to identify one of the attackers shown beating the minister. The wavy-haired man with a cigarette dangling from his lips, he testified, was a young Bobby Frank Cherry.

Then Birdwell, who was eleven at the time of the bombing, told of an afternoon visit to the defendant's home just days before the church bombing. Cherry and three other men, he recalled, were seated at the kitchen table as he entered to get a glass of water. "I heard them mention 'bomb' and 'Sixteenth Street,'" he told the jury. He also remembered seeing a white robe, similar to those worn by Klan members, draped across the couch in the living room.

Witness Michael Gowins recalled a mid-1980s conversation with Cherry, whom he had hired to clean carpets in a Dallas apartment complex he managed at the time. After the two men realized they were both originally from Birmingham, he testified, Cherry spoke openly of his involvement in the long-ago church bombing.

Retired FBI agent John Downey, who had interviewed Cherry a year after the bombing, remembered the defendant's repeatedly denying any involvement in the crime. However, he also remembers him saying that "the only reason I didn't do the church bombing was because someone beat me to it."

For the aging defendant, the testimony would only become more damaging in the days to come. His ex-wife Brogdon took the stand to repeat what she had earlier detailed for the grand jury. She told of a time shortly after their 1970 marriage when Cherry's car broke down near the rebuilt Sixteenth Street church. "I went to get him, and he said that was the church where he put the bomb," she testified. "He said he got out of the car and put the bomb under the stairs the night before. He said he lit the fuse."

Brogdon then told the jury that her former husband had expressed regret that the four children were killed, only to add, "At least they can't grow up to have any more niggers."

Then Teresa Stacy described sitting on the porch of the Cherry's Texas home and hearing her grandfather tell of "blowing up a bunch of niggers back in Birmingham." "He seemed rather jovial, braggish," she testified.

Defense attorney Mickey Johnson called two of Cherry's grandsons, who testified that they never heard their grandfather discuss the Birmingham tragedy. He then called a man whose testimony helped convict both Chambliss and Blanton, and that witness swore that he'd never seen Cherry with either of the men. Finally, he called a Texas minister, who told of a born-again Cherry joining his multiracial church in 1997.

Johnson, still voicing belief that his client suffered from dementia, chose not to put Cherry on the witness stand. Cherry, he argued, was but a scapegoat, being used to close the books on a dark period in Birmingham's history. "They [the prosecution] said, 'Here's someone who's easy to prosecute because he's the human equivalent of a cockroach,'" Johnson told the jury.

At the end of the weeklong trial, the jury deliberated less than seven hours over a two-day period before returning with a "guilty" verdict. The life sentence he was dealt and his failing health all but assured that he would spend all of his remaining time behind bars.

But if there is repentance for the crime of which he was convicted, even the bigoted attitude that finally caused his downfall, it is yet to come. Asked by the judge at trial's end if he had anything he wished to say, Cherry quickly lashed out at those who testified against him. "This whole bunch lied all the way through this thing," he said, pointing to the nearby prosecutors. "I told the truth. I don't know why I'm going to jail for nothing."

By then, Tom Cherry, subpoenaed as a witness but never asked to testify, was headed back to Texas, fearful that his father would be convicted and knowing that his family was irreparably shattered. Years ago his siblings, who stood firmly in his father's corner, issued a "you're with us or against us" ultimatum that he chose to ignore. As a result, they no longer speak to him. "I've got one sister I still talk to; that's about it," he says.

His relationship with his daughter Teresa is now strained. "We did finally have a long talk one night in Birmingham during the trial," he says. "I told her that despite everything that had happened, everything we'd disagreed about, I still want to be a part of her life and a part of my grandkids' lives. There were a lot of tears and we hugged." She told her father that she would be in touch after she returned home but has yet to do so.

And isn't likely to. "We talked [in Birmingham]," she says, "but it was all pretty superficial. My father wouldn't know the truth if it hit him in the face. He still seems to be able to forgive just about everything his dad ever did."

A stay-at-home mom, Teresa now looks back on her involvement in the prosecution of her grandfather as "a shameful experience" that she is glad to have behind her—but she quickly adds, "If there is justice in the universe, he will be shoveling shit in hell."

Which leaves little doubt about her feelings for Bobby Frank Cherry. But does she anticipate ever making that call to her dad? "No," she says.

Perhaps, her father suggests, the damage that has been done is too severe to overcome. "I think maybe there's been too much said," he somberly admits. "Too many lies have been told. A misunderstanding, I can understand, but a blatant lie I can't deal with.

"If it hadn't been for so many witnesses who I know lied," he reflects, "I'd have no problem [with the verdict]." Boyhood friend Bobby Birdwell, he insists, was never inside the Cherry home. "He told a bald-faced lie." And his father's ex-wife Brogdon "lied through her teeth."

But what of the damaging testimony from his own daughter? "She's let too many people control her," he says, refusing to elaborate.

Never, he insists, did he ever hear Bobby Frank Cherry talk of any involvement in the historic tragedy. But, did he ever directly ask his father if he committed the crime? "No," Tom says. Does the son feel his dad was, in fact, involved? He retreats to his standard answer: "I wasn't there."

THE AFTERMATH . . .

In the years leading up to his father's arrest, Tom Cherry testified before both federal and state grand juries, yet unlike other family members, he remained silent about what he had said. Still, a public perception, fanned by media reports, grew that it was he who had in fact provided the evidence that finally led to an indictment.

"Actually, they only asked me a few questions," he now explains. "They wanted to know what kind of father he was, and I answered as truthfully as I knew how. They wanted to know if he'd had nightmares or trouble sleeping in the days after the bombing or if he'd seemed remorseful. I told them no. They wanted to know things like if he had become more abusive after it had happened, and I told them I couldn't remember."

They asked what he remembered about that Sunday morning when the bomb went off. He told of accompanying his father to the Modern Sign Company near downtown Birmingham earlier that day and was helping him and several other men who were printing Confederate flags. "I told them all I remembered was hearing the sound of the explosion and Dad asking, 'What the hell was that?'" Almost immediately, he recalls, they left the sign shop and returned home.

When both investigators and the grand jury quizzed him about his father's alibi for the night before the bombing, Tom Cherry's recollection proved damaging. "As far as him being at home watching wrestling on TV, all I could tell them was that I knew it was what we did just about every Saturday night back then." But when asked about his father tending his sick mother that night, he testified that she hadn't learned that she was suffering from cancer until much later. "That," he says, "was when they began checking hospital records."

Attorney Posey, a Birmingham native who was just twelve himself when the crime he was prosecuting occurred, admits empathy for the family members tarnished by the tragic legacy of Bobby Frank Cherry. "Tom," he says, "was willing to meet and talk with us, and I know that was difficult for him. But I can honestly say that I don't think anything that he told us was untrue, that in any way he attempted to sabotage our case. On the other hand, it was difficult at times to know where he stood on things."

The same, for that matter, applies today. He has private thoughts, the divorced Cherry says, that he has no intention of sharing with anyone.

Still, he insists that he really had little information that would have dramatically advanced the state's case. Since he had been financially compensated as a consultant for the FX television movie *Sins of the Father* (in which Tom Sizemore was cast in the role of Tom and Richard Jenkins played his father), there was concern that his credibility would be called into question by the defense.

Relieved that he was not called as a witness, Cherry offers no apology for his involvement in the project that was based on a 2000 *Texas Monthly* article written by Pamela Colloff. "They [the producers] contacted me to say they were going to do the movie, with or without my input," he says. "I thought about it for a long time, and when they finally agreed to let me be a consultant, I decided to get involved. I didn't want them just lambasting him."

Having now seen the movie, which initially aired last January and has since played several times, he says he is "comfortable with it" despite its harsh portrayal of his father.

There is, for that matter, a sense that Thomas Frank Cherry, a likable man whose mood runs from outgoing to pensive, is comfortable with himself, despite his proximity to that nightmarish event of 1963, despite the family's ill-feelings and the haunting questions and troubling memories he lives with.

Walking to the side of the house, he leans against an old boat he's recently had refurbished. He lights another cigarette and remembers when he and his dad would fish the lake together for sand bass and yellow cats.

It was, he recalls, when they were out on the water together that they had many of their best times.

HOW CONSUMMATE CON ARTIST HENRY LEE LUCAS RESURRECTED THE DEAD AND WENT LOOKING FOR A SUCKER. HE ALMOST FOUND ONE.

DEAD WRONG

...northern Denton County, Texas
Victim: Frieda Lorraine
("Becky") Powell, w/f, 15

In June 1983, Henry Lucas described to officers that he and the victim were in Denton County...He and the victim began arguing, and she slapped him, at which time he drew his knife from his belt and immediately stabbed her...After killing her, he had intercourse with her and then dissected her body.

— From a Texas Department of Public Safety summary of offenses cleared by Henry Lucas

On a recent spring morning, the man once viewed as the most diabolical serial killer in

American history was put to rest in a Texas prison cemetery. With a dozen of his fellow inmates on hand to perform the dead duties of grave diggers and pallbearers, the body of

BY CARLTON STOWERS

64-year-old Henry Lee Lucas, claimed by neither family nor friends, was buried in a simple wooden coffin.

The perverse and unlikely celebrity from the impoverished hills of western Virginia had died quietly in his Ellis Unit cell just

north of Huntsville, having told his last lie never again would he embarrass law enforcement and reporters as he had done consistently for almost two decades.

Uncheated though he might have been, he was a con man con fide. I know. Like most journalists who for years had dutifully followed his exploits and listened to his nightmarish stories, I was suckered by the sick games he invented. I wasn't alone, since

the same embarrassment had visited everyone from television network big shots to lauded investigative reporters.

For a time, before his star faded in the shadows of the next celebrity murderer, Lucas' story chilled the nation like no other had before him. His was a bizarre, vivid and gruesome accounting of a coast-to-coast series of murders that staggered the imagination. A fifth-grade dropout with an IQ that didn't reach triple digits, he became an instant household name in 1983 when he stunned a sparsely attended hearing in Montague County, Texas, by announcing that he had killed 100 people probably more.

Journalists from around the country came running. By continued on page 2:

ILLUSTRATION BY MICHAEL HOGUE

3

DEAD WRONG

Date: 8-24-82
Location: Denton County, Texas
Victim: Frieda Lorraine (Becky) Powell, w/f, 15
In June 1983, Henry Lucas described to officers that he and
the victim were in Denton County. . . . He and the victim
began arguing and she slapped him, at which time he drew
his knife from his belt and immediately stabbed her. . . . After killing her, he had intercourse with her and then dissected her body. . . .

—From a Texas Department of Public Safety
Interoffice Memorandum Summary of Offenses
Cleared by Henry Lucas

On a spring morning, with an unseasonable chill in the air and with
threatening clouds serving as an appropriate canopy for the event,
the man once viewed as the most diabolical serial killer in American
history was put to rest in the Texas prison cemetery. With a dozen of
his fellow inmates on hand to perform the duel duties of grave diggers
and pallbearers, the body of sixty-four-year-old Henry Lee Lucas,
claimed by neither family nor friends, was buried in a simple wooden
coffin.

The perverse and unlikely celebrity from the impoverished hills of
western Virginia had died quietly in his Ellis Unit cell just north of
Huntsville, having told his last lie, never again to embarrass law enforcement and members of the media as he'd done with rare consistency
for almost two decades. Uneducated though he might have been, he was
a con man cum laude. I know. Like most journalists who for years had

39

dutifully followed his exploits and listened to his nightmarish stories, I was suckered by the sick games he invented. However, I found myself in good company, since the same embarrassment had visited everyone from network big shots to investigative reporters with all manner of citations attesting to their talents.

For a time, before his star would fade in the shadows of the next celebrity murderer to creep into the nation's spotlight, Lucas' story chilled the nation like no other before him. His was a bizarre, vivid, and gruesome accounting of a coast-to-coast killathon that staggered the imagination. A fifth-grade dropout with an IQ that didn't reach triple digits, he became an instant household name back in 1983 when he stunned a sparsely attended hearing in Montague County, Texas, by announcing that he'd killed one hundred people, probably more.

Journalists from around the country, alerted to this new criminal curiosity, came running. By the time Lucas' death count rose to 360, he was staring into television cameras and from the pages of newspapers and magazines the world over. He was also being courted by hundreds of law enforcement officers from throughout the United States, each hoping he might help with some of their unsolved homicides. Even the Royal Canadian Mounted Police came calling after Henry described a series of north-of-the-border murders. He gave all who came what they wanted, confessing to homicides in twenty-six states and Canada. He was, by his own admission, "the most worst serial killer in history."

A special task force, manned by the late Williamson County sheriff Jim Boutwell and members of the legendary Texas Rangers, was formed and assigned the duty of helping other agencies sort out the stream of horrors to which Lucas couldn't confess fast enough. Soon he was being jetted all over the country to lead investigators to crime scenes and recount the terrifying manner in which his victims met their fates.

"I done it every way imaginable," he liked to say. "Shootings, stabbings, strangulations, drownings. Killing somebody, to me, was just like walking outdoors." For good measure, he occasionally added details of postmortem sex or experiments in cannibalism.

In retrospect, the most interesting aspect of the eighteen-month period in which he was at the height of his crime-clearing binge was the fact that in no instance was Lucas tied to a murder by anything other than his own admission. Physical evidence—a weapon, a witness, finger-prints, even a hair sample—simply never existed.

Admittedly, there were now-and-then signs that maybe he was stretching the truth. He said he'd been the one who killed legendary teamsters leader Jimmy Hoffa; he'd delivered the poison to James Jones for his infamous religious cult's mass suicide in Guyana; and, oh yeah, he was a member of a Louisiana-based Satanic cult that called itself the Hand of Death and delivered babies into slavery in Mexico. So physically draining was his murderous odyssey, he once told a New York journalist, that "to regain my strength I'd sometimes cut out (the victim's) heart and hold it in my hand." Never mind what he meant; it made for the kind of headline that tabloids live for.

By early 1984, the body count of his alleged killing spree went completely off the charts, climbing to the six-hundred range. Yet, that was Lucas' story, and he was sticking to it. And why not? In his George-town, Texas, jail cell—where the task force watched over him and sched-uled his interviews with parading law officers—there was carpeting on the floor, a color television with a cable hookup, midnight milkshakes on demand, art lessons, and home-cooked meals served by a friendly lay sis-ter named Clemmie Schroeder. Son of a prostitute from Blacksburg, Vir-ginia, and a double-amputee father who sold pencils from a hat, Lucas was finally living the good life.

Books were being written, and a movie, *Henry: Portrait of a Serial Killer*, which was based loosely on his homicidal rampage, quickly de-veloped a cult following. A Japanese documentary film crew came to tell his story, and he was featured on his very own "Serial Killer Trading Card." Then, thanks to the Pulitzer-nominated investigative efforts of *Dallas Times Herald* reporters Hugh Aynesworth and Jim Henderson, Lucas' obscene bubble burst, and law enforcement—and other members of the media—were wiping egg from their faces. Retracing Lucas' movements from the time he'd been paroled from a Michigan prison (where he'd served a sentence for the admitted murder of his mother) to the day he was arrested in Montague County (charged with killing an elderly woman named Kate Rich), they methodically debunked the Lucas legend. With work records, they proved that he was in Florida when the dozens of faraway crimes he'd confessed to had occurred. The reporters found receipts showing where Lucas had been selling blood in one state on the same day a murder had occurred in another. Short of owning his own private jet, there was no way he could have made his way from one murder site to another in the unaccounted time available to him.

Lucas just flashed a toothless grin at the new revelations and changed his story to a better one. He'd always despised people in law enforcement, he explained to baffled reporters, and had made it his life's goal to embarrass them. The bogus confessions, he explained, were his way of getting back at them and committing a strange form of slow suicide. The confessions, he said, were fashioned from information fed him by investigators too anxious to clear their books. They described the crimes, showed him photos, left reports lying around for him to read—then he simply told them what they wanted to hear. Cases closed.

As late as 1999, he was telling of his fascination with the infamous deeds of Rafael Resendez-Ramirez, the so-called Railroad Killer charged with at least eight murders in Texas, Kentucky, and Illinois. "You know," Lucas said, "if this was 1983, I'd be claiming them murders, too."

By then it was too late. His game had ended. Conviction of the murder of an unidentified female in Williamson County resulted in a death penalty verdict. Yet, it was only after months of gentle persuasion from investigators that he'd finally agreed to admit to that particular murder. Did he actually do it? "Nope," he told me.

I had, in fact, tagged along with Aynesworth on one of his many interview visits to the Georgetown jail and listened as the reporter asked Lucas about how many people he actually murdered. Lucas pondered the question briefly then held up three fingers.

From that day forward I was convinced that this simple-minded con artist was responsible for (1) the death of his mother, (2) the killing of eighty-year-old Kate Rich, and (3) the slaying of his teenage traveling companion, Frieda (Becky) Powell. Bad enough, but far shy of the hundreds he'd once claimed.

Lucas, however, could never stick to any one story for long. In time he decided to reduce the count to a paltry "one." He began to insist that the only person he'd ever killed was his mother. He said he had no idea who murdered Mrs. Rich, and the last time he'd seen Becky, the love of his life, she was being driven away by a long-haul trucker.

My fascination with the story began to wane. The truth, hidden somewhere at the core of a monumental Gordian knot, seemed impossible to reach. Henry Lee Lucas was a headache I didn't need. Still, throughout the eighties, it remained a modern-day tar baby impossible to escape. At the urging of a grand jury, the Texas attorney general's office began to investigate claims that dozens of Lucas' confessions weren't worth the paper they were written on. Verbal warfare erupted between keepers of the task force and a controversial McLennan County district attorney named Vic Feazell, who was hurling charges of corruption at those clearing cases. When word leaked that Attorney General Jim Maddox's report was going to be highly critical of the Lucas task force, things really hit the fan. The matter evolved into a political football that caused Feazell more trouble than he'd ever bargained for. When suddenly the target of a federal investigation himself, he insisted that it was in retaliation of the investigation he'd encouraged. "None of this would have happened," he said, "if I hadn't stepped on some big toes."

The once-popular prosecutor found himself the target of an investigation that resembled alphabet soup. For months he was dogged by the FBI, IRS, Texas Department of Safety, and Waco police, finally charged with bribery, conspiracy, and mail fraud. Tried in Austin in June 1991, he was acquitted of all charges. Later, in response to a series of reports about his alleged misdeeds aired by Dallas' WFAA-TV, Feazell won a stunning $58 million judgment against the Belo Corporation and its station.

Meanwhile, questions about Lucas only begged more questions. Was this guy really smart enough to have duped so many? Were we all guilty of being too eager to believe his impossible stories? Could it be that dozens, perhaps hundreds, of killers remained free, their crimes assigned to a man willing to take on the sins of the world? Had so many lies been told that the truth would, in fact, forever remain hidden?

For months I continued to follow the twists and turns. I spoke with a mother and father in Lubbock who were certain Lucas had nothing to do with the death of their daughter despite the fact he'd confessed to her murder. I learned of an alert Dallas homicide investigator who put together a fabricated crime, then listened to Lucas happily confess to it. I begrudgingly stayed in touch with Henry Lee, replying to his rambling letters, accepting his occasional long-distance phone calls, all in hopes of one day being able to write some defining end to the strange tale. In retrospect, I'd have been better off to cut my losses.

In the fall of 1994 I first began to hear the suggestions that Becky Powell, one of those I was sure Lucas killed, was alive and in hiding. Feazell, by then in private practice and having signed on as Lucas' newest lawyer, said he was determined to find her. I gave the matter little thought until I received one of those invitations a reporter can't refuse: Did I want to interview Becky who, at that very moment, was in Feazell's Austin home and who was ready to tell a story that would not only put all the lies to rest but even provide Lucas an alibi for the one homicide for which he'd received the death penalty?

How could I say no? It certainly wouldn't be my first wild-goose chase since first hearing Lucas' name.

She sipped a Coke and chain-smoked Cambridge cigarettes, her hazel eyes pinched as if to somehow help her remember small forgotten details. Frail looking at five-foot-seven and 109 pounds, she looked older than the twenty-seven she claimed to be, a fact she attributed to a three-pack-a-day habit and a hard life. For years, she explained, she had hidden her past, calling herself Phyllis Wilcox. "But you can call me Becky," she added.

She shared childhood memories of her prostitute mother dying of a drug overdose, being raped by her stepfather, and finally being sent away to a children's home. Later there would be an unhappy common-law marriage, an addiction to painkillers, and minor run-ins with the law. Hardly a happy story. Still, she looked remarkably good for someone who had been officially dead since age fifteen, remembered only as one of the hundreds of victims Lucas had originally claimed. She had a smile on her face, mirroring the excitement she was feeling for a trip she planned for the following day. She was going to pay a visit to the man who long ago confessed to killing her.

"I've asked him why he said all those things," she noted in a voice that sang with childlike innocence, "and he explained that he did it to protect me."

Now, it seemed, she was about to come to Lucas' rescue. For starters, the fact that she was alive would automatically eliminate one of the thirteen murders for which he'd received life prison sentences. If true, the story she had to tell could well prompt second thoughts about the lone death sentence he'd received.

On the night of October 31, 1979, the body of the unidentified victim was found in a culvert just off Interstate 35 near Georgetown, nude except for a pair of fuzzy orange socks on her feet. For four years the case remained unsolved until Lucas was asked if it might, in fact, be one of "his." By then a virtual confession machine, Lucas claimed responsibility, was tried and convicted, and was sentenced to death by injection.

Now, however, this woman swearing to be Frieda (Becky) Powell was explaining that it had been in 1979 when she met Lucas after her uncle, Ottis Toole, had brought him to the Jacksonville, Florida, home of her grandmother. She recalled in great detail how Lucas had taken her and her younger brother, Frank, trick-or-treating the first Halloween he lived there—the same night the "Orange Socks'" body was found in Texas.

"There's no way he could have committed that crime," she insisted. "He was with me and my brother."

In many of Lucas' most outlandish confessions, he included Toole as an accomplice on his cross-country murder rampage. In prison in Florida on charges of his own, Toole happily agreed with whatever story Lucas told. Both men routinely told authorities that Becky and Frank Powell accompanied them on their travels. Henry said he'd often used Becky as a decoy to gain entrance into strangers' homes, sending her to the door to say their car had broken down, that they were out of gas, or that they were cold, hungry, and looking for a place to stay for the night.

Reminded of that, the woman only shook her head. Never happened, she said. Her story of life with Lucas differed remarkably from that police officials had been hearing for years.

"While he was living in Jacksonville," she said, "he would take me with him to pick up scrap metal and junk. Sometimes we'd go through people's trash before the garbage trucks came. You can find a lot of good stuff that way—like lamps and things that Henry could fix up and sell.

"We became real close. He acted like he was my daddy, very protective."

Though raised by her grandparents, she recalled a time when she and her brother briefly lived with her mother and stepfather. "My stepfather raped me," she remembered, "and I was put in a girls school. Frank went to a boys school. I hated it and ran away, back to Henry. That's when he told me that he was afraid they (the authorities) would come and take me back, so we decided to leave." Ottis Toole, she said, accompanied them.

The strange threesome, joined by the girl's pet Chihuahua ("I had a little dog named Frieda," she said, "and my brother had one named Frank," she recalled), traveled westward in an old Oldsmobile driven by Lucas. After two weeks they arrived in Texas, and Toole, already weary of the road, turned back to Jacksonville, never to again be seen by Lucas or Becky. She told of how she and Henry Lee continued on despite growing hardships. He would, she remembered, regularly sell blood at local blood banks for gas money.

"Finally, somewhere in Texas the old car ran out of gas, and we just left it on the side of the road and started hitchhiking," she said. Ultimately, they were given a ride by a truck driver named Jack Smart and wound up in Hemet, California, in January 1982. For several months she and Lucas lived with the Smarts. (Smart and his wife would later insist that Lucas had, during a four-month period, never been out of their sight for more than a day. Meanwhile, police in other parts of the country used later Lucas confessions to clear eight murders that occurred during that same time period.)

"I remember one time when Jack and his wife, Obera, took us with them over to Palm Springs to go to a bunch of flea markets. That was the only time I remember ever leaving Hemet until we decided to come to Texas."

Their new destination was the tiny North Texas hamlet of Ringgold where Obera Smart's aged mother, Kate Rich, lived. "Mrs. Smart said her mother needed someone to take care of her and help her around the house. They gave us some money, put us on a bus, and off we went."

The arrangement: In exchange for room and board in Rich's home, Becky would cook and clean while Henry did repairs to the house.

"Ringgold was a tiny little ol' place," she recalled. "Sneeze as you pass through and you'll miss it. All it had was a grocery store. I hated it." She remembered eighty-year-old Kate Rich as being "kinda crazy," her house filthy, littered with dirty clothing, dirty dishes, and cat feces.

She recalls a daughter living in a nearby town who took an immediate disliking to the visitors. "She came to see Kate and said that we weren't taking care of her. She claimed we were spending her money and sleeping too much and that the house was still a mess. So she threw us out."

Next stop, a ramshackle religious retreat just a few miles down the road called the House of Prayer. Taken there by Reverend Ruben Moore, Henry and Becky took up residence in an "apartment" modeled from an old chicken barn. "It didn't even have a kitchen," she recalls. "We had to go into the church dining room to have our meals."

Still, it was a place where the wandering Lucas felt comfortable, tinkering with old cars and working at occasional roofing jobs. For Becky, fourteen at the time, life wasn't much fun. She would watch Lucas work on cars, at times allowed to drive them around the grounds once he had them running. She played on the piano inside the church. In time she began longing to return to Jacksonville. "I was tired of being broke and hungry," she says.

And that's where her story and Henry's reached a dramatic crossroads.

In one version, Lucas told authorities that he'd finally agreed to return with her to Jacksonville, so they set off hitchhiking. They got only as far as Denton before nightfall and decided to sleep in an open field just off the highway. They had argued; Becky had slapped him; and in what he described as an instinctive reaction, he pulled a knife and stabbed her to death. In an attempt to hide his crime, he'd dismembered her body and buried it in several shallow graves dug with the knife he'd used to take her life.

In yet another version, he recalled Becky's running away and his leaving later to search for her. At any rate, he eventually returned to the House of Prayer, where he tearfully told friends that Becky had left him, hitching a ride with a truck driver.

Now, I was hearing a new version: "Yes, I was homesick and wanted to leave," she said, "but Henry didn't. So a guy who lived at the House of Prayer named Gilbert Beagle gave me a ride to a truck stop in Bowie." All her belongings, she remembers, were stuffed into a grocery sack.

It was there, she recalls, that a long-haul trucker named Curtis Wilcox offered her a ride that would dramatically change both their lives. In a videotaped deposition, which I later viewed, Wilcox took up the story: He promised to drive the teenager to Jacksonville, but by the time they got there Becky had cooled on the idea of returning to relatives and possibly being sent back to the girls home.

"I was already regretting leaving Texas," she says, "and wanted to go back to Henry. But I couldn't ask Curtis to drive me back." Instead, she says, she and Wilcox rented an apartment in Jacksonville where they resided for several months.

To hide her real identity, she said, she took the first name Phyllis and assumed Wilcox's last name. "After a while Curtis suggested that we go live in Cape Girardeau [Missouri], where he had family." Frieda Lorraine (Becky) Powell then disappeared, and Phyllis Wilcox came into a generally unhappy existence. As the years passed, she would have two children, get her GED, and work for years as a cashier in a Texaco station eight miles down the road in Jackson. Putting her previous life behind her, she never attempted to contact her family. Or Henry Lee Lucas.

Clearly no student of current affairs, she insisted that it wasn't until 1991 that she learned of Lucas' murderous claims, recantations, and serpentine legal tangles. "I was in a bookstore one day," she remembered, "and saw Henry's picture on the cover of a paperback." The title: *Henry Lee Lucas: The Shocking True Story of America's Most Notorious Serial Killer.*

"It scared me," she said. "As I read it, I couldn't believe it was saying that Henry had done all these terrible murders. It even said I had been with him and helped him bury bodies. It just wasn't true."

Curious, she made some phone calls, located the prison in which Lucas was being held, and began to write him, always signing her married name. She even traveled to Texas to visit him and in time began to drop hints that she knew where Becky might be. With his date in the Huntsville Death House fast approaching, Lucas finally confided to Feazell that there was someone who might know where Becky was hiding. If she could be found, Lucas said, she could provide him an alibi that might help stay his scheduled execution.

Not convinced, Feazell nonetheless scheduled a trip to the Cape Girardeau address Lucas provided him. "I knocked on the door," he recalls, "and this woman I assumed to be Phyllis Wilcox answered. I asked where I might find Becky Powell. She smiled at me through the screen door and said, 'I'm Becky.'"

The stunned lawyer spent hours listening to her story, mentally matching it to facts he knew about his client's wandering life. Her detail and recall were remarkable. Her husband, whom he also interviewed at length, didn't seem at all reluctant to fill in the blanks about Becky's long-ago disappearance, nor did he demonstrate concern over the fact that his wife admitted she never stopped loving Henry Lee Lucas. "It was all pretty strange," Feazell remembers, "but that kind of thing had always swirled around Lucas. Everything about him seemed to come out of the twilight zone."

Would she, he asked the woman, accompany him back to Texas and submit to a polygraph test? "If it will help Henry," she replied. She passed with flying colors.

Later I looked over the questions and her responses: Is your real name Frieda Lorraine Powell? Yes. Were you born February 27, 1967? Yes. Were you called Becky? Yes. Did Henry Lee Lucas ever hurt anyone when you and he were together? No. Were you and Henry Lee Lucas in Jacksonville, Florida, on October 31, 1979? Yes.

Okay, I was convinced. It all fit together like a child's puzzle: the story she told me as a tape recorder played, the physical resemblance (she even had a tiny scar on her upper lip, much like the one I'd seen in a photo of a younger Becky), the videotaped deposition from Curtis Wilcox, the results of the polygraph test. I had one hell of an addition to the never-ending Henry Lee Lucas saga and was ready to write—that is, until an embarrassed Feazell phoned a few days later to tell me it was all a lie, carefully constructed and coached by (who else?) the man who made a career of conning people. The attorney found a series of letters from Lucas to Phyllis Wilcox in which he provided her the details of the story she agreed to tell. Confronted, Wilcox tearfully admitted playing the role of his long dead Becky Powell.

Why? "Because I love him," she said. Go figure.

For a reaction to the latest scam, I phoned Phil Ryan, the former Texas Ranger who originally investigated the murder of Becky, who listened to Lucas' confession, and who located her skeletal remains in the field where Lucas had said the murder occurred. "Hey, that's just the way Lucas is," he said. "The guy is like a circus that won't leave town."

Phyllis Wilcox, it turned out, wasn't born in 1967 and wasn't twenty-seven. She was a forty-year-old housewife who spent her entire life in Cape Girardeau, working at menial jobs, married for nineteen years. Like so many weary-of-life women across the country, she became fascinated by the serial killers as pop-culture celebrities. She read everything she could find on Jeffrey Dahmer, John Wayne Gacy, and Ted Bundy. Then she'd happened on the book about Lucas. "There was something about him that really got to me," she said. "Soon, he was all I thought about. We started corresponding and then I went to visit him in prison. One thing led to another." After seeing that she resembled Becky Powell on their first face-to-face visit, Lucas proposed the plot. "I started thinking like Becky," she admitted. "I was beginning to believe I really was Becky. She took over my life."

In time, her sad story was of interest only to the supermarket tabloids. "Back from the Dead," screamed one headline. Then the story went on to detail the deception that occurred. After a couple of goofy television talk show appearances, Phyllis Wilcox's fifteen minutes of fame passed.

Of course, Lucas had his own explanation for it all. A new story. He told members of the press who made their weekly prison stop for inmate interviews that he was "hurt bad" by Wilcox's recanting. "Now," he said, "she's lying. I just don't get it. She knowed things we'd done together, things nobody else could have knowed." This time, however, he got little mileage from his weary listeners.

The furor of the latest Lucas scam attempt had already died when, one evening, I answered the phone to hear a long-distance operator say that I had a collect call from Lucas. "Will you accept charges?" she asked.

"No," I replied for the first time. Then, realizing that he was likely listening for my response, I added emphasis. "Not only 'no,'" I said, "but 'hell no.'" Finally, I had too belatedly realized, the time had come to put the life and lies of Henry Lee Lucas behind me.

A KILLER ABROAD

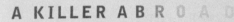

IN 1977,
TYLER NATIVE
HOLLY MADDUX
WAS MURDERED BY
EARTH DAY CREATOR
IRA EINHORN.
MORE THAN TWO
DECADES LATER,
HER FAMILY IS
STILL WAITING
FOR THE FUGITIVE
TO RETURN.

BY CARLTON STOWERS

Violence always marks the end of a relationship."
—from the journals of convicted murderer Ira Einhorn

On days like this, when the wintry skies signal a chill, she stands at her kitchen window looking out onto the rolling Tarrant County pasture where a couple of mares leisurely feed on the rain-browned grass. And a memory, nearing a quarter century old, comes rushing back for Elizabeth (Buffy) Hall.

Speaking in a soft, raspy voice, the 41-year-old mother of two recalls a long ago high-school-sponsored trip abroad that provided a surprise opportunity to briefly see her older sister, who was visiting London. There, as they spoke of friends and family, of old times as children growing up in Tyler, Texas, as they assured each other of their respective well-being, Hall had no way of knowing it was the last time she would see Helen (Holly) Maddux alive.

Or that soon one of the driving forces in her life and those of her siblings would be a seemingly endless demand for justice that has been glacially slow in coming.

Just a matter of days after Hall saw Holly, eldest of the five Maddux children, one-time John Tyler High School honor student, cheerleader and graduate of Bryn Mawr University, her sister disappeared. Eighteen months later, in March 1979, her mummified body, grotesquely withered from 110 to just 37 pounds, was found inside a steamer trunk, hidden away in the padlocked closet of her Philadelphia lover. The medical examiner's report indicated she had suffered at least six blows to the head "with an inordinate amount of force."

Arrested and charged with murder was Ira Einhorn, a controversial Philly celebrity whom Maddux had, during that long ago London visit, told her then-36-year-old suitor she was planning to leave. "She told me that day that she was going to return to the United States and begin a new life which did not include Ira," Buffy Hall remembers. "When I got home and told my parents, they were so thrilled they wanted to dance in the street."

continued on page 36

4

A KILLER ABROAD

Violence always marks the end of a relationship. . . .

—from the journals of convicted murderer Ira Einhorn

On days like this, when the wintry skies are gray and weeping, signaling the chill a new season will soon bring, she stands at her kitchen window looking out onto the rolling Tarrant County pasture, where a couple of mares leisurely feed on the rain-greened grass. On days like this, a memory nearing a quarter-century old comes rushing back for Elisabeth (Buffy) Hall.

Speaking in a soft, raspy voice, the forty-one-year-old mother of two recalls a long-ago high school–sponsored trip abroad that provided a surprise opportunity to briefly see her older sister who was visiting London. As they spoke of friends and family, of old times as children growing up in Tyler, Texas, and as they assured each other of their respective well-being, Hall had no way of knowing it was the last time she would see Helen (Holly) Maddux alive. Nor did she know that soon one of the driving forces in her life and those of her siblings would be a seemingly endless demand for justice that has been glacially slow in coming.

Just a matter of days after Hall saw Holly, eldest of the five Maddux children, one-time John Tyler High School honor student, cheerleader, and graduate of Bryn Mawr, her sister disappeared. Eighteen months later—in March 1979—her mummified body, grotesquely withered from 110 to just 37 pounds, was found inside a steamer trunk hidden away in the padlocked closet of her Philadelphia lover. The medical examiner's report indicated that she suffered at least six blows to the head "with an inordinate amount of force."

53

Arrested and charged with murder was Ira Einhorn, a controversial Philly celebrity whom Maddux had, during that long-ago London visit, told her then sixteen-year-old sister she was planning to leave. "She told me that day that she was going to return to the United States and begin a new life, which did not include Ira," Buffy remembers. "When I got home and told my parents, they were so thrilled they wanted to dance in the street."

Finally, the Maddux family had reason to believe, the disastrous and destructive five-year relationship Holly had fallen into was coming to an end. But not in the nightmarish manner that haunts them to this day. It was, in retrospect, a pairing that from the outset seemed as improbable as it was passionate.

Young Holly, pretty and smart enough to be eligible for Mensa membership, eager to break the bonds of her quiet Texas upbringing, ignored the pleas of her conservative, authoritarian father to consider enrolling at Texas A&M and traveled east. Leaving the class of '65 behind, she wanted to explore an outside world that included a more intellectual, free-thinking lifestyle. "She was," reflects former John Tyler classmate Jim Rex, "probably ten years ahead of everybody else in her thinking." While most of her classmates were content with the traditional southern mindset of Texas teenagers—dating, football games, pop music, and leisurely good times—she supplemented her academic successes with studies of ballet and judo, art and synchronized swimming.

In October 1972, having graduated from Bryn Mawr with a fine arts degree and in the process of determining the next step in her life, the petite blonde was introduced to Einhorn in a Philadelphia restaurant where the local celebrity often held court. Two weeks later she moved into his apartment, beginning a volatile relationship that, according to friends, was equal parts love and hate, always controlled by the enigmatic and charismatic Einhorn.

Seven years older, Einhorn, a Philadelphia native, was a product of and an active participant in the drugs-sex-and-rock-and-roll movement of the sixties. While Holly Maddux expressed her modest delight in being named salutatorian and a class favorite at her Tyler high school, Ira Einhorn flaunted his youthful rebellion by wearing jeans and tennis shoes instead of the traditional tuxedo to the Philadelphia Central High senior prom. By the time he'd earned his degree from the University of Pennsylvania, he was an advocate and spokesman for the growing drug culture. For good measure, Philadelphia's ego-driven answer to Abbie Hoffman and Allen Ginsberg wrote and lectured on subjects ranging from the environmental to his belief in UFOs, the ills of the Vietnam War to quantum physics, the paranormal to the benefits of LSD use. The bearded, long-haired hippie-turned-New-Age-guru authored a regular column for a local underground newspaper, signing his rambling, overwritten essays as "The Unicorn." At one time the man who delighted in referring to himself as a "planetary enzyme" even ran a half-hearted campaign for mayor of Philadelphia.

What propelled him from local oddity to full-blown avant-garde celebrity, however, was his involvement in the organizing and staging of Earth Day, a highly publicized celebration of environmental issues in 1970. From that point his mainstream credibility grew—to a point where local Fortune 500 business leaders sought his advice and offered consultant contracts in exchange for his expertise on a variety of social issues. Harvard even summoned him to serve as a teaching fellow, lecturing students on the counterculture of the day.

Thus Ira Einhorn, self-described pacifist and freethinker, had carved himself a high-profile niche. Through much of the seventies, girlfriend Holly Maddux alternately warmed in the glow of his fame while at the same time feeling it dramatically suffocate her own ambitions. Yet on the numerous occasions when she would be angered by Einhorn's domination, physical abuse, and regular infidelities and attempts to break away, the results were routinely the same. Promising change and devotion, Ira would lure her back. Always to the disappointment of Holly's family.

Meg Wakeman, forty-four, now a nurse living in Seattle, recalls the first time she met the man ultimately convicted of killing her sister: "She brought him to Tyler just once," Wakeman remembers, "and he went out of his way to be unpleasant to everyone. One evening as we sat down for dinner, he began eating and reaching across the table for food, even as my father was saying grace. Later, while we were sitting in the living room, Holly came in with the family photo album and asked Ira if he would like to see pictures of her when she was a child. He said, 'No, comb my hair.' I'll never forget the hurt look on Holly face as she put the album aside and went to find a comb and brush. He just smiled, as if pleased that he'd shown everyone in the room he was in complete control."

John Maddux, fifty-two, recalls Einhorn as "dirty and gross." "Everyone in the family was appalled," he says. Wakeman also remembers a letter received from her sister two years later, in the summer of 1977. "She wrote that she had decided to leave him and was so pleased that she'd finally realized she was not only capable of living on her own, but really looking forward to it."

That letter, she remembers, arrived shortly before her thirty-year-old sister vanished.

> In Ira Einhorn's mind, he is the only individual in the world
> with real intelligence. The rest of us are supposed to sit at
> his feet, spellbound by his every nonsensical word. . . .
>
> —John Maddux, Holly's brother

Despite the fact that their relationship had disintegrated into an ongoing litany of arguments and separations, Holly had, in 1977, reluctantly agreed to accompany Einhorn on a four-month research and lecture trip to Europe. Through Denmark, Sweden, and Norway they argued. Things got even worse as they arrived in London. On July 28, just days after her brief visit with her younger sister, Maddux finally asserted her independence and returned to the United States alone. Her plan, she told Einhorn, was to find an apartment and begin her life away from him.

As soon as he returned to Philadelphia, however, Einhorn began pressuring her to reconsider. When charm failed, he threatened to throw clothing she'd left behind into the street if she didn't immediately come to his apartment for her possessions. Once more she allowed herself to be lured back into the Unicorn's world. On the Saturday night of September 11, in fact, the couple, apparently reconciled, double-dated with friends, attending a movie in nearby New Jersey.

And then Holly Maddux disappeared.

In the days that followed, Einhorn's explanation would take on a mantra-like tone: He had, he said, been taking a bath when Holly decided to leave on a grocery-shopping trip to the nearby Ecology Food co-op. The next he heard from her was a phone call two days later. "I'm okay," she allegedly said. "Don't look for me. I'll call you once a week." That no further calls came did not seem to concern him. If Ira was distraught over his girlfriend's leave-taking, he hid it well, continuing with his ambitious social and professional schedule.

In Tyler, however, genuine concern quickly mounted. "All her life," says Buffy Hall, "Holly had been good about staying in touch with the family. Then, suddenly, the letters and calls stopped. So did the handmade cards she always sent us on our birthdays. There were three birthdays in the family in the month of October and no one heard from her."

When Liz Maddux phoned Einhorn to ask about her sister, she got little information. Though he was unusually polite and expressed concern (pointing out he'd called Holly's friends, hospitals, and the police when she did not return to his apartment), he expressed no real interest in attempting to find the young woman who had been living with him for five years. "I was left with the impression," Liz recalls of the ten-minute conversation, "that he felt she'd gone off somewhere to collect her thoughts and didn't want any of us to contact her."

By the time Christmas and New Year's Day passed without word, genuine fear that something ominous had happened to her was growing among Maddux's family. Her father, Fredrick, sought out retired Tyler FBI-agent-turned-private-investigator R. J. Stevens and hired him to find their daughter. The search would go on for over a year, eventually broadening to include investigators, police, and, finally, the district attorney's office in Philadelphia.

What would ultimately point the way to a resolution of the mystery were statements by college students living in an apartment directly below Einhorn and the offhand recollection of two of Ira's young female friends. For months after Holly's disappearance, the downstairs neighbors attempted every chemical they could think of—ammonia, Lysol, bleach—to mask a growing stench emitting from a dark liquid that oozed through the ceiling of their kitchen closet. One of the residents, a biology major, had even observed to his roommate that the smell was "much like that of dried blood." The odor, he suggested, was coming from the apartment above them. Months would pass before the smell finally began to wane.

Then there had been the September evening when Einhorn asked the two teenage girls if they would help him haul a trunk allegedly filled with "secret Russian documents" to the nearby Schuylkill River where he planned to dump it. The young women, arguing that their car was too small to accommodate it, refused. Finally, acting on the information collected by investigators, Philadelphia police detective Mike Chitwood, accompanied by six uniformed officers, knocked on Einhorn's door on the morning of March 28, 1979. In hand he had a thirty-five-page search warrant.

In his 1988 book on the case, *The Unicorn's Secret, Newsday* writer Steven Levy deftly reconstructed what occurred that day at the 3411 Race Street apartment:

> Almost as if Chitwood had no interest in the apartment itself—though in fact he had never seen a place with so many books, and it held a strange fascination for him—he brushed aside the maroon blanket covering the French door. He walked purposefully to the closet, stopped, and contemplated the thick Master padlock on the door. . . . The closet was 4 1/2 feet wide and 8 feet high, and a little less than 3 feet deep. . . . Inside some of the boxes he saw were labeled "Maddux." On the floor was a green suitcase. On the handle was the name "Holly Maddux" and a Texas address. Behind the suitcase on the closet floor was a large black steamer trunk. . . .
>
> Michael Chitwood took off his suit jacket. He was now ready to open the trunk. The foul odor was now much stronger. . . . Scooping away newspapers and a layer of Styrofoam and plastic bags, he at first could not make out what it was because it was so wrinkled and tough. But then he saw the shape of it—wrist, palm, and five fingers, curled and frozen in their stillness. It was a human hand. . . . He had seen enough.

The discovery of Holly Maddux's body and the arrest of Einhorn bumped even the potential nuclear disaster at nearby Three Mile Island from the lead position on the front page of the *Philadelphia Daily News.* "Hippie Guru Held in Trunk Murder," the banner headline read.

In Tyler, during a driving April rain, Holly Maddux was buried.

Meanwhile, Einhorn's explanation of the morbid discovery in his apartment was as vague as it was preposterous: The CIA and Soviet KGB, eager to shut down research he'd been doing on the military use of mind control, had sought to frame him, placing Maddux's body in his apartment. High-placed friends and devoted followers quickly spoke out, suggesting it was impossible that the colorful pacifist they so admired could have committed such a horrible crime.

Which served as good indication that they knew nothing of the Unicorn's dark side. In journals taken from his apartment, the authorities found detailed recollections of previous violence. He wrote of entering the college dorm room of one former girlfriend and strangling her until she passed out. In a fit of rage, he hit another in the head with a Coke bottle, knocking her unconscious.

Represented by highly regarded defense attorney Arlen Specter, now the well-known U.S. senator from Pennsylvania, Einhorn's bail was reduced from one hundred thousand dollars to forty thousand—his mother, Beatrice, put her house up as collateral for the paltry four thousand he would actually have to post—and a January 1981 trial was set. It was a date the defendant never intended to keep.

On the eve of his pretrial hearing, Einhorn fled the country.

The shattered Maddux family was left to deal with its grief and frustration. In 1988, Fred Maddux, the once proud and gregarious ex-member of the 82nd Airborne that had parachuted into Normandy on D-Day, took his own life. "He was depressed and angry," says daughter Buffy. "He just finally gave up. Through the last nine years of his life, he was racked with guilt, wondering if there was something he could have said or done to prevent Holly from going so far away from home. He never forgave himself." Five months pregnant at the time of her father's death, Hall has gone through a routine of intense therapy in an effort to cope with the family tragedies and Einhorn's escape from justice. "For a long time," she says, "I didn't handle Holly's death at all well. I tried keeping it all inside, and that was a disaster. Had I not had obligations to my own family, it would have been tough to even get out of bed."

Brother John, a former marine and Vietnam veteran, retreated to a solitary life on a small farm outside of Alvarado. He never married. "Holly's death is something I've never been able to turn loose," he says. "Most people my age are now grandfathers. But I've felt for all these years that my life is just on hold. I've just gone through the motions."

The Maddux family's youngest, Mary, thirty-eight and living in Stockbridge, Massachusetts, says John, still fights an ongoing battle with the pain and anger she feels over Holly's death and the fact Einhorn still remains free.

Two years after Fred Maddux's suicide, his wife, Elizabeth, died. "Ira Einhorn not only killed our sister," Hall says. "He took our parents away as well."

> If it is necessary, I'll be old and in a wheelchair, still chasing him.
> —Rich DiBenedetto,
> Philadelphia assistant district attorney

★   ★   ★

Convinced of his innocence, Canadian Barbara Bronfman, wife of one of the Seagram owners, financed Einhorn's escape. With financial backing, Einhorn fled to Ireland, a country that at the time had no extradition agreement with the United States, and there, he settled into an apartment in the Rathmines section of Dublin. To his landlord, he was Ira Einhorn. To others in his new circle of friends and benefactors, he alternately introduced himself as a writer named "Ben Moore" and, on occasion, "Ian Morrison."

It would be three years before Philadelphia authorities learned of his whereabouts.

When the couple from whom he was renting his apartment announced they were planning a vacation trip to the United States, the secretive Einhorn specifically requested that they not mention his name to anyone during their American visit. Collette and Dennis Weaire—both troubled by the mood swings and secretive behavior they'd witnessed during his stay—chose to ignore the request and instead made plans to see what they could find out about the boarder living on the third floor of their brownstone once they reached Chicago.

Shortly after their arrival, in fact, a firecracker-like series of events transpired. Mrs. Weaire told a friend about their strange tenant. The friend contacted a reporter at the *Chicago Sun-Times*. In turn, that reporter got in touch with a fellow journalist working for the *Philadelphia Inquirer* who, naturally, knew the trunk murder story by heart.

Upon learning the facts of Einhorn's background, Dennis Weaire contacted the Irish Consulate in Chicago and was told to immediately get in touch with the FBI. Within a matter of days he was being shown a photograph of Einhorn and quickly identified it as a picture of the man living in his home.

In mid-October 1981, a Philadelphia police sergeant assigned to the case flew to Dublin with a twofold purpose: He hoped to locate Einhorn and, more important, somehow convince the Irish authorities to allow him to be returned to the United States. The trip proved to be a waste of time. Before the officer's arrival, the Unicorn had moved from the Weaires' apartment to parts unknown.

For the next few years, Richard DiBenedetto, an extraditions officer in the Philadelphia district attorney's office, doggedly continued the search for the accused murderer with no success. His fugitive, it seemed, had simply vanished. Another five years would pass before DiBenedetto received word that his prey had again been sighted in Ireland, near the campus of Dublin's Trinity College where, under an assumed name, he was teaching. Encouraged by the fact that an extradition treaty with Ireland had recently been reinstated, authorities planned a trip abroad in hopes of arresting Einhorn. But even before arrangements could be made in that summer of 1986, word came that Einhorn had abruptly decided to leave the country, his new destination unknown.

The frustration in both Philadelphia and Tyler had become a dull, ever-present ache as the eighties drew to a close with Einhorn still a free man. When, finally, a tip that he was seen in Sweden with a wealthy woman named Annika Flodin resulted from a segment on the case aired by the television show *America's Most Wanted*, Stockholm police visited the address only to be told by Flodin that Einhorn no longer lived there. The trim, blond Swede, who bore a remarkable resemblance to Holly Maddux, soon disappeared herself. The Sweden sighting of Einhorn would be the last solid lead to cross DiBenedetto's desk for seven years.

In Philadelphia, meanwhile, the district attorney decided to exercise a newly established judicial process. Einhorn, it was determined, would be tried in absentia; in effect, a murder trial would be conducted during which the defendant, though represented by counsel, would not be present during the proceedings. In September 1993, a jury deliberated for three hours before finding Einhorn guilty of first-degree murder and sentenced to life in prison for the murder of Holly Maddux.

Memories of the nine-day trial still haunt Buffy Hall. "Sitting in that courtroom, listening to the medical examiner detail the blows that Holly suffered—and even suggest it was possible that she had still been alive when she was placed in that trunk—was one of the most difficult things I've ever experienced," she says. For weeks after, nightmarish images interrupted her sleep.

"Over time," she reflects, "your mind plays strange games. For whatever reason, I had always assumed Holly's death was the result of some fit of jealous rage. But hearing testimony that indicated Einhorn had done things like purchase the trunk just days earlier, something even more horrible soaked in. It had been premeditated. He was planning to kill her, even as they went out to dinner and a movie with friends that night."

In Philadelphia, assistant district attorney DiBenedetto renewed his vows to bring Einhorn back to American soil.

> He's still the arrogant, sarcastic jerk he was the day we found the body. He's all bullshit, a bum, a con man . . . a coward.
>
> —former Philadelphia detective Mike Chitwood

On his fifty-seventh birthday, Ira Einhorn's luck finally ran out. DiBenedetto, with help from Interpol, followed a paper trail of the Swedish woman whom Einhorn married in 1982, and he learned on May 15, 1997, that she applied for a driver's license in France. She told local authorities her name was Annika Flodin Mallon, giving an address on the outskirts of Champagne-Mouton, southwest of Paris, as her new home.

Several French undercover officers, posing as tourists and fishermen, visited the quaint village and determined that Annika Flodin was indeed living in a restored mill with an American who generally fit Einhorn's description. The man, who was known locally as Eugene Mallon, said he was a writer. A bit thinner than he'd been in his glory days in Philadelphia, his hair was gray and cut shorter, the trademark bushy beard now only a stringy white goatee.

In the early morning hours of June 13, French authorities arrested Einhorn. Though arguing that some mistake had been made, a fingerprint comparison quickly proved he was, in fact, the fugitive for whom American authorities had been searching for sixteen years.

Upon hearing the news that her sister's killer had been arrested, Buffy Hall took flowers to Holly's gravesite. "I cried and I told her, 'We finally got him,'" she remembers. "And I began looking forward to seeing him returned to the United States to serve his sentence."

However, neither the Maddux family nor the Philadelphia district attorney's office anticipated the legal quagmire that would soon develop. Returning Einhorn to the United States, they soon learned, would prove to be every bit as difficult as finding him had been. As the convicted killer sat in Bordeaux's Gradignan Prison, his French legal team prepared to argue that his American trial in absentia was in violation of the European Convention on Human Rights. Under French law, he would have to be given a new trial. Back in Pennsylvania, state statutes offered no such provision; Einhorn had already been convicted and thus should begin serving his long-delayed life sentence immediately upon his return. Lending weight to the legal logjam was the anti-American mind-set of the French who viewed the United States justice system, which included the death penalty they so strongly opposed, as patently cruel and often barbaric.

Twice, members of the Maddux family traveled to France in anticipation of hearings, only to learn after their arrival at the Bordeaux courthouse that the decision on Einhorn's fate had not yet been reached. What they did learn, however, was that the French press was not only skeptical but also highly suspicious of their reason for being there. "The general attitude," recalls Buffy Hall, "was one of not being able to understand how, after twenty years, we were even concerned. I had several reporters ask why we were still upset over the matter; why we didn't just put it behind us and move on. The opinion seemed to be that after such a long period of time, Ira had certainly paid for whatever sins he committed and should be left alone.

"I think, in fact, that we were viewed as a pack of gunslingers from the Texas old west, come to town to assassinate the man who had killed our sister. The French seemed bewildered by our presence, totally oblivious to the obscenity of what this man had done."

Finally, at a December hearing before the French Cour d'Appeal (Court of Appeals), the extradition request was denied since American authorities could not legally agree to a retrial. In a matter of minutes, Einhorn was released from custody. The only time Holly's name was even mentioned, brother John says, was when Ira walked to a microphone in front of the bench to say, "I did not kill Holly Maddux." And then, John remembers, Einhorn laughed.

The lone restriction given Einhorn's freedom was a demand that he report his whereabouts twice a week to authorities investigating the possibility that he had violated French immigration laws by entering the country on a false passport.

Shortly before 4 A.M. on a Friday in Seattle, Meg Wakeman, unable to make another trip abroad because of her job, received news of the French court's decision. "Initally," she recalls, "I was shocked. Then I became angry. It occurred to me that in protecting Ira Einhorn's civil rights they had never even bothered to consider the civil rights of my sister. To that point I had been reluctant to really get involved in the matter. It was just too painful. But on the day they set him free, I decided to go into an activist mode. The whole family did."

"We got together," says Buffy Hall, "and came to a decision that we could do one of two things: We could roll over, or we could fight like hell. We decided on the latter."

Thus, while Einhorn and his wife shopped the markets in Champagne-Mouton, chatting with shopkeepers and smiling for news cameras and driving through town in their red Fiat, the Maddux family vowed to launch a campaign for justice that continues to this day. They began lobbying government officials from the White House to the State Department, initiated a website, and sought the ear of any member of the media willing to hear their story of unserved justice. Supporters of their cause were urged to wear holly-shaped pins and ribbons as a reminder of their sister's murder.

They quickly found they were not without allies. In Pennsylvania, state legislators, citing news reports of France's judicial decision, voted to revise the law, clearing the way for Einhorn to be retried if returned to the United States. A petition demanding the fugitive's extradition and signed by five thousand Philadelphians was sent to French government officials. Television news shows from NBC's *Dateline*, *20-20*, *Unsolved Mysteries*, and as far away as Germany reported on the nightmarish story that seemed to have no end. Network officials began plans to develop a made-for-television movie based on Levy's book on the case.

Learning that Einhorn had contacted an American publisher about a book he was allegedly writing about the case, the Maddux family decided to file a civil suit, charging him with the wrongful death of their sister. After a two-day trial in the summer of 1999, Philadelphia jurors found Einhorn guilty and ordered that he pay a staggering $907 million in damages. "We never expect to see a penny of that," says John Maddux, "but the trial served its purpose. Part of the ruling was that he would not be allowed to profit in any way from Holly's murder. And it sent a message to him that he was not going to be allowed to get away with what he did—and that we weren't going away."

In France, Einhorn did not respond to legal papers delivered to his home. But, in an interview with the syndicated talk show *Radio America*, he told an interviewer, "I am innocent of the crime and will declare that until my dying breath."

In February 1999, Buffy and sister Mary made yet another trip to France to attend a hearing on the requested extradition, this time accompanied by *America's Most Wanted* producer John Walsh, who planned to film yet another show on the serpentine case.

"I was fully expecting to hear an unfavorable outcome," Hall says, "so I'd prepared myself to be disappointed. All I had really hoped for was the opportunity to finally look Ira in the eye and let him know how I felt about him."

Again, she found, her memory had played tricks on her. "Oddly, my first thought upon seeing him was that he was not nearly as tall as I had remembered him to be. Over the years I'd come to think of him as a much bigger man. What I finally saw, though, was just a short, fat guy with a really bad haircut."

At one point during the proceedings, in fact, Einhorn stood no more than five feet from her but for some time refused to even make eye contact. "Finally," she remembers, "he turned to me with this evil smile on his face, as if he already knew what the court's decision would be."

Soon, however, that smile would vanish when the judge announced a ruling in favor of the extradition order. "I don't speak French," Buffy says, "and had no interpreter, so I didn't know what had happened until John Walsh leaned over and began hugging me, saying, 'You won. He's out of here.' All I can remember is bursting into tears."

The ruling specifically included the agreement by U.S. authorities that Einhorn would, upon returning to Philadelphia, be granted a new trial and that the death penalty would not be sought.

Though French prime minister Lionel Jospin finally signed the extradition papers in July, the victory has thus far been a hollow one. The court ruled that Einhorn could remain free while awaiting an appeal of the decision to the Conseil d'Etat (Council of State), and legal authorities in both France and the United States anticipate that the process will take two years, perhaps longer.

Thus, the long-running saga continues. Once encouraged by the court's ruling, Buffy Hall and John Maddux gauge the chances of the now sixty-year-old Einhorn's being returned to a Philadelphia court-room at "something like 80 percent—on good days."

"Who knows how long he and his lawyers can drag out the appeal process, what rabbits they can keep pulling out of the hat to keep him there," Hall says. "And, what concerns me even more is the very real possibility that once he sees things aren't going well for him, he will disappear again. I don't think anyone doubts that will happen."

Last spring in Philadelphia, a radio station, taking note of the fact it was harvest season for family gardens, sponsored an off-the-wall promotional contest asking that listeners submit any tomato that bore a resemblance to the man once lionized as a countercultural hero in the city. All entries would ultimately be thrown at a life-sized picture of Einhorn provided by the station. The oddball show of distaste for the city's fallen hero received considerable publicity. Holly's sister, Mary, had even traveled from her Stockbridge, Massachusetts, home to attend.

"My guess is," says Buffy Hall, "that when he got word of that kind of demonstration, frivolous though it might have been, it deeply bruised Ira's enormous ego. What they were doing was making fun of him, and that is something he could never tolerate."

Indeed, it must have had its effect. Following a recent—and again unsuccessful—attempt to convince the prime minister to reconsider extraditing him, Einhorn held a brief press conference. When a local reporter asked if he felt any compassion for the Maddux family, his reply was, "What I have to say about the Maddux family is: Let them eat tomatoes."

"That," says Philadephia district attorney Lynne Abraham, "is a perfect example of the arrogance and unrepentance of Ira Einhorn."

For Buffy Hall and her siblings, it is that psychopathic arrogance and unrepentant attitude that now fuels their cause, energizing their determination to see justice done for a sister who, if still alive, would have recently celebrated her fiftieth birthday.

"We're human," says John. "We get discouraged and tired, but it seems that every time one of us gets down, there's someone in the family there to lift us up." The Maddux siblings, he notes, lean upon each other a great deal.

"We may not be all that strong individually," adds Buffy, "but we like to think we have great strength in numbers."

She says that for a time the only mental picture she could summon of her deceased sister was the one burned into her memory during that long-ago trial in Philadelphia. "All I could ever see was Holly lying dead in that trunk," she says. "But now, after a lot of therapy and passage of time, things are different. When I think of her now, I see her alive and laughing, pretty and happy. And that helps a great deal."

No longer do thoughts of Ira Einhorn monopolize her life. Retired from a career in nursing, she helps her husband, a financial administrator at the University of Texas at Arlington, tend the quarter horses they raise and show and serves on the board of a Fort Worth women's shelter. She delights in the simple pleasures of watching her own children grow.

There is son Ian, born shortly after her father's death. And a daughter. Named Holly.

POSTSCRIPT

In July 2001, Einhorn was finally extradited to the United States. He appeared in a Philadelphia court and filed papers requesting a new trial. Now broke and displaying little of the arrogance that was once his trademark, he will be represented by a court-appointed attorney when he is again tried for the murder of Holly Maddux.

Seated on the front row of a crowded Philadelphia courtroom in October of 2002, John Maddux, uncomfortable in the slacks and coat he'd been wearing for the past two weeks, finally broke into a broad smile. For the quiet and reserved man who prefers jeans and the solitude of his rural Alverado home, it was a rare emotional demonstration. Beside him, his three sisters were crying, signaling relief that their long and painful odyssey had finally reached a just end.

Nearby, sixty-two-year-old Ira Einhorn, once the high-profile counterculture guru of Philly's hippie generation, the man who had called himself "The Unicorn" and boastfully took credit for everything from the Earth Day celebration to establishment of the Environmental Protection Agency, had been found guilty of the murder of their sibling Holly and sentenced to life in prison.

Justice had taken over two decades.

DALLAS

THE WEEKLY NEWSPAPER OF DALLAS ■ OCTOBER 31, 1991

Observer

The wimp factor

Laura Miller on school super Marvin Edwards, p.5

FATAL RAGE

THE LAST, ANGRY DAYS OF GEORGE HENNARD. BY CARLTON STOWERS *P.11*

Pixie schtick: Black Francis on bananas, *p.39*

DTC's breathtaking *Substance of Fire*, p.27

5

FATAL RAGE

She was squeezing lemon into her iced tea when the blue Ford pickup crashed through the front window of the cafeteria. Legal secretary Mona Deorsam's first thought was that the driver had lost control of his vehicle. But then came the horrifying sound of gunshots. For the attractive mother of two, a nightmare that still haunts her had begun.

"I had just gone through the service line," she remembers, "and noticed that one of the busboys was cleaning off a table near the front window. I asked the women with me if they wanted to sit up there, but one of them was a smoker, so we found a table near the rear of the building.

"We had just sat down when I heard this terrible sound. Suddenly, there was this truck coming to a stop in the middle of the dining area. Bodies were flying everywhere. Then this man stepped out and immediately started shooting people who were lying on the floor near him.

"We got down on the floor, under our table, crying and praying.

"One of the girls I was with whispered to me that he was there to rob everyone, so I slipped my wedding ring off my finger and put it into my mouth. Then I grabbed the hand of the woman I was next to and tried to see where he was. He was just walking around the room, shooting people. He seemed so calm; there was an almost casual manner about the way he was shooting people. I kept counting the shots, thinking he would run out of bullets and it would all be over.

"He came to our table and I just knew that I was going to die. Thoughts of my husband and my kids were going through my mind. Of all the ways to go, I never dreamed it would be anything like that. I was crying so hard my body was heaving, and I placed one hand over my face.

"Then I heard another shot and the hand I was holding went limp.

"He turned away and started walking back in the direction of his truck, shooting some more people along the way. But in a couple of minutes he came back in the direction of our table. I was sure he was coming to finish what he had started. There was nothing I could do. It was such a helpless feeling. We were just at his mercy.

"For whatever reason, he didn't shoot. He was close enough that I could have touched his shoes with my hand. I knew he was aware I wasn't dead because I couldn't stop crying. I looked up at him, and he stared down at me for a second then turned away.

"That was when a man threw himself through a window, providing an escape route. Suddenly, everyone was pushing and shoving, knocking each other down to get out. I looked up to see where the man was and saw that he was near his truck, shooting in the direction of those going out the window.

"There was an exit door right behind me, so I reached up and opened it slightly then crawled out on my hands and knees. I managed to get outside and hide behind a trash dumpster.

"I could see the people who had made it out the window, running in every direction. People were crying and bloody. None of it seemed real. It was like being trapped in a horror movie. I felt like I'd been through hell."

What Mona Deorsam had lived to tell about was, in fact, one deranged man's . . .

Dawn was just breaking as sixty-year-old Mary Mead began her long-established routine of opening the Leon Heights Drive-In convenience store for business. She brewed coffee, checked the pastry shelf and the contents of the cash register, then wiped off the counter before unlocking the front door and, as she'd been doing for weeks, frowned out at the construction work on Belton's Main Street. The detour signs and mounds of dirt had made it increasingly difficult for customers to reach her store. No question, she thought, the ongoing street work was hurting business.

The mazelike disrepair, however, did not deter the man who was riding in her direction on a ten-speed bicycle, coming from his nearby East Fourteenth Street home to buy his early morning junk-food break-fast. Mead recalls that nothing in the demeanor of the customer sug-gested he was on the brink of a violent explosion. He was, in fact, al-most pleasant when he purchased his doughnuts, candy bar, orange juice, sausage-and-biscuit sandwich, newspaper, and a pack of Winstons that morning. It was still seven hours before George Pierre Hennard—an angry, troubled, out-of-work seaman just one day past his thirty-fifth birthday—would write the bloodiest chapter in the nation's chilling his-tory of mass murders.

Shortly after noon on Wednesday, October 16, 1991, Hennard drove his blue Ford Ranger pickup through the front window of a Luby's Cafeteria in nearby Killeen and methodically set about killing twenty-three people and wounding twenty-seven others before taking his own life with the final bullet left in his Glock 17 semiautomatic pistol.

As he walked through the panicked crowd of an estimated 150 cus-tomers, many of them there in celebration of National Boss's Day, he yelled crazed obscenities about "viperous women" and it being "payback time." "This," he said again and again as his fifteen-minute killing spree went on, "is what Bell County has done to me. Was it worth it? Was it worth it?"

Before the rampage ended, fifteen of his trapped victims died from point-blank shots to the head. Others were shot in the chest and stom-ach, with several receiving multiple wounds. Repeatedly, he approached female victims hiding beneath chairs or overturned tables and cursed them before shooting. "Trying to hide from me, bitch?" he said to one before firing a single fatal shot into her face. When one man, seventy-one-year-old Al Gratia, rose from his hiding place to lunge at the gun-man, Hennard shot him in the chest. As Gratia fell to the floor, his wife rushed to him, kneeling over his body. Hennard stoically walked to the weeping woman and killed her.

"You could see the hate literally blazing in his eyes," recalls Sam Wink, forty-seven, a Killeen School District attendance officer, who was among the survivors. "He seemed to be enjoying himself."

In one moment he ended the life of Olgica Taylor, then, in a strange show of compassion, looked into the eyes of Taylor's daughter, a young mother named Anica McNeil, and told her to get her four-year-old child out of the cafeteria. McNeil fled through the same window through which Hennard had driven his truck. Still, it was, in every sense of the word, an indiscriminate act of maddening, wholesale slaughter.

Witnesses say that the death toll would have climbed even higher had it not been for the heroic action of a six-foot-six, three-hundred-pound auto mechanic named Larry Vaughn, twenty-eight, who, in a moment of desperation, hurled his body through a plate glass window in the rear of the cafeteria, finally creating an escape route for dozens.

For quiet little Killeen (population 63,500), the central Texas city that had seen neighboring Fort Hood send twenty-six thousand troops off to Operation Desert Storm and welcomed all but ten of them safely home, Hennard's mindless rampage begged a litany of questions: How could a tragedy one might more likely expect from the lunacy of New York or Los Angeles, even Dallas, be played out in their small community? What dark demons could have triggered the massacre of so many innocent victims? Who was this man who took all the answers with him when he committed suicide during a shoot-out with Killeen police officers?

"Obviously," says Dr. James Grigson, noted Dallas forensic psychiatrist, who has interviewed hundreds of murderers during his career and followed events in Killeen with great interest, "he was a raging volcano, ready to explode."

During the last two decades, the controversial Grigson has served as an expert witness in numerous death penalty cases, most often for the prosecution. That his testimony has helped convince judges and jurors to sentence over one hundred murderers to die has earned him the nickname "Doctor Death" in some judicial circles. Dr. Grigson testified in the highly publicized Randall Dale Adams case that the defendant would kill again if set free. Adams, who spent more than a decade in a Texas prison for the murder of a Dallas police officer that another inmate later confessed to, was eventually exonerated and freed. Grigson, meanwhile, remains convinced of Adams' guilt. He is also convinced that the signs indicating that George Hennard was headed down a deadly path had been evident for some time.

Long before she saw him for the last time, convenience store cashier Mead had become accustomed to Hennard's strange behavior. "He'd been coming in for a year or more, off and on," she says. "I never saw him smile. In fact, I only knew his name because he would sometimes sign his ticket and come back later to pay me. That morning [of the shooting] he told me that he'd be back in the afternoon.

"The man seemed like someone who had the weight of the world on his shoulders; he was such a sad person. Frankly, he scared me."

Mead recalled an incident a few months earlier when a female customer was at the counter writing a check when Hennard walked hurriedly into the store. He went to the soda cooler then approached the counter, where he pushed the check-writing woman aside. "He didn't say 'Excuse me,' or anything," Mead remembers. "He just shoved her out of the way, glared at her for a second, paid his bill, then walked out like he hated every single person in the world."

On another morning, Mead continues, "he told me, 'I want you to tell everyone if they don't stop messing with my place they're going to be in bad trouble.' That's all he said then turned and walked out. I had no idea what he was talking about."

On the morning of October 16, however, the six-foot, brown-eyed Hennard seemed less tense, less harried than she had ever seen him. "For some reason," she observes, "he seemed almost calm, almost friendly for the first time I could remember."

The attitude, notes Dr. Grigson, is telling. "By that morning he had apparently resolved the conflicts he'd been struggling with for some time. He had finally made up his mind that he was going to do something drastic, something that would call attention to himself. For some, the conflict involved in making a decision of this nature takes a long time; for others, it is almost a snap decision.

"In Hennard's case, I'd guess that he had been working on it for quite some time."

The sketchy biographical information available on George Hennard paints a portrait of a man whose life had been a strange, dark, and solitary journey, one fueled by a love–hate relationship with a domineering mother and an often-absent father; a hatred for women, gays, and ethnic groups; alcohol and drug abuse; self-disappointment and rejection. Those acquainted with him use adjectives like "troubled," "combative," "rude," and "loner" to describe the handsome, Pennsylvania-born man whom most knew as JoJo, a nickname given him as a child to distinguish him from his Swiss-born father.

Tony Movsesian remembers Hennard as a moody youngster, quick to anger. "He had no real friends," says Movsesian, who met Hennard after his family moved to Las Cruces, New Mexico, where George's father, an orthopedic surgeon, was on the medical staff at the White Sands Missile Base. "I had some run-ins with him myself. Once, he thought I'd stolen a hat from him, and I could not convince him I hadn't done it. He would come over to the house and stand in the front yard, yelling that he wanted to kick my ass. That went on for two weeks."

Few who knew him express surprise that his life finally ended in a burst of insane violence.

"When I heard about what had happened," says Jamie Dunlap, who shared a Temple apartment with Hennard for a brief period of time in 1982, "it didn't surprise me. He was weird. He hated blacks and Hispanics. He hated gays. He said women were snakes, that they were always after your money. He always had derogatory things to say about women, especially after he and his mother would get into a fight. I think a lot of his problems stemmed from the relationship he had with his mother."

Hennard, Dunlap recalls, often spoke of wanting to "choke his mother to death."

Before she and Dr. Hennard divorced in 1983, Gloria Jeanne Hennard owned two antique shops in the Belton–Killeen area. She was known as a fastidious woman whose house was always spotless.

Matt Movsesian, who attended Las Cruces' Mayfield High School with Hennard, recalls that neither George nor his younger brother, Alan, were allowed to venture into the living room of their home. "They were afraid of getting it dirty and angering their mother," he says. "Their house was always immaculate. Everything was just right, and the living room was their mother's showcase.

"I don't ever remember any interaction between the mother and father and the children," he says. "They seemed really alienated from each other."

"His parents didn't seem to care about him," says former Las Cruces neighbor Paul Crowe. "They were never around."

Another classmate, Lou Catoggio, recalls an event that seemed to have a dramatic effect on Hennard. "He and his dad got into this big argument over the length of his hair. The next day, JoJo came to school looking like he'd been mauled. It looked as if his old man had taken a butcher knife and cut his hair. He was never the same after that.

"That was when we were in about the seventh grade. By the time he got to high school, you never saw him with any girls or hanging around with anybody. He'd changed into a completely different guy."

After offering brief reactions immediately following the Luby's shooting, both of Hennard's parents have refused to publicly discuss their son. His father, who now resides and practices in Houston, said at the time of the incident that he had not seen his son in over a year. Curiously, his mother's apparently well-ordered life had already taken another strange turn earlier in the year. According to Travis County records, she was charged with shoplifting $184.50 worth of panties, bras, sheets, and pillowcases from an Austin mall. In June, the Class B misdemeanor was dropped when she agreed to plead guilty to a lesser charge—a Class C misdemeanor for theft of less than twenty dollars. County records show that she paid a $100 fine and $17.50 in court costs.

Her "loner" son enlisted in the navy shortly after graduating from high school in 1974. He served twenty-eight months before being honorably discharged as a Seaman First Class in February of 1977.

Later that same year he traveled to Houston and joined the merchant marines, working primarily in the Gulf of Mexico until the fall of 1981. In November of that year, he moved west and shipped out of the California port of San Pedro on the first of thirty-seven overseas voyages that would take him to exotic ports around the world. If George Hennard had a true love, it was the sea.

His career, however, was punctuated by a series of recurrent problems. Aboard the *John Lykes* in May 1982, he and a black shipmate got into what was reported as "a racial argument." His seaman's papers were suspended for six months, and he was placed on a year's probation. Then, in May 1989, while serving as a boatswain on the cargo ship *Green Wave*, he was caught with a small amount of marijuana in his cabin. Earlier, in October 1981, he was arrested in El Paso and pleaded guilty to marijuana possession, receiving a one-year probated sentence.

The marijuana possession resulted in the loss of his mariner's license. A month later Hennard enrolled himself in a substance abuse program at St. Joseph's Hospital in Houston and continued treatments as an outpatient until the fall of 1989. The program, records indicate, had been recommended to him by the National Maritime Union, which had suspended his license. In October of that year, he made his final formal appeal to have his seaman's license reinstated, pleading to the U.S. Coast Guard tribunal that life at seas was "all I've got."

Ike Williams, Wilmington–San Pedro branch agent for the National Maritime Union of America, remembers Hennard as a hard worker who loved the sea but found it impossible to establish any personal relationships. "He was hot-tempered and always looking for ways to even the score with people," Williams recalls. "He was very vindictive, acted like he didn't trust anybody." Williams, like everyone else, was keenly aware of Hennard's hatred for women.

When his reinstatement appeal was denied, Hennard spiraled downward into a state of depression from which he apparently never recovered. "That," observes Dr. Grigson, "was just another in a sequence of rejections for him. By then it had become a pattern in his life. Losing his license was, without a doubt, a major blow. Probably the only time he ever felt like a man was when he was at sea. It was a macho sort of thing he could glamorize to himself and others. Yet, I find it interesting that even in his most ideal setting he remained generally isolated from those he worked with."

Hennard's journey in the last two years of his life became one with little direction. He drifted from one construction job to another, living part-time with his mother, who had moved to Henderson, Arizona, and at the Belton home on East Fourteenth, which she had received as part of the divorce settlement.

Between September 1989 and October 1990 he lived in Austin, working as a day laborer and playing drums in obscure rock bands with names like Illegally Blind and Missing Lynx. "I think the only thing in the world that he valued," says fellow musician James Aldridge, "was his drum set. He told me it had cost him five thousand dollars.

"He was a lonely person. He kinda wanted friends, I think, but he just couldn't get along with people."

During his stay in Austin, Hennard made frequent trips back to Belton. "I remember him telling me that he had some problems with some rednecks and cowboys in Killeen," says Aldridge, "and he seemed to think that people were always out to get him."

In February, just months before his killing spree, while visiting his mother in Nevada, telling signs began to surface. Hennard purchased two handguns—a Ruger P89 and a nine-millimeter Glock 17—from Mike's Gun House in Henderson. Passing all legal checks, he registered the weapons with the Las Vegas police department.

"If you look back on those days immediately prior to his purchasing the guns," Dr. Grigson says, "you're going to find something that really sent him into a deep depression. There are very few reasons for buying those kinds of weapons. He had begun thinking seriously about killing someone—most likely himself. That's where it all started."

During a final visit to Nevada that June, Hennard's problems grew beyond his control. Indeed, an event that transpired shortly thereafter lends credence to the psychologist's observation. On June 1, 1991, Hennard was arrested in the Lake Mead Recreation Area near his mother's home and charged with possession of loaded firearms in a vehicle and being under the influence of alcohol in the park. "Very likely," Dr. Grigson offers, "he was there, contemplating suicide."

Then there was the rambling, angry letter written that same month to two Belton girls who lived just a few blocks from his Texas home. "I came in from work," says Jane Bugg, mother of nineteen-year-old Jana Jernigan and twenty-three-year-old Jill Fritz, "and there was this frantic man's voice on my answering machine. He said, 'My name is George Hennard and I'm calling from Las Vegas. I need you to call me back because there's been a terrible mix-up. It's a mess. I mailed a letter to your daughters, and I sent it to the wrong address. I sent it to the house next door. Please go next door and get the letter because I've enclosed some pictures. Please call me back.' Then he left a number."

Having no idea who the caller might be, she dialed the number and found herself in a bizarre, frightening conversation with a stranger who she finally realized was the weird-acting man she had occasionally seen in the neighborhood. "He kept talking about this terrible mistake and how badly he wanted the girls to have the letter. Finally I asked why he was writing my daughters, and he said, 'Well, I've been watching ya'll for about three and a half years and I think it's time that I got to know you.' It scared me. I told him not to call anymore and hung up."

She did, however, go next door and get the five-page, almost nonsensical letter in which Hennard asks that the girls afford him "the satisfaction of someday laughing in the face of all those mostly white, tremendously female vipers from those two towns [Belton and Killeen] who tried to destroy me and my family." The letter, addressed to "Stacy and Robin" (apparently Hennard did not even know the girls' names), makes reference to the author's delusion that the two were "groopie fans" who had followed him to Austin four years earlier.

The distraught mother turned the letter, the five photographs of Hennard standing in the Nevada desert that had been enclosed, and the recording from her answering machine over to the Belton police department. A few days later she was told that a check revealed only the minor marijuana arrest in El Paso on Hennard's record. Since there was nothing of a threatening nature in the letter or phone conversation, there was nothing they could do.

"Looking back," says Bugg, "I wish I'd pressed the matter more, maybe gone to the sheriff or even the FBI. But the police made me feel I'd bothered them with something trivial. I decided maybe I'd overreacted."

But in the days to come her worries grew. When Hennard returned to Belton shortly after the letter was received, he made no attempt to contact either Jill or Jana. He did, however, begin to regularly shoot them the finger as they drove past his house. Both girls were aware of his following them on trips to the grocery store. On one occasion he stopped into the bank where Jill worked.

Others in the quiet, pecan tree–shaded neighborhood had also begun to take greater notice of Hennard's strange actions. A woman across the street from him went out of her way to avoid what she called his "cursing and hateful glares." Another remembers his rushing into the street, yelling and waving his arms wildly, as she passed by in her car. Jill Fritz and Jana Jernigan were not the only ones to whom he made obscene gestures from his front yard.

"The last time I saw him," says the girls' mother, "was one afternoon when he was out riding his bike. I'd stopped at the corner, and he came roaring up beside me from the direction of that little convenience store. He made this swerving turn by my car, looked at me for a second, then went on."

It would, however, not be the last time Jill and Jana saw George Hennard. On the morning of October 16, as they were returning from classes at Temple Junior College, they saw him in his driveway, standing by his pickup. He seemed very calm, Jill remembers, and did not yell out or make any gestures in their direction. The time, she recalls, was shortly before noon—approximately forty minutes before he drove his truck into the front window of the Killeen Luby's, seventeen miles away.

"By the time he wrote that letter to the young women," Dr. Grigson says, "he had begun to go through the stages I've seen so often in those who just snap and go on a killing rampage.

"First, there was the hatred for his mother, which likely had begun during early childhood. Then, as he reached the age of puberty and became interested in girls, that hatred was transferred to them, making it impossible for him to establish any kind of positive relationship, regardless of how badly he might have wanted to. Even as he was trying to say nice, flattering things to the girls in that letter, he still had to lash out at all other women in town. He was long past any hope of having a normal relationship with any woman. So he was faced with yet another rejection."

In retrospect, there were others in the community who, in the weeks preceding his murderous rampage, had seen signs that Hennard's grip on reality was fast slipping away.

A week and a half earlier, he picked up the paycheck owed him by a cement company in nearby Copperas Cove and announced to several members of his work crew that he was quitting. "He started talking about some people in Belton," says Edward Hawkins, "certain women who he said were giving him problems. And some men, too. Then he asked us what we thought would happen if he was to kill somebody. When nobody seemed to take him seriously, he said, 'Watch and see, just watch and see.'

"I tried to laugh it off and told him that knowing the kind of guy he was, he'd never make it to the pen if he did do something like that. He'd have to kill himself if he got in trouble. He told me he'd do whatever he had to do.

"JoJo always acted pretty paranoid. We'd be driving along and would pass somebody and he would say, 'Hey, did you see that guy flip me off? Let's go back and kick his ass.' Stuff like that all the time." Hawkins recalled a night when he and Hennard had gotten into a bar fight with two other men, and Hennard later talking about "going back and taking care of them."

"I knew he kept those guns in his pickup, so I talked him out of it."

A rap song that Hennard played frequently, Hawkins says, was one titled "(Bitch) Ain't Nothing but a Word to Me," whose sexually explicit lyrics addressed acts of violence toward women. Hennard was also fond of the music of the heavy metal group Metallica.

For Belton businessman Ted Potter, Hennard's killing spree offered a bizarre twist. An acquaintance of the Hennard family, he saw George occasionally, when he would stop by the office to say hello. Hennard, in fact, paid Potter such a visit two days before the Killeen tragedy.

Potter compared Hennard to a junior high classmate he had known while growing up in Dallas, a mass murder named Richard Speck who killed eight Chicago nurses in 1968. "Both [Hennard and Speck] were loners and had hot tempers," Potter recalls. "Speck was a guy who didn't like women. George was the same way."

On the evening before the killings, Hennard stopped in at the Nomad Turnaround, a convenience store/grill on the outskirts of Belton, where he had regularly eaten cheeseburgers and nacho dinners in the previous three weeks. The television was on, and the reports of the Senate's approval of Clarence Thomas to sit on the Supreme Court were being aired. When University of Oklahoma law professor Anita Hill, the woman who accused Thomas of sexual harassment, appeared on the screen, Hennard went into a tirade.

"He just went off, threw a real tantrum," says Bill Stringer, the store manager. "He jumped up and started pointing at the TV, screaming, 'You dumb bitch! You bastards opened the doors for all the women!' He was pacing around the store, hollering and cussing until I told him we didn't tolerate that kind of language. He apologized and sat down to finish his burger."

Stringer says that it was the only "incident" with Hennard he ever experienced during the seven months he visited the store. "Oh, he was always complaining about something, usually the taxes he had to pay the city. He always said that, for a little town, Belton had the highest taxes in the world, and he didn't know if he was going to keep paying them."

Was something so simple as the annual $1,962 in taxes charged on the red-brick, two-story, colonial-style home on East Fourteenth Street enough to trigger the final act of Hennard's troubled life? Could an argument he had over a water bill with a city official weeks earlier have caused him to seek such bloody revenge?

Absolutely not, says Dr. Grigson. "I don't think there is any question that Hennard had a motive for what he did. But it had little or nothing to do with anything the communities of Belton or Killeen might have done to him. He wasn't mad at Belton or Killeen or Bell County. He was angry at the world in general.

"His motive was that anger which had been building over a long period of time. What caused the tragedy in the cafeteria was the long-running series of rejections he had been dealt throughout his life: what he had experienced as a child, the lack of any close friendships as an adult, the loss of his seaman's license. He was a man whose hatred began with his mother, grew to include all women, and finally everyone and everything around him.

"Placing blame on the community was just the manner in which he rationalized his actions."

Although fourteen of the Luby's victims were female, Dr. Grigson doubts that Hennard entered the cafeteria with a specific plan to kill only women. "In all likelihood, he hadn't decided who, specifically, he would kill when he went in there. Several who were shot were apparently people who moved or gave some indication they were trying to escape. The reason they were shot was because their actions, their movement, presented a threat to the control he wanted to feel over the situation.

"Had Hennard not been interrupted by the police, he would have methodically continued to kill until he got down to his last shot. And I have to believe that, from the start, it was his intention to use that last bullet on himself."

Questions haunt the boarded-up restaurant on the outskirts of Killeen. "We may never know why he did what he did—what caused him to snap," admits local police chief Francis Giacomozzi.

Perhaps there is no simple answer to the question.

Perhaps, as Dr. Grigson suggests, there was no single, handily isolated event that drove George (JoJo) Hennard to his final act of bloody destruction. More likely, it was the culmination of a lifetime of rejections and growing angers whose combined weight finally became too great to bear.

DALLAS

Observer

HIGH-PROFILE P.I. BILL DEAR BELIEVES HE KNOWS WHO KILLED NICOLE SIMPSON? IT'S NOT WHO YOU THINK.

O.J.
CONFIDENTIAL

BY CARLTON STOWERS

FREE

6

O.J. CONFIDENTIAL

On a June Friday in 1994, Dallas private investigator Bill Dear, dapper as ever in his three-piece suit, monogrammed shirt, and alligator boots, completed his speech to the National Conference of Investigative Reporters and Editors and remained in the St. Louis Convention Center to answer questions.

On that day, however, attending journalists seemed less interested in a litany of recollections of high-profile cases he'd worked during a colorful—and sometimes controversial—career that spanned three decades. Never mind the investigations that had been spun into critically acclaimed books; the fascinating tales of dangers faced and bad guys put behind bars; the bigger-than-life persona that Dear had long perpetuated. The topic of the day, clearly, was a crime that occurred thousands of miles away, in an upscale California residential area known as Brentwood.

There, in the world of Los Angeles' rich and famous, the slain bodies of Nicole Brown Simpson and Ron Goldman had been found. The savage murders that occurred in the doorway of Nicole's Bundy Drive condo only five days earlier had been locked onto the front pages of newspapers throughout the world and were the around-the-clock concern of the electronic media. The prime suspect: the murdered woman's ex-husband, O. J. Simpson, Heisman Trophy winner, NFL Hall of Famer, movie star, and pitchman for everything from rental cars to orange juice.

What, the famed private investigator was asked, did he think about the case?

"I told them what I believed to be true, based on what I'd heard and read," Dear remembers. "O.J.'s blood was found at the Bundy crime scene. Nicole's blood was at Simpson's home on Rockingham. Ron

83

Goldman's blood was in Simpson's Ford Bronco. This, I said, looked exactly like what it was: O.J. was guilty."

Later, as he stood in the convention center lobby, Dear noticed a strange look on his son Michael's face. Having accompanied his father on the trip, the young man sat in on the question-and-answer session. "You've never done that before," he finally said.

"I didn't have to ask what he meant," the elder Dear recalls. He had, in a from-the-hip reply to a reporter's question, joined the nationwide chorus that was proclaiming O. J. Simpson guilty even before the investigation was complete and before a single legal wheel had turned. The credo he had sworn to throughout his career—never assume, always verify—had been violated. Three weeks later—after watching the live coverage of the bizarre slow-speed chase along a Los Angeles freeway that finally ended in Simpson's arrest, after reading and rereading every news report he could lay hands on, after filling a legal pad with questions he wished answered—Bill Dear was on a plane to Los Angeles.

Though he had been talking of slowing the frantic pace of his career and moving into semiretirement, he was off on what would turn into a six-year odyssey. It became, he admits, an obsession. Working independently, without assistance from Los Angeles law enforcement or the "Dream Team" of lawyers assembled to defend Simpson, Dear went in search of a truth he was convinced had not yet surfaced. Unlike most, he saw reason to doubt that O.J. was, in fact, guilty of what was being called the Crime of the Century.

- If the crime scene had been the horrific bloodbath described by media reports, why was it that such small amounts of blood were found in Simpson's Bronco? If he had made his getaway from Nicole's home and driven directly home to make certain he caught a scheduled late night flight to Chicago, didn't it stand to reason there would have been blood on the vehicle's gas pedal, brake, or steering wheel? Why, in the wall-to-wall beige carpeting inside Simpson's home, was there no blood left by a man who, just minutes earlier, had stabbed and killed two people? In a limited time frame, how had he disposed of bloody clothing? If he'd done so, why would he have overlooked the one sock later found in his bedroom with a single droplet of blood on it? And what of the murder weapon?

- Why, after what authorities assumed was a violent struggle with victim Goldman, did Simpson have no bruises or scratches except for a small cut on the knuckle of one finger? If the finger had, in fact, been injured during the murders, why was it that there was no cut on either of the gloves Simpson was supposed to have worn?

Then there was the most troubling question of all: If Simpson was wrongly accused, who else might have committed the horrific crimes?

Today, after dozens of trips to California, visits with world-renowned forensic specialists in the United States and Europe, interviews with people whom the Los Angeles police department and the Los Angeles County district attorney's office showed little or no interest in, and reviews of previously uncovered medical records, Dear is convinced that there is a strong suspect who was never considered.

"What I initially set out to do," he says, "was make the list of people who were considered among the inner circle—family and friends of O.J., Nicole, and Ron Goldman—and see who could be eliminated."

In time, all but one was.

In his self-published book, *O.J. Is Guilty, but Not of Murder,* Dear presents a provocative case that O.J.'s troubled son, Jason, twenty-four at the time of the murders, should have been viewed as a prime suspect. "I'm not accusing him of murder," Dear says, "but this is a man with a history of mental problems, a man who was seen carrying a set of sharp chef's knives on the night of the murders, and one who obviously lied about his whereabouts at the time of the crime. At the very least, he should have been questioned."

Instead, he points out, Jason Lamar Simpson was apparently never even interviewed by investigators. As proof, Dear pulls a copy of a deposition given by Jason prior to the 1996 civil trial in which his father was found responsible for the crimes. In response to questions from attorney Daniel Petrocelli about his ever being questioned about the murders by the LAPD or the district attorney's office, the young Simpson's answers were "No."

That is but one of many things Dear found troubling as his investigation progressed. Why was it, he asks, that unidentified fingerprints discovered in Nicole's condo were compared to fifteen others yet there was never any attempt to match them to Jason?

"My investigation," he writes, "uncovered the fact that the day after the murders . . . O.J. retained a high-profile criminal defense attorney who specialized in death penalty murder cases to represent Jason Simpson. Why would [he] hire a criminal attorney to represent Jason, who was not even a suspect at the time?"

The police, Dear says, had, from the outset of their investigation, been convinced that Jason had an "air-tight alibi" for the time—shortly after 10:15 P.M.—when the murders were committed. A chef at a trendy Beverly Hills restaurant called Jackson's, he had allegedly worked until 11 P.M. then was picked up by a girlfriend who was driving his Jeep. They went directly to her apartment to watch a movie on television.

Investigators learned the alibi, Dear says, not directly from Simpson but, instead, from attorney Johnny Cochran, a member of O.J.'s defense team. However, when Dear located the girlfriend and interviewed her, she told a different story. Because business was slow that evening, she said, Jason closed the kitchen early and left work at 9:45. According to her account, Jason left her place at approximately 11 P.M.

Then, in his civil deposition, Jason provided yet another version: He indicated that he left the restaurant between 10:00 and 10:30, drove his girlfriend to her apartment, kissed her goodnight in the Jeep, then went directly home where he watched television alone until three in the morning.

"All three versions," Dear points out, "can't be right."

Why, he asks, did those assigned to the case not bother to check Jason Simpson's background? "If someone had done so," he says, "it would certainly have raised some red flags."

In his 339-page book, copies of which he recently sent to the California attorney general's office, the Los Angeles County district attorney, and the Los Angeles police department, Dear offers evidence that the young Simpson was, in fact, on probation for aggravated assault at the time of the Bundy Drive murders, having attacked a former employer. Medical records obtained by Dear list a lengthy history of mental problems, suicide attempts, and excessive use of drugs and alcohol. On at least two occasions, Jason Simpson, diagnosed by his doctor as suffering an intermittent rage disorder that was being controlled by the drug Depakote, had physically assaulted ex-girlfriends. One, who Dear quotes at length, described Simpson as being gentle and loving at one moment, then angry and out of control the next.

In the book she describes one of many violent incidents that occurred between them: "He [Jason] grabbed me and pinned me down on the bathroom floor. Then he grabbed for my braids. He started whacking off my hair with his chef's knife." Several times, she told the private investigator, Simpson had attempted suicide. On one occasion, she recalled, he had broken a plate glass window, picked up one of the shards, and began slashing at his wrists. "He was yelling, 'See what I'm going to do? I'm going to kill myself.' It was all so crazy. He was acting like a madman, somebody else, somebody I didn't know."

The violence and anger, she said, generally occurred when Simpson was not taking his medication. She told Dear that she had seen Jason two months before the murders occurred, and he had told her he was no longer taking the Depakote. "I asked him," Dear quotes her as saying, "and he told me, 'No, that medication was fucking me up in the head. I'm not taking that shit anymore.'"

As one forensic psychologist who reviewed Dear's findings stated, Jason Simpson was, at the time of the Bundy murders, "a walking time-bomb."

The den of the sixty-four-year-old Dear's quiet Midlothian home is a testimony to the fervor he's attached to his lengthy—and expensive—effort to prove that the investigation done by the LAPD and district attorney's office amounted to little more than "a relentless rush to judgment." He estimates he's spent six hundred thousand dollars on his marathon fact-finding mission. Exercise equipment now shares space with large trunks filled with the files he's accumulated. In a bookcase are copies of forty other books that have been written on the Simpson case. Photographs and legal documents related to the murders are spread across a pool table on which a game hasn't been played in ages.

Still, it is a setting far different from the one in which you would have found the flamboyant private investigator in another time in his career—back when the swimming pool adjacent to his sprawling south Dallas County mansion had a canal that extended into the master bedroom, when his closet was filled with two hundred suits and a like number of custom-made boots, and the jet black Corvette he drove had personalized license plates.

In those days Dear was in Canada one week, Europe the next, working at a breakneck pace to earn the millions that people were willing to pay for his expertise. It was a time when he owned a popular steakhouse and a thriving western-clothing store; when he watched over his own school for wannabe private eyes and wrote books on his most fascinating cases. Hell yes, he admits, he loved it when *Playboy* was comparing him to Sherlock Holmes at the same time the British tabloids labeled him "the real James Bond."

Bill Dear, it seems, was one of those born to warm in the spotlight. As a fifteen-year-old growing up in Florida, he witnessed a robbery while making his morning paper route deliveries. Following the getaway car on his bicycle, he took down the address it eventually pulled into and phoned the police. Proclaimed a hero in the next day's paper, he was soon being followed by another car that twice ran him off the road. Assuming someone was attempting to scare the youngster from testifying, police provided him a daily escort on his paper route until the trial was over. By seventeen, he was the youngest sworn police officer in Florida history. One of the first things the young patrolman did was cite legendary teamsters union leader Jimmy Hoffa for a traffic violation. More headlines. He's been there ever since.

In the midfifties he left Florida for Dallas, convinced that a career as a private investigator offered more excitement and considerably better paydays than carrying a badge. Adopting a workaholic routine, he was soon busy investigating homicides, helping clients collect on insurance settlements, and locating children who had either run away or been kidnapped. Soon his reputation began to spread. So did his business.

By 1979, he was on the campus of Michigan State University, delving into the Dungeons and Dragons–playing background of a sixteen-year-old prodigy named James Dallas Egbert III, who had disappeared into a labyrinth of steam tunnels beneath the school. Two months passed before Dear finally located the troubled youngster hiding in Morgan City, Louisiana. From the experience came his first book, *The Dungeon Master*.

Then there was the bizarre murder case in Bath, Ohio, where Dear moved into the home of millionaire victim Dean Milo, even wearing his clothing and sleeping in his bed in an attempt to gain some "feel" for the crime. As unorthodox as his practices might have seemed, his investigation resulted in the convictions of no less than eleven conspirators, including the victim's brother—and another book, this one titled *Please . . . Don't Kill Me.*

Or, how about the time when, after being hired by the Tarrant County grandparents of a missing five-year-old, he managed to track her to a small town in Nebraska, where she was being held by her mentally unstable father? The story's happy ending featured Dear and the little girl stepping off a plane in Dallas as the minicams recorded the joyful reunion. Remember when, at the urging of a British journalist, the body of accused presidential assassin Lee Harvey Oswald was exhumed? Bill Dear was hired to oversee the grim task. Each round of publicity, he quickly learned, resulted in a new wave of calls from prospective clients.

Those were the days when he was at his self-promoting best, a time when he was lionized by some and labeled more sizzle than steak by others. His detractors were quick to point out that the gushing newspaper and magazine profiles never bothered to mention the cases he *didn't* solve or that much of the legwork credited to him was actually being done by the sizable staff he employed. At one point a rumor circulated that his license had been suspended after a dissatisfied client complained to the Texas Board of Private Investigators. Never happened.

Says Richard Riddle, a former Dear partner who now has his own agency, "Sure, Bill's got a big ego. Doesn't even try to hide it. But he works his tail off for his clients. I don't know how many missing kid cases he's worked for a dollar. On top of that, I've seen him spend thousands of dollars of his own money on cases when the client couldn't afford to pay."

While the self-assuredness—the sizable ego—remains, today's Bill Dear says he is no longer chasing the brass ring of fame and fortune. Members of the staff that once worked for him have gone off to set up their own investigative agencies. He now takes only those cases that interest him, enjoys the simple pleasures of being a grandfather, and might even occasionally venture out in public without a suit and tie. It's his version of "semiretirement."

Now, however, the unanswered questions surrounding the Simpson–Goldman murders have his motor running like the old days. The Los Angeles police, he says, "screwed up." Since O. J. Simpson was acquitted of criminal charges, the murder cases officially remain open.

"It needs to be resolved," Dear says.

Certainly the portrait of Jason Simpson drawn from Dear's investigation is one of a young man battling myriad problems. The files assembled from the investigator's research are proof.

In 1990, police records show, Simpson was charged with driving under the influence of alcohol and drugs and placed on summary probation. Two years later, there had been the assault charges, which were filed after Jason attacked the owner of a restaurant where he worked as the prep chef. Pleading no contest to a reduced charge of disturbing the peace, he was again placed on probation, this time for twenty-four months. The only other brush with the law Dear was able to find occurred in 1994 when Simpson rammed his Jeep into the back of a pickup in the wee hours of the morning and fled the scene. A witness had taken down his license plate number, and he was later charged with leaving the scene of an accident and driving with a suspended license.

The medical and psychological records obtained by Dear document a series of suicide attempts, drug use, brief stays in psychiatric hospitals, and ongoing visits with a counselor. Dear, in fact, traced Jason's erratic behavior back to the age of fourteen when he was first admitted to the hospital following a cocaine-induced seizure. One time an enraged Simpson took a baseball bat to a bronze statue of his father that was located on the grounds of the Rockingham home. According to family friends that Dear quotes in his book, an ongoing battle, both verbal and physical, existed between O. J. Simpson and his son.

On at least three occasions, Jason attempted to take his own life. In one incident he cut his wrists with the glass from a broken window after an argument with his girlfriend, on another occasion he stabbed himself in the abdomen, and on yet another, after a night of drinking tequila and beer, he swallowed thirty Depakote tablets, over ten times the recommended dosage prescribed to prevent epileptic seizures.

Dear quotes Dr. Burton Kittay, the psychologist who treated Simpson on numerous occasions, as saying that his patient did, in fact, have mental problems. He did not, however, believe Jason could have committed the murders of Nicole Simpson and Ron Goldman. Yet even the young man's behavior at the funeral of Nicole Simpson puzzles Dear. "I remember seeing in the book *Raging Heart*, written by Sheila Weller, that as O.J., his daughter Arnelle, and Jason approached the casket," he says, "Jason suddenly turned and ran out of the funeral home. Despite coaxing from his father and several others, Jason refused to view the body."

The foremost question, however, focuses on motive. Why should Jason be considered a suspect in the murder of a former stepmother he obviously cared for and a waiter whose only apparent reason for being at her home that Sunday night was to deliver a pair of eyeglasses left behind by Nicole's mother? Clearly, the young Simpson had been close to Nicole. Dear writes that it was Jason who often volunteered to take Nicole, who loved to dance, to local clubs when his father begged off. According to Dear, Jason and Nicole remained good friends even after her breakup with O.J. But, Dear speculates, she embarrassed him on the day before she died.

"You'll remember that the family was to attend a school dance recital that afternoon," Dear explains. "Jason wasn't going to be able to attend because he was scheduled to work. He'd talked to Nicole about it, suggesting they all come to Jackson's Restaurant for dinner afterwards. She'd agreed that it was a good idea."

Jason, he surmises, was excited about the prospect of demonstrating his cooking talents for Nicole and her family. He'd made reservations and even bragged to fellow employees that they would be stopping in for dinner. At the last minute, however, Nicole phoned to say they had decided to go to Mezzaluna, a less expensive neighborhood restaurant, instead.

Dear suggests the possibility that Jason, angered and embarrassed over being stood up, drove to Nicole's condo after dropping his girlfriend off at her apartment. Perhaps, he writes, there was a confrontation during which the young Simpson's rage boiled over. Maybe Ron Goldman arrived just as that rage, no longer held in check by doses of Depakote, peaked. End result: two people dead.

Taking his theory a step further, Dear suggests the possibility that Jason, frightened by the realization of what has occurred, places a call to his father to tell him what happened. O.J. rushes to the Bundy Drive address and sees that there is nothing he can do—except try to protect his son.

Even the controversial DNA evidence presented at O. J. Simpson's criminal trial comes into question in Dear's book. The blood chemistry of fathers and siblings, he points out, often have similar genetic characteristics. And what of the footprints allegedly left by the Bruno Magli shoes owned by O.J.? Writes Dear, "O.J. and Jason have approximately the same size feet. Jason also had access to O.J.'s clothes closets and was known to have taken items of clothing from his dad at will."

Once his investigation was completed, Dear took his case to experts. Skeptical at first, they agreed after reviewing the private investigator's findings, that Jason Simpson should, in fact, have been considered a suspect. Among them was James Cron, former commander of the Dallas County sheriff's crime scene unit. "Dear's theory," he said, "is extremely plausible and believable."

Well-known British crime-scene experts Terry Merston and Peter Harpur reviewed Dear's findings and concluded that O. J. Simpson was not the killer of his ex-wife and Ron Goldman but was likely at the crime scene at some time after the murders. Additionally, their twenty-four-page analysis concluded that the stab wounds on the victims were more likely to have been inflicted by a sharp knife with a single-edge smooth blade rather than the long-bladed, double-edged stiletto supposedly owned by O. J. Simpson and described by the prosecution as the murder weapon.

Several psychologists who reviewed Dear's evidence concluded that Jason Simpson should have been considered a suspect. Wrote one, "After reviewing all of the history of suicide attempts, failed relationships in which isolation and moods of violence and dependency were interwoven, it seems more and more likely that Jason psychologically could have been a very reasonable suspect in the murders."

Among the material Dear asked doctors to review was what he refers to as the "Dear Jason" letter. Over a four-month period during which the investigator tracked Simpson's movements, a weekly routine of checking the contents of the young man's trash developed. Among the items collected were numerous liquor bottles, empty prescription bottles, and, on one late Tuesday night, a wadded page from a three-ring notebook. "At first," Dear says, "it looked like a letter that had been written to Jason then marked over by a series of lines and circles." It took him hours to decipher the block letter writing beneath the scribbles.

"Dear Jason," it began, then meandered through a sad stream-of-consciousness message. "I want solace . . . now I am a failure . . . alcohol is the root of all my shortcomings . . . I know I'm a good guy somewhere but I cannot find him . . . I had so many plans but now what . . . will and integrity absent . . . I do know what to do but don't have the will to do it. . . . In short I'm fucked . . . walking on broken glass. . . ."

The more he read the tormented words, the more Dear was convinced the letter had not been written to Jason but, rather, by him. Taking it to expert handwriting analyst Don Lehew along with samples of Simpson's writing from discarded documents that had been found in the young man's curbside trash container, Dear was told that the handwriting on the letter was Simpson's.

As one listens to Dear, reviews the material he's collected, and reads his book, there is no single revelation that causes one to view Jason Simpson as a suspect. Rather, it is the accumulation of facts that give credibility to his case. What he has accomplished is not a resolution of the case but, rather, a starting point for an investigation.

"That," he says, "is all I set out to do."

Meanwhile, he's back in the public eye. The BBC recently aired a documentary titled *O.J.: The Untold Story*, in which it introduced much of Dear's evidence. Radio talk shows are now calling almost daily to interview him about his new book. Recently, a *60 Minutes* producer phoned to discuss the possibility of taking yet another look at the case.

Even in "semiretirement," the spotlight continues to shine in his direction.

POSTSCRIPT

For a time Bill Dear's book generated a renewed interest in the case. Callers to radio talk shows found his investigation fascinating; so did the tabloids and several members of the Hollywood entertainment community. But the Los Angeles County district attorney's office showed little interest. Not inclined to give up on the case, Dear says he still hopes to convince the California attorney general to open a criminal investigation of Jason Simpson. "I won't rest," Dear says, "until there is a confession from either Jason or O.J. about what happened that night." To date, none has been forthcoming.

DALLAS Observer

Penetration and
ink: Dallas vice
cops go after
naughty comics
BY JOE PAPPALARDO

Hey, good buddy:
So our Texas
boy is going to
Washington.
Who's he taking
with him?
BY MIRIAM ROZEN

Film:
Steven Soderbergh
fights the
unwinnable
drug war with
his brilliant,
sprawling *Traffic*
BY ROBERT WILONSKY

Dish yearns for
the mainland
after a trip to
Caribbean Red
BY MARK STUERTZ

January 4-10, 2001
FREE
Volume 931
dallasobserver.com

THE ANGEL OF JUAREZ

HUNDREDS OF POOR WOMEN HAVE BEEN ABDUCTED, RAPED, AND MURDERED ON THE STREETS OF CIUDAD JUAREZ, THEIR CRIMES FORGOTTEN AND LARGELY IGNORED BY AUTHORITIES UNTIL ESTHER CHAVEZ CAME ALONG.

BY CARLTON STOWERS

7

THE ANGEL OF JUÁREZ

Seated behind her desk at Casa Amiga Centro de Crisis, sixty-six-year-old Esther Chavez Cano fills the room with laughter as she attempts to quickly get to the punch line of her story. Executive director of the first and only rape crisis center operating in Ciudad Juárez, Mexico, a city of a million and a half people, she laughs and smiles often, with a genuine warmth that, at least for the moment, blots out the pain and suffering that threatens to suffocate the world in which she has chosen to live.

For the moment she is reflecting on the days immediately following the grand opening of the unique storefront facility located just a short walk from the fast-beating heart of downtown. No sooner in business, she recalls, the center was burglarized, and its new computer, the most vital and valuable piece of equipment in the small adobe building, was taken. The thief, she says, also stole away with several chairs.

Then she gets to the punch line: "He even took my toothbrush," she says. With a booming laugh that can't possibly come from a person who stands just five feet tall and weighs only ninety pounds, she adds, ". . . so at least he was a robber with concern for good hygiene."

In the grand scheme of human injustice that she sees and speaks out against on a daily basis, a lost toothbrush, even a computer is a trifling setback. They can be replaced. Lost lives and stolen dignity can't. These are the matters for which she reserves her genuine anger. Here, but a stone's throw from American prosperity, people live in fear, poverty, and homes fashioned of crumbling adobe, discarded plywood, and cardboard boxes while the bright lights of El Paso wink down on them from the Texas side of the Rio Grande.

This cruel state of affairs silences Esther Chavez's laughter and drives her through fourteen-hour days focused on gaining new recognition for the rights of the downtrodden and abused; seeking justice for the hundreds of young women who continue to travel to Juárez in search of the forty-dollar-a-week dream the maquiladoras assembly lines promise, only to wind up dead and discarded in the isolated canyons of the nearby Chihuahua Desert.

A woman who never planned to make this border town her home, who at one time fully intended to devote her life to the pursuit of business-world big bucks, Chavez is today the most recognized voice of Juárez's impoverished, the champion of those grieving for their raped and murdered loved ones. They hear her speaking out in their behalf on the radio. They read her weekly column on human rights in *Dairio de Juárez*, the city's largest circulation newspaper. They see her on television, lashing out against what she views as corrupt government, chauvinistic mind-sets, and less-than-aggressive police work. They see her at the front of marches and rallies. They see her walking their dusty, unpaved streets and in their homes where there is no running water, no electricity, no sewer system. While the horrible living conditions trouble her, it is the lack of hope she sees all around that causes her greatest pain. What progress she has witnessed has come in increments almost too small to measure.

"Improvement," she says candidly, "is slow in coming." Yet even in an atmosphere that forces her to live in a constant state of frustration, she continues the fight on a battleground she had only planned to visit, never to call home.

The daughter of a rancher who died when she was just two, Esther grew up in Guadalajara with five sisters and two brothers. "We all worked," she says. She had her first full-time job at age fourteen, working as an accountant for a group of Catholic priests. In time, armed with a high school diploma and a few college credits, she worked her way up to a position with Kraft Foods in Mexico City as a globetrotting financial advisor for two decades.

So focused was she on her career, so driven to enjoy the business-world perks, that there was little time for anything else. She never married. "I was always too busy to think about anything but my work," she admits. Today the rows of photographs that sit atop a table in her Casa Amiga office are not of her own children but, rather, forty-three nephews and nieces. "They are my family," she says.

The same might be said for literally hundreds of other children—offspring of many of the lost souls of Juárez—whose lives she has touched in a variety of ways. That she is where she is today, assuming the responsibility of spokesperson for thousands of abused Mexican women, is the result of another kind of mercy mission made years ago. Because there were so many children in her family, Esther was raised by an elderly aunt who, at age ninety, announced that her last wish was to live her final days in her hometown of Juárez. "She wanted to come here to die," Esther says, "so I moved here with her in 1982, expecting to stay a year, maybe two."

Chavez's aunt lived to be 102, dying in August 1989. By then, Esther, the woman just passing through, had become a successful businesswoman and civic leader. Juárez had become her home and her cause. "I will never leave now," she says, "because there is so much work to be done here. This will always be my home."

For ten years she worked as general manager of a local business that made and sold bathroom fixtures; then she opened her own small dress shop in Juárez's mercado publico. "I did nothing but lose money," she admits. Not because there weren't customers but, instead, because she found it impossible to properly manage her store. The dark plights of needy women, accelerated in 1992 when the state proposed outlawing abortion, began calling out for more and more of her attention. "There simply was not enough time to do everything," she reflects. "I enjoyed owning the store, but I was always having to close up so I could rush down to the police station or the hospital to check on someone or go to a school and speak to the children about the dangers awaiting them on the streets."

Ultimately she had to make a decision: Be a businesswoman or devote herself to a full-time fight against social injustice. Esther Chavez chose the latter. Shutting down her shop, she organized a women's group that lobbied for tougher penalties against sexual assault, fought for abortion rights, and began writing her controversial newspaper column. Long before the nightmarish series of murders of young Juárez workers began to draw the attention of the national media, Chavez was picketing police stations, counseling distraught family members, and pleading with the owners of the factories for increased security measures and fair treatment of women employees.

That females applying for jobs were forced to take physical exami-
nations that included pregnancy tests they were not told of was another
wrong she vowed to right. "Of course," she says, "the women are not told
that a pregnancy test is a part of their physical, but the fact is if they are
pregnant, they simply are not hired. That is not right." She saw a need to
speak out about the cramped living conditions in the city's *colonias*—the
one-room, dirt-floor shanties—wherein an epidemic of abuse, family violence, and incest festered.

Yet today, as the war continues, victories still remain few and far between. "We have to fight very hard to alter society," she admits, "to get
past the 'macho' attitude that has been passed down for generations. For
instance, in our culture, marital rape is considered a man's right. If a
woman does go to the police or a doctor to report what has been done
to her, she can only expect to receive a rape of a different sort. She is crit-
icized for the way she dresses, the places she goes, or for not treating her
husband with proper respect.

"These are the attitudes we are fighting, step by very small step."

To date, she points out, a rare rape conviction results in a penalty of
only two to eight years in prison. Nowhere in the laws of her land is there
any penalty for the crime of domestic violence. Her latest battlefront is
Casa Amigas, opened in February 1999 when Juárez mayor Gustavo Eli-
zondo agreed that the city would pay rent for the building and modest
salaries for Chavez and two assistants. The Mexican Federation of Private
Health and Community Development Associations provided twenty-five
thousand dollars in grant money, and the neighboring Texas attorney general's office agreed to fund the training of rape crisis volunteers.

With sixty-four thousand dollars raised from a recent telethon, Chavez
has been able to add two psychologists and an additional social worker to
her paid staff. A businesswomen's organization in El Paso donated five thousand dollars for the printing of needed educational materials.

"We are," the energetic director proudly says, "here to stay."

"Here" is where she gets a firsthand view of the tragic parade of
abuse that has a stranglehold on Mexican society. "Women come to us,"
she says, "with bruises and cuts, cigarette burns on their arms and breasts.
Often they bring their children who have also been badly abused. In this
center we see the hatred every day." And she and her coworkers reach
out to help.

"This," says a twenty-year-old client who did not wish to have her name used, "is the first time someone has listened to me." Her story is heartbreaking. Her two young daughters, she says, are being raped by their father.

The women of Juárez, Chavez knows, are afraid. Particularly the young girls—some barely teenagers—who have migrated north from their poverty-stricken homes to seek the four-dollar-a-day wages offered in the maquiladoras, the three hundred assembly-for-export plants, half of which are owned by companies with corporate headquarters in the United States (3M, DuPont, Honeywell, Amway, etc.). Since 1993, a year after the maquiladoras program was established, allowing manufacturers to take advantage of cheap Mexican labor, local law enforcement officials have counted over two hundred women workers who have been murdered. Most were raped before they were killed, their bodies discarded either in the sand-blown desert outside the city, in the foul-smelling vacant lots adjacent to the city's nightspots, or along the railroad tracks that wind through the most downtrodden parts of Juárez.

Chavez, who keeps a list of every victim in her computer and quickly e-mails members of the media each time a new body is discovered, is convinced the death toll is far greater than the official law enforcement count. As she lobbies for more aggressive investigations of the deaths, she routinely angers and embarrasses people in high places.

"For a long time, the managers of the plants didn't want to talk to me," she says. "The governor didn't want to talk to me. The police didn't like me. But I have to say what is true."

One of Chavez's primary targets has been Arturo Gonzalez Rascon, attorney general of the state of Chihahua, who has, in the past, seemed to place at least some of the blame on the victims themselves, suggesting they have put themselves in harm's way by dressing provocatively and frequenting unsavory after-hours nightclubs. Rascon's comments infuriated Chavez. "He is not an attorney general," she once said. "He talks like an old priest. He's stupid. He has to learn to respect women."

Plain-speak, then, is Esther Chavez's sharpest sword, and slowly but surely it has reaped results. Owners of the maqualidoras now work with her, even briefly shutting down assembly lines when she arrives to conduct seminars for the workers. The attorney general she once lashed out against recently paid a visit to Casa Amiga, leaving the center with positive comments and promise of help. The police have begun to embrace her efforts. And after Mexico's president Vicente Fox took office, Chavez and several other feminist leaders were summoned to a meeting with him in Mexico City to discuss the problems of equality for women. "He assured us," she says, "that he planned to work hard against the violence."

Feminism, once viewed as a curse word by much of Mexico's male population, seems to be finally gaining some degree of acceptance. "We're no longer the enemy," Chavez says.

"Esther gets on people's nerves, but she's respected," says Brian Barger, forty-seven, a former CNN investigative reporter who, after viewing the conditions in Juárez, resigned his job in 1998 to establish his nonprofit International Trauma Resource Center in Silver Spring, Maryland, which is dedicated to the establishment of trauma facilities like Casa Amiga in all Mexico border towns. He had, he says, become weary of "parachuting" into troubled areas, reporting the story, then moving on to the next assignment. Listening to Chavez's woeful stories, he decided to see if he could help her make a difference. "The politicians and police might not like everything she does and says, but, at least privately, they admit that they have a great deal of respect for her.

"I've been in constant contact with her since we began to formulate the idea for the rape crisis center, and as I've come to know her I'm more convinced than ever that she is a woman uniquely qualified to play the advocacy role for the women of Juárez. That kind of responsibility takes a special person, and Esther Chavez is special."

Indeed, by Mexican standards, the advancements she has nurtured seem remarkable. To date, over eighty volunteer workers have been trained in the counseling of abused women and children, and they are now available twenty-four hours a day to respond to police calls involving domestic violence and sexual abuse. The staff psychologists conduct daylong group-counseling sessions for victims each Saturday. Local attorneys have begun offering legal aid to victims, and churches and hospitals have joined the cause as well. Alcoholics Anonymous chapters throughout the city now offer help to those accused of drunken abuse of spouses and children.

Twice a month, Juárez municipal police officers gather at the police academy or the Calle Peru Norte facility for daylong sensitivity workshops conducted by volunteer members of the El Paso police department's crimes against persons unit. "What we do," says El Paso detective Millie Hinojos, "is ask that they [Juárez officers] examine their own views about criminal sexual conduct then work toward building new trust between victims and the police." Adds her training partner, Detective Peter Ocegueda, "The point we're trying to make is that the police department needs to start reaching out to the public, not wait for it to reluctantly come to it." Help has been provided to over one thousand sexually abused clients since Casa Amiga's opening.

Helenmarie Zachritz, executive director of the nonprofit Mexican Federation of Private Health and Community Development Associations, says none of it would have happened had it not been for the stubborn efforts of Chavez. "Esther is one of those incredible people who draws others to her and her cause. The government, I'm sure, still looks at her as a bothersome fly in the ointment. And, yes, she drives people crazy with her persistence. But believe me, she drives them crazy in a way that is good and positive.

"When you see her out front in the women's marches, carrying a cross bearing the name of one of the murder victims, you immediately know that she is a sincere, concerned person who wants nothing more than justice and a better way of life for women. I've known her for years and have grown to admire her more and more with each passing day."

Adds Guadalupe Ramirez Lopez, director of a Juárez human rights group: "Years ago, Esther was the only one with the courage to speak out. She was the only person who dared to demand equal treatment for women and better investigations into the horrible crimes being committed. Now that remarkable courage has rubbed off on others who are involved in her efforts."

Six hundred to one thousand new people arrive in Ciudad Juárez daily, many lured by hope of finding prosperity in the sprawling montage of maquiladoras on the outskirts of the city. Despite the fact that the manufacturing plants employ over 160,000 people (60 percent of them women), jobs seem always available. Production goes on around the clock. Twenty-four hours a day. Three eight-hour shifts.

These factories, where everything from sandals to jeans, television sets to automobile cruise-control systems are produced, are a by-product of an agreement that allows foreign-owned companies to avoid paying tariff on the goods they produce.

At the end of each shift, thousands of workers, many of them teenage girls still wearing their maquiladora smocks, climb onto the buses provided by their employers for the ride back into the center of Juárez. While there is a rule that one must be at least sixteen to work in the factories, it is not uncommon for girls two and three years under age to have made arrangements to purchase fake identification even before leaving their farms and villages to seek a job.

Juárez authorities say that danger arises when the buses reach the plaza in the heart of the city. From there, the young women can catch connecting busses to the *colonias*, but to do so requires that they walk several blocks past brightly lit cantinas and discos and corners where men with too much time on their hands and too much alcohol and drugs in their systems stand in wait.

For many of the young women, experiencing the bright lights of Mexico's seventh largest city for the first time, the urge to stop in for a drink, a dance, and a flirtation is understandably strong. For a brief time they can forget the long hours of work and the dismal homes they must return to; they can disassociate themselves from the aching loneliness that haunts them, the tired diets of beans and tortillas they survive on. Bathed in the big-city bright lights and the brassy sounds that call out to them, they can have fun for an hour or two before they step back onto a treadmill taking them nowhere. Innocent in the ways of city life, most do not know much of the society of pimps and prostitutes, the street gangs and drug dealers they are walking among. Nor are they aware that it is their naiveté, their vulnerability, on which such underworld people prey.

And so, in recent years, many of them have suddenly disappeared, only to be found long after their deaths, the tattered remains of their work smocks covering nothing more than sun-bleached bones left after packs of coyotes and wild dogs have had their grotesque feasts.

Names of the young victims are seared in Chavez's memory. Like that of thirteen-year-old Irma Angelica Rosales, whose nude body was found in a drainage canal not far from her workplace, raped and suffocated to death by the plastic bag that was still over her head when two youngsters happened upon her. Just weeks earlier Rosales had traveled to Juárez to live with a brother and sister-in-law, paying the going rate of twenty dollars for fake identification papers that indicated she was sixteen so that she could find employment on the Electrocomponentes de Mexico assembly line. In the short days before her death, she had earned twenty-seven dollars.

Chavez tried to comfort the girl's family, to help them in negotiations with profiteering coffin vendors, and to deal with the political red tape necessary to have the victim's body returned home for burial. "The anguish of those poor people," she says, "tore at me. It was a nightmare. I felt a volcano of pain for them."

Such images haunt her, and it is the criticism of those who locals so often refer to as the "maquiladora girls" that angers her to tears. When those in authority suggest that many of the murders could have been avoided had the young women simply gone directly to the safety of their homes, avoiding the temptations and dangers of Juárez nightlife, she fumes. "That a young woman wants to go dancing or that she chooses to wear a mini-skirt should not be seen as an invitation to her death. They [law enforcement officials] are doing nothing but minimizing the crimes and placing blame on the victims.

"Women here have not been liberated by any means. We have more and more single mothers being forced into the workplace, but when they get jobs, they are resented by men who see them as suddenly independent. There is a strong patriarchal backlash that has led to many of these horrible crimes."

When the first bodies of young women were found in the desert, there was little cause to assume them evidence of anything more sinister than the senseless violence that visits all major cities. But soon the number grew at an alarming rate. From 1995 until 1997 alone, the bodies of 104 women were discovered, and a pattern became obvious. The majority of the victims were young women who had disappeared after leaving their jobs on the maquiladoras assembly lines.

Yet Esther Chavez and the growing number of women's rights advocates she had rallied were concerned that the authorities were not taking the horrors they were seeing as seriously as they should. Despite the growing number of bodies, the police gave little indication that they saw the same terrifying pattern that those in the feminist movement did. Almost without exception, those murdered were young, pretty, and poor, and they had worked the late shifts in Juárez's industrial park.

In time the local media—bombarded by complaints from Chavez, other feminists, and families of victims—began to pressure the police for answers. Were they, in fact, aggressively investigating the murders? Did they have suspects? When might they anticipate making arrests?

Initially, the popular assumption among both law enforcement and concerned citizens was that the city had a crazed serial killer running loose, making some demented game of abduction, rape, murder, and the tossing away of bodies like so much garbage. At first there was resistance from authorities to the public pressure. "The press is giving too much attention to the homicides of women," Ernesto Garcia, spokesman for the State Judicial Police in Juárez said in a 1998 press conference. "For us, homicides of women, men, and children are all important."

But as the demonstrations at the police station grew in number and volume and as local media attention was followed by reporters dispatched from such faraway places as New York and Los Angeles, the pressure to solve the crimes and stop the killings mounted. Chihuahua attorney general Rascon began taking an active role, summoning additional manpower to assist in the Juárez investigations and publicly stating that his office had made solving the murders a priority. Clearly, the wave of crimes against the women of Juárez had become a political hand grenade, thanks in no small part to the likes of Chavez and her growing legion of supporters. When Patricio Martinez Garcia took office as governor last year, it was said that he won his election by criticizing his predecessor for the mismanagement of the investigation and offering a five-thousand-dollar reward for information leading to the identify of the person or persons responsible for the murders.

Even after an Egyptian chemist named Omar Latif Sharif Sharif, a man with a twenty-five-year history of sexual crimes throughout the United States before finding his way to Juárez, was arrested in 1995 and initially charged with the murders of nine women, the attorney general's office sought the input of outside experts in an effort to *(a)* further aid the still ongoing investigation and *(b)* publicly demonstrate that the crimes were indeed being taken seriously.

First to visit and consult with local authorities was Robert Ressler, a retired member of the FBI's celebrated behavioral science unit. Ressler, the agent who in fact had first coined the term "serial killer," spent two weeks reviewing reports, visiting crime scenes, and talking with investigators. After helping the police set up a database on which to log all the investigative information collected, Ressler made the judgment that the murders were not the act of a lone killer. "It was my opinion," he says, "that there is the possibility of one or more serial killers who could account for as many as twenty of the cases I reviewed. There was also strong evidence that some were the result of gang activity. Many, however, seemed to be the random, one-on-one homicides that are almost always the end result of a rape or drug transaction gone bad."

While Sharif remained in the Juárez Ceresco prison, appealing a thirty-year sentence for the 1995 rape and strangulation of a seventeen-year-old factory worker named Elizabeth Castro Panda Garcia, he quickly grew into something of an urban legend—even as the killings continued. Strange stories of his orchestrating unspeakable crimes from behind bars were embraced by local journalists.

In April 1996, a dozen members of a Juárez gang calling itself "Los Rebeldes" (The Rebels) were arrested following an intense undercover investigation and linked to the ongoing string of slayings. Composed primarily of men in their midteens to early twenties, the gang's leader was a twenty-eight-year-old nightclub security guard named Sergio Armendariz. His street name was "El Diablo." According to the authorities, he and his fellow gang members had a lengthy history of luring women from downtown streets and bars, taking them to local hotels and homes where they were gang-raped, killed, and their bodies taken into the desert and dumped.

Police, saying they felt "Los Rebeldes" might be responsible for as many as fifty unsolved murders, added a new twist to the already bizarre story: The jailed Sharif, investigators suggested, was the mastermind of the gang and had, even while in custody, been paying its members to commit murders so it would demonstrate that he was not responsible for the killings authorities thought he might have committed. From his jail cell where he was awaiting appeal of his sentence, Sharif denied involvement with the street gang and labeled the police's theory absurd. Ultimately, "El Diablo" and several of his fellow gang members were convicted and sent to prison, clearing seventeen previously unsolved homicides.

But since that time an additional fifty Juárez women have been raped and murdered. In fact, more women were killed in 1998 than in any year since 1993. And the homicides continue. The problem, clearly, is far from resolved. So Chavez and her feminist counterparts—bearing organizational titles like the Citizens Committee against Violence and Mujeres por Juárez (Women for Juárez)—continue to speak out, gathering each Monday at police headquarters on the southern edge of the city to sit quietly in the lobby in silent protest. Once a month they are joined by family members of victims to walk in the desert, searching for bodies of the still missing.

Today even the grieving relatives have a collective name: Voces sin Eco (Voices without Echo). On the telephone and light poles along Juárez's main streets, they leave their mark—a black cross painted on a pink background—as a public reminder of the dead and missing.

"It is necessary," says Mujeres por Juárez leader Victoria Caraveo, "for us to work harder and scream louder so the community will not see these killings as something to ignore."

Last spring, five experts from the FBI's National Center for the Analysis of Violent Crime were summoned from Quantico, Virginia, by Mexican authorities, this time to attempt to provide local authorities with a profile of the killer or killers still on the loose. After four days of reviewing seventy-eight unsolved cases, they released a prepared statement to the press: "The team determined," it read, "that the majority of the cases were single homicides, each committed by a different individual. It is too premature and irresponsible to state that a serial killer is loose in Juárez."

Less than a month after the FBI's visit, the most shocking twist in the already serpentine case occurred. A maquiladora bus driver, Jesus Manuel Guardado Marquez, sexually assaulted a fourteen-year-old factory worker and left her for dead. The girl, who admitted that she had used falsified documents indicating she was older to get her job, survived to report her attack to the authorities. Like many earlier victims, police later said, she had been the last passenger remaining on the bus when her attack occurred. Guardado came to the attention of the police after his pregnant wife had filed abuse charges against him. While giving her statement, Maria del Carmen Flores told authorities that her husband had talked with her about killing other women and had, in fact, kept some of his victims' clothing.

Once in custody, Guardado wove an incredible story that implicated others in the murders. He and three other bus drivers, he said, had killed seven young women at the urging of a twenty-eight-year-old El Paso resident named Victor (El Narco) Moreno Rivera. Moreno was immediately arrested along with drivers Agustin Toribio Castillo, Jose Gaspar Ceballos Chavez, and Bernardo Hernandez.

Again, the already jailed Sharif was labeled as the ringleader who set the murder plots in motion. Authorities say that Sharif paid for murders carried out by the drivers between June 1998 and March 1999. The exchange of money—reportedly twelve hundred dollars for two murders each month—was allegedly made when Moreno visited Sharif in jail. Police said that Moreno showed the Egyptian the pieces of jewelry taken from the victims as proof they had been killed. Once more the theory was that Sharif paid the bus drivers to commit the murders in an attempt to steer suspicion away from him.

Quick to shoot down the bizarre theory was Sharif's attorney, Irene Blanco, who pointed out that her client did not even have money to pay for the copying of legal documents, much less thousands of dollars for murders. Too, she pointed out, there was no record indicating that Moreno had ever paid a jail visit to Sharif. "He has become the police's scapegoat," Blanco says.

"We're still investigating how he [Sharif] was able to obtain the money," Chihuahua prosecutor Manuel Esparza told the media, "but we are told that he had initially asked that four murders be committed each month, but the bus drivers told him that was too many." As to the suggestion Moreno's jail visits to Sharif never occurred, authorities surmise only that he might have used another name.

What has become increasingly difficult is to distinguish fact and fantasy. Just as did the gang members earlier arrested, the bus drivers and Moreno would later tell the press that their confessions had been made only after severe beatings from those who interrogated them. Sharif again summoned the press to scoff at the new theory. "They accuse me of everything," he said. "I am not a psychopath. I am not a criminal. I'm only a scapegoat from Egypt." He insisted he knew neither Moreno nor any of the jailed bus drivers."

Still, Steve Slater, a public safety advisor for the state of Chihuahua, is among the believers. "This character, Sharif, is an evil man. He wanted to continue the killings, but since he was in jail he couldn't. So he hired others to do them for him. That's how he got his thrills."

While skepticism abounds, it mixes with a widespread sense of relief that police work on the cases moves forward. Authorities are firmly convinced Sharif is a killer. So, too, are the convicted members of Los Rebeldes. The bus drivers are suspected of being responsible for at least seven murders, perhaps as many as a dozen.

"The idea that this one man [Sharif] is responsible for all the death is foolish," Esther Chavez says, "but it is a sign of progress. There are now criminals in jail, which is good. But there is much more to do. Young women are still dying. They continue to disappear. They're still being beaten and raped."

Blame, she says, is also due to the owners of the maquiladoras. "How in the world could they have hired such people to drive their buses?" she asks. "No background checks, no controls?"

In a strange postscript to the arrest of the bus driver Guardado, the assembly plant that had hired his fourteen-year-old victim filed a legal complaint against the girl. Motores Electrios (owned by Milwaukee-based A. O. Smith) alleged that the girl had provided false information about her age on her job application. The only comment on the matter from A. O. Smith officials came from company spokesman Ed O'Connor, who said only that, "It is not our policy to hire anyone under sixteen."

Such insensitivity only heightens Chavez's frustration. "This girl," she says, "has six brothers and sisters and lives in a shack with a dirt floor. She has only a sixth-grade education. She has been severely traumatized and needs help with medical and psychological treatment, not to have legal action taken against her.

"Her family is poor, which is why she needed a job. There are many people who believe she should have received the governor's five-thousand-dollar reward for coming forward like she did."

During midafternoon, the dust devils play in the unpaved street that winds through one of the Juárez *colonias* that has become such a part of Esther Chavez's world. It is a heartbreaking eyesore of abject poverty. Though less than a mile from the U.S. border, within shouting distance of American affluence and busy commerce, it is a place so wretched that no human being should be forced to call it home. The residences are no larger than the storage sheds that many on the other side of the border use to house gardening equipment and useless items that won't fit into the attic. Made of misshapen adobe bricks and scrap metal, discarded pieces of plywood, and faded cardboard, many accommodate families of five, six, or more. Those fortunate enough to enjoy the comfort of electricity do so by stealing it, stringing electrical cords to an outlet that is several broken-down houses away. Those who live in that house have, in turn, strung cords to another. And another. No one will say where the origin point of the pirated electricity is located. But neither does anyone worry that authorities will find them out. The police, they have learned, rarely venture into their part of the world.

From several open doors, toddlers clad only in diapers or boxer shorts peer suspiciously through wide brown eyes into the sunlit world but do not venture outside. Some look malnourished. All are dirty, the grime and dust of the powered dirt street having settled onto their coffee-colored bodies.

In a neighborhood so populated with young children there should be noise—laughter, arguing, even crying—but there is none. The troubling silence is broken only by the gentle whistle of the always-blowing wind as it sneaks its way through cracks in the walls and the holes in the sheet metal rooftops.

Standing near her car, dressed in jeans and tennis shoes, Chavez squints her eyes against the afternoon sun, watching as a steady parade of youngsters walk home from school on the dusty street and along the adjacent railroad track. The carcasses of three dead dogs, in various stages of decay, draw flies and block the children's route.

Esther is not smiling. She nods at a few young passersby then points toward a nearby pile of rocks. "There," she says, then turns away, focusing her attention on the blue, cloudless sky. She doesn't want to look toward the tracks again. And for good reason. Months earlier, the body of a young woman had been dumped there by some still unknown assailant. Chavez despises these trips to the landmarks of her city's inhumanity.

They rekindle an anger that spreads across her face and into her voice. "This," she says, making a sweeping wave at the neighborhood she is visiting, "is not a third world country. It is a fourth world country."

With that she is quickly back in her car, driving away. A few children wave as the tireless little woman so determined to help them passes. She will, they know, be back.

Because the grief and suffering goes on. And the murders continue.

DALLAS Observer

INNOCENCE LOST

WAS THE CASE AGAINST LACRESHA MURRAY,
THE YOUNGEST TEXAN EVER TRIED FOR CAPITAL MURDER,
A RUSH TO JUDGMENT OR A STORY OF JUSTICE DENIED?

BY CARLTON STOWERS

8

INNOCENCE LOST

With a lost and haunting look on her face, she was too young, too unworldly to understand the darkness that had swept into her life. Lacresha Candy Murray, only twelve years old, was seated in an Austin courtroom, her frightened brown eyes darting among a forest of strangers. Found guilty of murdering a small child, she listened as a judge sentenced her to twenty-five years in prison. Whatever emotion might have welled inside her at the moment was masked by a blank expression. Not so with her adoptive grandparents, R. L. and Shirley Murray, who sat in the gallery nearby, holding hands, shaking their heads in disbelief.

Lacresha, a jury earlier decided, had killed two-year-old Jayla Belton while the toddler was being kept in the home of Lacresha's grandparents on the afternoon of May 24, 1996. Travis County prosecutors had outlined a nightmarish scenario wherein Murray dropped the baby then kicked her with enough force to break several ribs and rupture her liver. Those severe internal injuries, medical experts determined, led to the child's death—and to the charges that triggered one of the most volatile and controversial cases in Austin history. Before all was said and done, an entire nation was taking notice—and taking sides. As far away as London, newspaper accounts would compare the case to that of teenage British au pair Louise Woodward, also charged with the death of a small child.

This, in fact, was the second time the youngster had found herself seated at a defense table generally reserved for adults. First tried at age eleven, earning her the dubious distinction of being the youngest capital murder defendant in Texas judicial history, she had been convicted of the lesser charges of negligent homicide and injury to a child and was given a twenty-year sentence. Then, on the court-granted second attempt to plead her case, things had only gotten worse: the charge elevated to murder, her sentence increased.

What would emerge from all the accusations and countercharges, all the public outrages, and all the cries for justice was a story tragic beyond belief and still shrouded in unanswered questions. Even now, five years later, after a quiet has finally settled, after all charges have been dropped, and after Lacresha has been set free, there remains a great division of thought among those who prosecuted and defended her. What actually happened to Jayla Belton, and who was really responsible? Was Lacresha, in fact, guilty as a jury had decided in 1996 and again in 1997? Or was she nothing more than an unfortunate pawn in a political power play; an expendable young black girl who served as an ideal campaign rally cry for a district attorney seeking reelection and a city fed up with juvenile crime?

Is it a textbook tale of a rush to judgment? Or one of justice denied?

It began on a springtime Friday morning when sixty-five-year-old Shirley Murray, who routinely kept several children in her home despite having no license to conduct day care, was away, enjoying a bus tour through Louisiana and Mississippi that was a combined Mother's Day–birthday gift from her niece. In anticipation of the Memorial Day weekend outing, she had contacted the parents of children she normally watched over to tell them she would be away. Some showed up anyway, including toddler Jayla Belton, who was brought by at approximately 8:30 A.M. by Derrick Shaw, the then twenty-three-year-old boyfriend of the child's mother.

Shawntay Murray, seventeen at the time and the oldest of the adopted children living in the Murray household, answered the door to see Shaw, a cook at a local restaurant, standing on the porch with little Jayla and her ten-month-old sister Jasmine. He and Judy Belton had been bringing the children to Shirley Murray's home for the previous six months. "He woke me up," Shawntay would later recall. "I told him that my grandma was gone, but he said he needed to leave them for just a little while." Shawntay was basically in charge of the younger children in the house in her grandmother's absence: Jayla and Jasmine, three small children left off by a woman named Alicia Turner, as well as her five siblings.

Shaw never returned, instead going to work.

Though he would later tell a jury that Jayla had "been playful the morning I dropped her off," the recollection of Shawntay was quite different: Normally active and a voracious eater, Jayla seemed lethargic that day and had no appetite. Soon after arriving she began to sweat profusely then vomited. Thinking the child might be suffering from a flu virus, Shawntay gave Jayla a Tylenol tablet. The Murray teenager recalls the child slept most of the day and was still asleep when she left for her job at a local pharmacy just before 3 P.M.

Thereafter, the only adult in the home was her grandfather. R. L. Murray, who has walked with the aid of crutches since his legs were paralyzed by polio in childhood, had been there throughout the day, except for a brief period of time earlier in the morning when he'd taken his car in for minor repairs.

The day, in fact, passed routinely until shortly after 5 P.M., when eleven-year-old Lacresha came in from the backyard and briefly joined her twelve-year-old sister, Cleo, in watching television in the elder Murrays' bedroom. Leaving to visit the bathroom, Lacresha passed the adjacent room where Jayla Belton lay on Shawntay's bed. The baby, Lacresha would later tell authorities, was acting strangely. According to transcripts of a taped interview conducted by an Austin police homicide detective, she said, "I heard Jayla crying. She was shaking, so I went in there, picked her up, and ran to my grandpa and asked him what was wrong with her."

Alicia Turner had just arrived at the Hansford Drive home to pick up her children when she saw the condition of the baby and urged the sixty-seven-year-old grandfather to place a call to 911. Instead, R. L. Murray and Lacresha got into the family van and hurried the convulsing child to nearby Breckenridge Hospital. A barefoot Lacresha was the one who carried the baby's limp body into the emergency room. After twenty minutes of intensive CPR, Jayla Latre Belton was pronounced dead.

She was still lying on a gurney, a tube in her mouth and electrodes attached to her tiny chest, when Judy Belton, alerted at her job as supervisor of a local bookstore, and Derrick Shaw arrived at the hospital. "She was so cold," the mother remembers. "I just kissed her, rubbed her head, and told her that I loved her."

Kent Burress, a social worker at the hospital at the time, would later testify that he had escorted Belton and Shaw to the child's body and found Shaw's behavior unusual in light of the circumstances. While the distraught mother lingered over Jayla, Burress remembered, Shaw seemed more concerned with getting a parking sticker for his automobile.

An autopsy, performed by Travis County medical examiner Dr. Roberto Bayardo, ruled that the child had died from a severe blow to the liver. During his examination he also found thirty bruises scattered over the child's head, legs, and torso, a three-quarter-inch abrasion near the base of the skull, and four broken ribs. A blunt force injury to the abdomen, he ruled, had broken the ribs and severed the liver. The fatal injury, he said, had taken place no more than fifteen minutes before the child's death.

R. L. Murray would later insist that he had seen no bruises on Jayla Belton's body when Lacresha brought her to him. However, the mother who was there to pick up her children told a jury that she noticed what she thought were bruises on the two-year-old's stomach as she was being carried from the house for the trip to the hospital.

In Dr. Bayardo's opinion, a homicide had occurred.

Within days, the focus of the investigation centered on eleven-year-old Lacresha. Large for her age, Lacresha was child with an outgoing personality; she was a happy-go-lucky girl who enjoyed playing basketball, singing in the church choir, and taking evening walks through the neighborhood with her grandmother. The primary reason to assume her the most likely suspect: She was the last person known to have been in the company of Jayla before it became necessary to rush her to the hospital.

Ironically, it was a sworn statement to the police by her grandfather that helped focus suspicion onto her. He was sitting in the living room, he recalled, when Lacresha came inside from the backyard to go to the bathroom in the rear of the Murrays' east Austin home. "I heard a thumping noise," he said in his affidavit. "It sounded like someone throwing a ball against the wall. I called out to Lacresha and asked her what was going on. She said that she was playing ball, and I told her she knew better; she is not supposed to play ball in the house.

"About a minute later she came into the hallway and said that [Jayla] was shaking and throwing up. That's when I told her to bring the baby to me."

After the frantic trip to the emergency room and the pronouncement that little Jayla was dead, the elder Murray told police, "If Lacresha did this, I want to see her get some help."

As the investigation got underway, police requested that Child Protective Services officials remove Lacresha and her siblings (sister Cleo and three younger brothers) from the Murray home—standard procedure in such cases. Isolated from her family at the Texas Baptist Children's Home in nearby Round Rock for four days, she was finally interviewed by Austin police department homicide detective Ernesto Pedraza for almost three hours with neither a lawyer present nor with the grandparents, whom she'd lived with since age two. She repeatedly insisted that she had done nothing to harm the baby. On no less than thirty-nine occasions during the interview, Lacresha said that she did not know what had happened to cause Jayla's death. Finally, calling on twenty years' experience at investigating homicides, Sergeant Pedraza began to question Lacresha along less accusatory lines.

Sergeant Pedraza: I know it's real hard, Lacresha. It's hard when something like this happens, but you know there's a reason, there might be a reason why this happened. You know, you might have been carrying the baby and the baby might've fallen from your arms, or fell off the bed, or something like this . . . but until we hear it from you, we won't know. We need to get your side of the story.

Lacresha: I just told you.

Sergeant Pedraza: . . . You're not telling me all of it.

Lacresha: Yes I am.

Sergeant Pedraza: . . . I have a doctor who says those injuries happened at the time. You know where it leads us to? To you. And like I was explaining to you, there are reasons why the baby sustained those injuries. There's always an explanation to everything. . . . Things happen, we make mistakes. I make mistakes all the time, you know. But I don't try to hide them. . . . You're a young girl. You still have your whole life ahead of you . . . we can correct things. Do you understand what I'm saying?

Lacresha: Yes.

Sergeant Pedraza: When you picked up the baby . . .

Lacresha: I was picking her up and I was coming to take her to Grandpa. She did fall a little bit. She fell, her head hit the floor, her body hit the floor, and then I picked her up and run to Grandpa.

Sergeant Pedraza: Do you recall picking up anything that might have caused an injury right there? Take your time. You don't recall using a belt?

Lacresha: For what?

Sergeant Pedraza: To maybe discipline the baby . . .

Lacresha: I don't hit kids . . .

Sergeant Pedraza: . . . and maybe left an injury there.

By the end of the session, Lacresha had agreed with the detective's suggestion that it was "possible" she might also have accidentally kicked the child. Sergeant Pedraza soon had her childlike signature on a document indicating that her statement was not only true and correct but had been given voluntarily. The admission that she had dropped the baby was enough to place her under arrest, charged with capital murder.

Two months later, she was in court, her prosecution overseen by Travis County district attorney Ronnie Earle who, while having held the office since 1976, was in the midst of a tough bid for reelection, facing an opponent for the first time in two decades. Among the incumbent's campaign promises was a tougher, more aggressive stance on juvenile crime. Detractors insisted that the hurried trial of Lacresha Murray provided the needed publicity that fueled his election-day victory.

Earle bristles at the politically motivated, rush-to-judgment criticism, noting that it had long been standard procedure for local judges to quickly adjudicate juvenile cases. In Travis County, he noted, the average juvenile court case went to trial within sixty-two days following an indictment. "The truth of the matter is," he said, "we felt we were rushed. If the decision had been ours to make, we'd have liked longer to prepare our case." Additionally, statistics bore out many of Earle's concerns. Travis

County was receiving five thousand child abuse and neglect calls annually. One study indicated that 18 percent of children who were victims of abuse were later arrested for violent crimes.

Following the second conviction, seated in his second-floor office on the edge of downtown, Earle wearily reflected on the case, the trials, and the steady barrage of angry accusations levied at him and his staff. "Child abuse prosecution has always been one of our primary focuses," he said. "Any time we have a child abuse case or a child death case, I am kept apprised of every step in the progress of the investigation. When I first learned of Jayla Belton's death, I, like everyone else, immediately assumed that some adult was responsible. When I was told that all the evidence pointed to Lacresha, I was as shaken as anybody."

Prosecutor Gary Cobb, who would twice plead the state's case against Murray, had the same first reaction. "I just knew an adult must have done it," he recalled. "There was no way an eleven-year-old female child could have done something like this. Even after reviewing all the material presented to me, I didn't want to believe it. But the fact was, there was only one person who could have committed the crime." By her own admission, Lacresha was the last person to be near Jayla before she was rushed to the hospital. The coroner ruled that the fatal injuries had occurred during that brief period.

On August 9, 1996, a jury of six men and six women returned a guilty verdict, and Murray was sentenced to twenty years under the Determinate Sentencing Act, which provides for juveniles to be committed to the Texas Youth Commission until they become adults. Thereafter, the remainder of the sentence would be served in an adult prison.

The outrage erupted. From the headquarters of Amnesty International to local radio talk shows to the editorial pages of the *New York Times*, a volley of criticism was aimed not only at prosecutor Earle and the Austin police department but the already battle-scarred Texas legal system. Leading the nation in death penalty executions was one thing, critics argued. Trying and convicting children was quite another.

So intense did the public criticism become that a motion for a new trial was soon granted by 250th District judge John Dietz. In January 1997, Lacresha was again found guilty, this time sentenced to twenty-five years. Represented by a young public defender in her first trial, she was provided a three-person legal team that had attempted to deflect the blame to Derrick Shaw, but with little success. Among the accusations they wished the jury to hear was that Shaw had been drinking on the morning he left Jayla at the Murray house, that he was a drug user, and that Jayla was often left unsupervised for lengthy periods of time.

Judge Dietz, however, refused to admit such testimony, noting that police had interviewed both Shaw and Judy Belton extensively and eliminated them as suspects. Expert witnesses summoned by the defense noted that the bruises on her body—many apparently inflicted days before her death—offered evidence that Jayla had long been physically abused. Weighing less than twenty pounds when she died, she was seriously malnourished. The symptoms she had displayed on the morning she was left at the Murray house were strong indicators that she was already in shock when she arrived.

Ultimately, the jury was forced to make its decision after hearing dueling testimony from forensic experts. The child, Dr. Bayardo testified, had received the fatal blows only minutes before her death. Additionally, the prosecution put on famed San Antonio pathologist Dr. Vincent DiMaio, who testified that the groove pattern on the sole of a running shoe, known to have been worn by Lacresha the day the crime occurred, matched the bruises on Jayla's abdomen.

Dallas forensic pathologist Dr. Linda Norton saw things differently. Court-appointed to serve as a defense witness—despite the fact she most often testifies for the prosecution—she reviewed autopsy photographs and reports and soon became convinced that her colleague was wrong. Today, years later, she is still outraged by the guilty verdict. "Lachresha Murray did not kill that child," she says. "She had nothing to do with that little girl's death. It was a gross miscarriage of justice."

During her testimony, Dr. Norton had pointed out that many of the bruises on the victim's body were far too old to have been caused on the day she died. Some, she suggested, had likely been the result of being struck with a broom handle and a belt. The child, she explained to the jury, was badly malnourished. The toddler's sweating, nausea, and lethargic behavior—all classic symptoms of shock—were strong indicators that much of the damage to her ribs and liver had already occurred before she arrived at the Murray home.

That damage, complicated through the day, had only been compounded in the emergency room, she noted. In an effort to revive the child, doctors had pressed against Belton's tiny chest as many as one thousand times. "With CPR on a child," she says, "you're talking about one hundred very powerful compressions a minute, to a body that was very frail to begin with." That well-intended effort, she believes, added to the damage Dr. Bayardo found during his autopsy. Cracked ribs were further damaged, and an already hemorrhaging liver was severed. Drs. Bayardo and DiMaio argued that Dr. Norton's preexisting-injury theory was physically impossible, testifying that anyone suffering the intense pain such internal damage would cause could not stand or walk—something several witnesses had seen Jayla do that day.

"Dr. Bayardo is not a malicious person," Dr. Norton responds, "but that doesn't make his opinion any less a mistake."

Additionally, defense attorney Keith Hampton, forty-one, introduced into evidence a letter from the Texas Department of Safety forensic laboratory to the prosecutors. In the letter, criminalist Juan Rojas wrote that after reviewing photographs of marks on the victim's body and of a pair of shoes allegedly worn by Lacresha Murray, "we were unable to testify that the marks on Belton's body were made by these shoes due to insufficient general characteristics." Rojas suggested that the district attorney's office seek the opinion of another expert.

The jury, however, was not swayed. As was the case in the first trial, it voted unanimously to convict. Even now the verdict haunts the former member of the Dallas County medical examiner's staff. "I had a terrible time dealing with it," Dr. Norton admits. "For months afterwards it was the first thing that entered my mind when I woke. It crushed me, and all I could do was wonder what I might have done that would have made a difference in the outcome of the trial." This from a woman who once explained, "If I let every case get to me, I'd go stark-raving mad. You build a wall between yourself and your cases and just hope it holds up." This one, she admits, didn't.

Barbara Taft understands. She was earning fifty thousand dollars a year as a legal secretary for the Austin firm of Fulbright and Jaworski when she read about the first Murray trial during a bus ride to work. What she read in the morning paper angered her. The photo of Lacresha that accompanied the article broke her heart. That night she and her husband talked about the case late into the night; they rose the following morning to picket in front of the courthouse in protest of the ongoing trial. "In my heart I knew two things," Taft remembers. "I knew that Lacresha was innocent and that I was supposed to do something about what was being done to her." On nothing more than a gut feeling, she went to work.

In the years to come, Taft, who had not known Lacresha Murray or her family prior to the tragedy, became the accused girl's most dedicated and outspoken champion. In time, she developed a close friendship with Lacresha. Resigning from her job to pursue her new cause wasn't a decision Taft made casually, in light of the fact her boss, Mary Dietz, wife of the judge hearing the controversial case, was also a longtime friend. "She was shocked by my decision," Taft recalls, "but she understood that I was serious."

Ending a thirty-year career, Taft formed an organization called People of the Heart, its sole purpose to see justice for Lacresha. She took a part-time job as an office manager at a real estate agency and sold vacuum cleaners door-to-door. Most of her time, however, was focused on People of the Heart, directing its fund-raising efforts, maintaining its website, encouraging the media to look more closely at what she was certain was a travesty of justice, and leading monthly protests in front of the courthouse, outside the district attorney's office, or on the grounds of the state capitol.

"My life began to revolve around what had happened to Lacresha," she says, "because there simply was no one else to do it." As she lobbied for support, she never failed to point out that her concern was also for Jayla Belton. "From the very beginning," she says, "this was a matter of child abuse in America. There's no doubt she was an abused child."

It is an accusation Judy Belton and Derrick Shaw, now married, have repeatedly denied. In the last interview they gave, Derrick told Dave Harmon of the *Austin American-Statesman* that the accusations "still bother me a lot." "As I told everybody before," he said in March of 1999, "I would never do anything to hurt a child." In the same interview, Judy expressed concern that her daughter's death had been obscured by the publicity campaign generated by Lacresha Murray's supporters.

"Though Lacresha was physically and mentally healthy," Taft continued, "she was also abused—by the judicial system. All the Travis County district attorney and medical examiner wanted was a child killer case, and they got it with an eleven-year-old girl. Lacresha was taken from her home, hidden from her family, and questioned until she said what they wanted her to say. All you really have to tell an eleven-year-old is she isn't going home until she tells you what you want to hear. Under those circumstances, she'll say anything."

Ultimately, after Murray had spent three years in Texas Youth Commission facilities, first in Corsicana, then in Giddings, the Austin-based Third Court of Appeals agreed. The conviction was reversed and remanded again to Travis County after it was determined that Lacresha's statement to the police could have been "the product of fright and despair" since she was so young and separated from her family. An immediate appeal to the Texas Supreme Court by the district attorney's office fell on deaf ears.

Thus in April 1999, Lacresha was released and returned to the court-ordered supervision of her grandparents, there to await the district attorney's decision whether she would be tried a third time. Earle, still convinced of her guilt, insisted that if Jayla's mother was prepared to endure yet another courtroom battle, he would continue the fight.

The decision took two years and wound through a maze of negotiations that Murray's lawyer found mind-numbing. "Finally," recalls Hampton, "the D.A. agreed he would consider dropping the case if I could bring him some kind of solid evidence that would point the finger of guilt away from Lacresha." He returned to his files and reviewed findings Dr. Lloyd White, the Nueces County medical examiner, had been prepared to testify to in the second trial. At the time, the defense team had concluded that jurors had grown weary of highly technical medical testimony and thus opted not to call the veteran pathologist to the stand.

Dr. White, a practicing physician for a quarter century, had examined cross-sections of the victim's liver under a microscope and discovered inflammation in the tissues. A sizable collection of neutrophils (white blood cells that collect in response to injuries and bacteria invasions) were found in the damaged liver. "So long as one's heart is pumping," his colleague Dr. Norton explains, "those neutrophils continue to collect at an injury site. The sheer number [of neutrophils] told us that the liver injury had been there a considerable length of time prior to death."

Hampton thus went to Ronnie Earle with the findings, arguing that the initial damage to Jayla Bolton's liver had occurred, not fifteen minutes before death, but more likely eighteen to twenty-four hours earlier. The child, slowly bleeding internally, was, he said, dying before she ever arrived at the Murray home.

Finally, last August, the tragic saga ended in a draw. Earle, citing the fact that his case was seriously weakened by the ruling that Lacresha's statement would no longer be admissible and the fact that Judy and Derrick Shaw had expressed the wish that the matter be closed, opted against a third trial.

All charges against Lacresha Murray were dismissed, her record wiped clean.

On a recent Sunday afternoon, two black ministers cast in the role of mediators entered the Dispute Resolution Center in north Austin, joined by the Shaws, Lacresha, and her grandparents for an hour-long meeting. The purpose, to do what the legal community had been unable to—finally put the issue of Jayla Belton's death to rest.

Emerging after just over an hour, the media-shy Lecresha was at first hesitant to speak, then, in a whisper, finally said, "I told them they have my sympathy." Today, she says, she harbors no resentment for the legal system. "I put that stuff behind me. I just go on with my life." The Shaws would not discuss what had transpired in the closed meeting. "We have to come to some closure, some healing," was all Jayla's mother said.

With that they went their separate ways: Lacresha, now seventeen, to prepare for her junior year at Reagan High School; the Shaws, back to nearby Killeen, where they live with their three children. Weary of television cameras and reporters' tape recorders, everyone agreed there would be no more interviews, no more public reliving of their respective nightmares.

While still residing at the Texas Youth Commission facility in Giddings, Lacresha spoke of looking ahead to the day she would again be free. She talked of her faith, of how she missed her grandmother's cooking, and of her eagerness to again play basketball with her brother, Jason. And she spoke of a future. "When I was younger," she said, "I thought I wanted to be a policewoman when I grew up. But not anymore. I think I want to be a lawyer, a juvenile lawyer, so I can help kids who might be in the same situation I found myself in."

And so a story with all the elements of a Greek tragedy abruptly concluded with no real ending. For all the scarred lives, pain, and lost innocence, there remains the unsettling fact that questions regarding Jayla Belton's death are destined to linger for the ages.

There will, no doubt, forever be those convinced they know the answers. Assistant district attorney Gary Cobb, the lead prosecutor in both Murray trials, remains convinced that Lacresha committed murder. "Absolutely, no doubt about it," he says. His boss, Ronnie Earle, agrees. Though police sergeant Pedraza, who conducted the controversial interview that led to the first indictment, says he has no opinion on the dismissal, the Austin police department has now adopted new procedures for dealing with juvenile suspects. Before a child is questioned without a guardian present, a judge must be notified. Meanwhile, Barbara Taft, who says she can finally scrape the "Free Lacresha" bumper stickers from her pickup, never for a moment doubted Murray's innocence. Nor did Dr. Norton and a number of others who stationed themselves firmly in the girl's camp.

Lacresha, closely watched over by her grandparents, school officials, and a small circle of friends, is happy to be home, concentrating on her studies and earning a spot on the varsity basketball team. She no longer talks of the time spent as a Texas Youth Commission inmate. On the rare occasions when she overhears whispers about her past, she chooses to simply ignore them. "I just want to get on with my life," she confided to Taft.

Those who know her best reflect on the youngster's tragic journey and find it difficult to believe she ever became the central figure in such a horrific story. One of seven children born to a mother now living in Oklahoma and adopted by the Murrays at age two, Lacresha has a shyness about her that has always been one of her most notable personality traits. "She's a quiet child," says Reverend O. S. Davis, pastor of the Ulit Avenue Missionary Baptist Church attended by the Murray family. "She's always been involved in youth activities and had an even temperament. She's a lovable child." Deidra Raney, one of four teachers who testified in Lacresha's second trail, remembered her as "a great kid." "She was always a bit of a tomboy," Raney said, "and seemed to suffer some from low esteem because she didn't feel as pretty as the other girls." None of the instructors remember her as being aggressive or quick to anger. The worst complaint he ever heard from teachers, R. L. Murray adds, was that Lacresha and one of her friends sometimes talked too much in class and that Lacresha seemed to have some difficulties with her math lessons.

Shirley Murray, who returned from that long-ago holiday bus trip to learn that Jayla Belton had died and that her own children were being temporarily held by Child Protective Custody, never doubted Lacresha's innocence. "She's always been kind-hearted and loved little kids. Even when someone did or said something that hurt her feelings, she just ignored it."

The time when her adopted child was in custody, Mrs. Murray says, was agonizing. "Even though I saw her every weekend and talked to her on the phone every night, it didn't take the place of having her at home where she should have been. There was a hole in our family. What should have been a fun time in a child's life—playing, going to school, singing in the church choir, being with family—was taken away.

"But through it all, Lacresha kept her Bible nearby. She told me time and time again that she knew God would work things out."

In his Austin office, Keith Hampton reflects on the years that have passed since he was first introduced to a client who had just celebrated her twelfth birthday. He insists that he did not take long to know that he would be representing someone wrongfully accused. While he celebrates the fact Lacresha is finally free, it pains him to review the destruction that occurred. "I can only hope we've all learned something from this," he says. "A good investigation is one where you're led by the evidence rather than deciding someone's guilt and then building a case against them. That's how innocent people wind up in prison."

Surprisingly, there is no residue of ill will for the district attorney who was for so long his adversary. "It's ironic, I suppose, but the fact of the matter is I've always had a great deal of respect for Ronnie Earle. He's a good D.A. and a good man. I voted for him and probably will again.

But in this case he just allowed the big picture to get lost in a bureau-cratic mind-set."

With that, he pauses, then adds, "Despite all that has happened, the investigations, the trials and negotiations, we still really don't know what happened to little Jayla Belton.

"And that, to me, will forever be the saddest footnote to this case."

DALLAS
Observer

THE WAY OF
THE GUN
THE UNTOLD
STORY OF
WHY LENELL
GETER WAS
FREED

BY CARLTON STOWERS

November 15-21, 2001
FREE
Volume 976
dallasobserver.com

9

THE WAY OF THE GUN

I was a forerunner to racial profiling. . . .

—Lenell Geter

In those days, before the cancer would spread and finally claim his life, longtime law-enforcement officer Billy F. Fowler could recount old cases worked and old criminals encountered with recall that suggested something akin to a photographic memory. A member of the Dallas police department for two decades, he had been the partner of J. D. Tippit. Fowler was off duty on the day Tippit was shot and killed by Lee Harvey Oswald as he fled toward the Texas Theater in the aftermath of the Kennedy assassination. From the Dallas police department, Fowler had moved to the Dallas County district attorney's office where he spent a couple of years working as an investigator. Then for a time he'd been self-employed, investigating cases for several high-profile Dallas attorneys. He was serving as a lieutenant with the suburban Midlothian police department when he died in March 1992.

During Fowler's days in Midlothian, I was researching the murder of undercover officer George Raffield, spending a great deal of time recording Fowler's recollections. As routinely happens, the subject often veered off to other times, other cases—like the 1984 investigation he'd conducted in the infamous matter of Lenell Geter, a man falsely accused and convicted of a robbery and sent to prison for life.

"It's a shame," he confided before his death, "that Geter was never told what we learned." His message, though unspoken, was clear: Some day the story should be written. As if aware that I would need more than just his memory, however good, he handed me a bulky envelope. Like many old-time cops, Fowler had kept copies of files from some of his most interesting cases. The Geter story was all there—the paperwork, from handwritten notes, phone records, and typewritten reports—verifying every detail I'd earlier tape-recorded. Later, visiting with then–assistant district attorney Norm Kinne, he acknowledged that the story was as Fowler had told it.

When I learned that Lenell Geter would be returning to Dallas for a few days to promote a book, it seemed time he should hear it

It was, and remains, one of the dark and troubling moments in Dallas judicial history, spread to a head-shaking nation first by an investigative team from CBS's *60 Minutes*, then by a made-for-television movie produced by the same network. The prestigious *National Lawyer* magazine explored it in critical detail in a story titled "Lazy Justice," and newspaper editorial writers throughout the country used it as a platform to heartily condemn what they perceived as Dallas' quick-draw style of criminal prosecution.

Even as he was being eulogized recently, his life and career celebrated by the city's legal community, the glowing obituaries of longtime Dallas County district attorney Henry Wade were required to remind that among his many triumphs was a dark and lingering mistake. The wrongful prosecution of a black man named Lenell Geter has, for almost two decades, remained an indelibly tarnished spot on his thirty-six-year career.

Though the U.S. Fifth Circuit of Appeals would eventually rule that the Dallas County district attorney's office was shielded by governmental immunity and could not be sued for any violation of civil rights related to the case, it would haunt the public conscience in much the same way a nightmarish occurrence in Dealey Plaza had years earlier.

Geter, then a soft-spoken, twenty-four-year-old engineer working for E-Systems in nearby Greenville, had been arrested and convicted of the August 23, 1982, armed robbery of a Balch Springs Kentucky Fried Chicken (KFC) restaurant. Despite no previous criminal record, the South Carolina native was sentenced to life in prison.

For sixteen months, he remained behind bars while his lawyers continued to argue his innocence and a team of investigative reporters at the *Dallas Times Herald* raised provoking questions about Geter's actual involvement in the crime. Wade, meanwhile, stood firm in his insistence that the right man was in prison. Only after the airing of the *60 Minutes* investigation and a new trial was ordered did the legendary prosecutor, counting the remaining days until his retirement, have the Geter matter reopened. He assigned first assistant Norm Kinne, who had not been involved in the original prosecution of the case, to reinvestigate.

As the late Billy Fowler, a former investigator, and the now retired Kinne would later describe it, the following is how it was in fact the district attorney's office and not the media that ultimately proved Geter's innocence.

As soon as it was announced that a new trial would be granted, Kinne and assistant prosecutor Jerry Banks began traveling to E-Systems' headquarters, interviewing employees in an attempt to trace Geter's actions on the day of the robbery. What they learned was immediately troubling.

"Many of the people we spoke with," Kinne recalls, "had never been interviewed before. Three of Geter's coworkers—people who had not testified during the first trial or had even been interviewed by Geter's own lawyers—had testimony that when combined would have put Geter at work at the time of the offense.

"I soon realized that he had a much stronger alibi than the first jury had heard. And I knew at some point during the upcoming retrial I was going to have to tell the court that I was in possession of what I considered strong alibi evidence that the defense had not uncovered."

Kinne, a man who had long enjoyed his reputation as a fiery, aggressive prosecutor, was beginning to have doubts about the strength of the case he was scheduled to prosecute that coming April. Meanwhile, Fowler, a longtime Dallas police officer who had begun working as an investigator in the district attorney's office, made several trips to various units in the Texas prison system to talk with inmates who had, in the wake of the *60 Minutes* report, begun writing to say they had vital information about the robbery for which Geter was convicted.

What Fowler routinely encountered were inmates eager to use his visit to avoid prison work for the day. No interview, he recalled, had gone more than ten minutes before he was convinced there was nothing that would shed new light on the case.

"One afternoon as Fowler and I sat in my office, reading through the transcripts of the original trial," Kinne remembers, "I told him that I'd done absolutely everything I knew to do and wasn't able to break

Geter's story." Though neither mentioned it, both had privately begun to share the belief that Geter, indeed, might be innocent.

Then, on the afternoon of March 15, 1984, David Kirkland, a captain with the Lufkin police department, placed a call to Kinne that would turn the investigation into a frenzied search that would ultimately result in the truth: The man who had robbed the KFC was not Geter but, instead, was apparently a former Dallas resident named Curtis Eugene Mason.

What transpired during a remarkable six-day investigation—a journey that ultimately returned an innocent man to the free world—not even Geter knew until told the story by the *Observer* during a visit to Dallas to promote his new motivational book, *Overcome, Succeed and Prosper.*

Captain Kirkland had told Kinne of receiving a call from a former Lufkin city official who insisted to him that the Balch Springs robbery had been committed by his cousin's boyfriend, who was currently being held in Houston's Harris County jail. The Lufkin officer gave Kinne a telephone number where the informant could be reached.

On Friday, March 16, 1984, Kinne summoned Fowler into his office to tell him of the previous day's conversation with the Lufkin police captain. "Give this guy a call," he said. "It may be nothing, but just in case it is, I want to keep it quiet."

"At that point," Kinne remembers, "the Geter matter was the biggest story in town. There were reporters walking up and down the halls of the D.A.'s office constantly. I didn't want them, or the defense, to get wind of what we were looking into. If we did have the wrong man, I wanted it to be us who cleared the matter up. I just felt the fewer people who knew what we were doing, the better off we'd be."

Thus Fowler returned to the office he shared with several other investigators and waited until they had left for lunch before he placed his call to Lufkin. The ex-official's wife answered, explaining that her husband was at the dentist's office. She promised to have him return the call, and Fowler gave her numbers at his office and home. Then, while he waited, he checked to see if there was any existing record of Dallas crimes committed by Curtis Mason. He soon learned that just weeks prior to the Balch Springs KFC robbery, Mason had been arrested on a drug charge. Ironically, the codefendant in the case was a known drug dealer who had provided Fowler information that had helped him make numerous cases during his days as a narcotics investigator with the Dallas police. Fowler immediately drove to the home of his old snitch.

The man admitted that he and Mason had been snorting cocaine when the arresting officers had arrived and that they had blown the residue of the drug off the table and into the carpet before the police entered the room. "The only evidence seized," Fowler says, "was the razor blade used to cut the coke. The two men spent a couple of days in jail and were released." The investigator also learned that Mason had remained in Dallas for several days after he was set free.

"This guy told me he had no proof that Mason had been involved in any robberies," Fowler recalled, "but he did tell me that he would occasionally 'disappear' for a day or so, then return with a lot of money in his pocket."

The investigator also learned that the apartment where Mason had been living at the time the robbery was committed was located only a few blocks from the fried chicken restaurant Geter had been accused of robbing.

Returning to his office late in the afternoon, Fowler telephoned Wilbert Alexander, one of the chief assistants in the Harris County district attorney's office, and asked to speak to the person assigned to the Mason case. Karen McAshen was the prosecutor in charge, he was told, but had left for the day. "I'm not familiar with the details," Alexander volunteered, "but there are apparently several cases, and all of them have to do with robberies of Kentucky Fried Chicken restaurants."

Fowler hurried across the hall to tell Norm Kinne what he had learned.

"I think maybe we need to make a trip to Houston on Monday," the prosecutor said.

That Friday evening the mysterious Lufkin connection telephoned Fowler at his Midlothian home and began to elaborate on the story he'd earlier told the local police captain. "My cousin," he said, "was living in Dallas with Mason when the robbery took place."

"But what makes you think he committed the particular robbery we're interested in?" Fowler asked.

"Because he told my cousin he did it," the man responded. He went on to explain that she and Mason had moved to Houston soon thereafter and that he'd been arrested for a series of robberies there. "She called me the other day after an attorney representing him on the Harris County charges had come to her to house, saying that Mason had indicated she could provide an alibi for him. She's scared to death. She doesn't want to have to get on the stand and lie for him."

"I'll need to talk with her," Fowler said.

"She says she doesn't want to get involved, but I'll ask her about it and get back to you." The caller refused to give Fowler his cousin's name or say where she was living. The investigator waited up until past midnight, hoping for a return call, but the phone never rang. On Saturday morning, however, Fowler was mowing his yard when his wife summoned him to the phone. It was another long distance call from Lufkin.

"He told me he had spoken with his cousin and that she had said she didn't want to get involved. I begged and pleaded for him to give me her name and number, but he refused," Fowler remembered.

The caller did, however, provide the investigator with additional information on Mason. About a week after the Balch Springs robbery, Mason had stolen his cousin's car and taken it to Beaumont. While there, he had been in an accident. "One night he was crossing the street and a car hit him, breaking his leg and knocking out several teeth."

Fowler listened with only casual interest, having no idea how a pedestrian–auto accident might figure into the investigation he was conducting. Then a statement jolted him to attention. "The blue canvas bag and the pistol you've been looking for," he said, "are in the possession of the Beaumont police department. Mason had it with him when the car hit him. The police took it when they investigated the accident."

During the first Geter trial, the investigator knew, witnesses to the robbery had testified that the gunman had been carrying a blue canvas bag with white stripes and a white handle. They had also described the weapon as being "large and black." Neither the bag nor the gun had ever been found.

"Did you ever see the gun?" Fowler asked.

"Yes, he showed it to me one time when he was visiting in my home. All I can remember was that it was black and had a long barrel."

The caller went on to say that after Mason was released from the hospital he had traveled to Baton Rouge, Louisiana, to stay with a sister. "That's when he contacted my cousin, and she went over there to be with him. She told me they had stayed with Mason's sister for a only a few days before he cut the cast from his leg and they drove to Houston."

Shortly thereafter, Mason was arrested for a series of Kentucky Fried Chicken robberies there.

Aware that he had sparked Fowler's interest, the caller interrupted his narrative. "Before I go any farther," he said, "I want to know how lucrative this is going to be."

Surprised that the man was evidently interested in selling his information, Fowler said he wasn't sure. "I'll have to talk with my boss about it."

"Is he Geter's lawyer?" the man asked.

"No sir, he's a prosecutor with the Dallas County district attorney's office," Fowler replied. For several seconds there was a stunned silence on the other end of the line. "I guess I'm talking to the wrong people. Could you give me the name of Geter's lawyer?"

Fowler hedged, saying that he understood Geter had several attorneys but that he did not know their names. He said he could get their names Monday when he returned to the office.

"By then I was convinced that the information he had was certainly worth looking into," Fowler said, "and I knew Norm [Kinne] wouldn't want the defense attorneys to know about it before we had a chance to check it out. I begged the guy who had called to not talk with anyone else until Monday. Though I had absolutely no authority to do so, I told him I'd see what we could do about paying him for his information."

The informant reluctantly agreed to wait. Fowler immediately phoned Kinne at home to tell him about the conversation. "We need to go to Houston right away," the assistant district attorney said, instructing Fowler to meet him at Love Field in time to catch a 1 P.M. Southwest Airlines flight. Upon their arrival at Hobby International, they rented a car and drove directly to the Houston police department, where they spent an hour and a half reading through reports of seven aggravated robberies, all attributed to Curtis Eugene Mason. Attached to the files were reports of two armed robberies of Beaumont Kentucky Fried Chicken restaurants.

Though Mason had, during the later robberies, been armed with a shotgun instead of a pistol, the manner in which the November–December crimes were carried out bore a striking resemblance to that described by witnesses to the previous August's Balch Springs robbery. The only marked difference was that on each of the Houston reports the robber was described as "having a limp" and "several front teeth missing."

From the police department, Kinne and Fowler went to the Harris County jail and had Mason called down to one of the interview rooms. The man Kinne interrogated for over an hour looked nothing like Lenell Geter. He was five-foot-ten and weighed 150 pounds while Geter was six-feet-even and 180 pounds. Mason wore his hair in an Afro and had a goatee. At the time of his arrest, Geter's hair was short and he was clean-shaven.

Despite Kinne's best efforts, Mason refused to admit any involvement in the Balch Springs robbery. Finally weary of the prisoner's denials, Kinne angrily told him that he and Fowler would be back on Monday to transport him to Dallas where he would be placed in a lineup to be viewed by witnesses to the Balch Springs robbery. Mason just shrugged and said he'd be looking forward to seeing them again.

As Fowler drove the rental car back toward the airport, Kinne told him, "I want you to go on over to Beaumont and see what you can find out there." At 10:30 on Saturday night, the investigator arrived at the Beaumont police department and explained to the desk sergeant that he was looking for information on a year-old accident involving a man now suspected in a robbery investigation.

"Their traffic division was already closed," Fowler recalled, "so they had to call an officer in to locate the files." On the evening of September 6, 1982, it stated, a man named John Davis had been driving his 1979 Ford Futura eastbound on College Street. As he entered the intersection, Curtis Mason had suddenly walked into the path of his car. However, nothing in the report suggested that the victim carried any kind of athletic bag or pistol.

Near midnight, Fowler, having checked into a Beaumont motel, sat reviewing the accident report. Reading the telephone number of the driver of the car, he ignored the hour and phoned John Davis. Davis remembered the incident well. He described in great detail how Mason had run in front of him. "Was he carrying anything?" Fowler asked.

"Yes," Davis remembered. "He had this blue and white bag. It flew up and hit my windshield. I remember thinking that it was going to come through the glass." He went on to tell how the bag had been lying near the curb when police and the ambulance arrived. "I pointed it out and told one of the officers that it belonged to the man I'd hit.

"I thought it sort of strange when he [Mason] denied that the bag was his. The police took it, though."

"Did you ever see what was in the bag?" Fowler asked.

"Yeah, a pistol. One of the officers took it to his patrol car and put it in the trunk. I was standing right beside him when he unzipped the bag and looked inside. It was a really nice-looking black pistol."

Fowler thanked Davis and apologized for the late night call. Frustrated that he would have to wait until morning to return to the Beaumont police department and see if the bag and gun might still be in the property room, the investigator could not sleep. Soon he was back in his rental car, driving in the direction of the intersection where the accident had taken place. Upon his arrival he checked the diagram attached to the report and determined where Mason had run into the street. He had, the diagram indicated, apparently been coming from the driver's left.

Fowler mentally traced the path the victim had taken before the automobile had hit him. Then his eyes traveled to the corner, less than a hundred feet from where Mason had been hit. Pulling a pencil from his jacket pocket, he added his own notation to the diagram. On the corner was a Kentucky Fried Chicken restaurant.

Fowler smiled. "He was on his way to rob the place," he said aloud.

Early the following morning a sergeant in charge of the Beaumont police department's property room checked his files and found an invoice indicating that the bag and a .45 Smith & Wesson Colt revolver had been received on September 7, 1982. The invoice was signed by the two officers who had investigated the accident.

Unlike Dallas, where confiscated firearms are destroyed, the Beaumont police had a policy of issuing usable handguns to its officers once they were released by the courts. The .45, records showed, had been issued to a patrol sergeant. The bag had been one of many small items that the department placed in "grab bag" type boxes that were sold during periodic public auctions. They had no way to trace who might have purchased it. The officer, however, dialed the number of the sergeant to whom the gun had been issued then handed the phone to Fowler. Soon thereafter, the officer arrived with the handgun and signed it over to the investigator's custody.

By midafternoon Fowler was back in Dallas, bringing with him serious doubt that Lenell Geter had in any way been involved in the robbery for which he'd already served over a year of his life. He phoned Kinne at home and said, "I've got the gun that was used in the Balch Springs robbery."

On Monday he arrived in the district attorney's office with the pistol in his briefcase and took it directly to Kinne's office. "Pick someone to go with you," the prosecutor said, "and go back to Houston and get Mason."

Still adamant about keeping the investigation secret, Kinne instructed Fowler to go to the court of district judge Ron Chapman and get a bench warrant to have Mason returned to Dallas County, not as a suspect but as a "witness."

With the warrant in hand, Fowler sought out misdemeanor-investigator Bob Whitney and asked if he would accompany him to Houston to pick up a prisoner. Eager for an opportunity to get out of the office for the day, Whitney agreed. "What's going on?" he asked.

"I'll tell you when we get on the road," Fowler replied.

At just after four in the afternoon, they arrived at the Harris County sheriff's department and presented the paperwork authorizing them to take Curtis Mason to Dallas. "I'm not sure I can release him," the lieutenant in charge said. "He's scheduled to go to trial in two days. You'll have to get the judge's approval."

At Fowler's urging, the officer phoned the judge assigned to hear Mason's case and was told he would not approve release of the prisoner. If Dallas wanted Mason, the judge said, it would have to first get approval from the prosecutor. Thus the next call went to Harris County assistant district attorney Karen McAshen. "Fortunately," Fowler recalled, "she was still in her office. I explained that I wasn't authorized to give her any details but assured her as best I could that we needed Mason very badly. I asked her to try and persuade the judge to pass the case to a later court date.

"She was a little miffed by the fact I wouldn't explain what was going on but finally agreed to call the judge." By late in the afternoon the judge had signed off on the release.

When Mason was brought down from his jail cell, Fowler didn't immediately recognize him. He had shaved off his goatee and no longer wore his hair in an Afro, obviously preparing himself for the lineup appearance Kinne had warned of just two days earlier. The handcuffed

The district attorney looked at Fowler, then Kinne, saying nothing. Then he turned to walk to a nearby secretary's desk. "Schedule me a press conference for 4 P.M.," Wade said.

Billy Fowler and Norm Kinne stood against the wall in the back of the room, listening as the district attorney told members of the media that new evidence had come to light that indicated Lenell Geter was, in fact, innocent of the crime for which he'd been convicted. As Wade spoke, a secretary approached Fowler and whispered that he had a phone call. It was, she said, from someone in Lufkin.

In a troubled voice, the now familiar voice explained that his cousin had been receiving threatening phone calls from Curtis Mason since Fowler and Kinne had first visited him in the Harris County jail. The calls, he said, had continued following his transfer to Dallas. "He's threatening to kill her or have someone kill her because she's the only one he ever told about that Balch Springs robbery. She wants to talk to you."

Though Fowler and Kinne had, while reading reports during their visit to Houston, learned the name of the woman with whom Mason had been living and assumed she was, in fact, the cousin that had been mentioned, Fowler pled ignorance.

"You've never told me her name or where I can reach her," the investigator said. After being given the woman's name and phone number, Fowler hung up and immediately called the jail to request that Mason not be allowed further use of the phone. He then dialed a number in Houston.

While Wade was addressing the media across the hall, Mason's former girlfriend was telling Fowler a story that removed any lingering doubts. When she and Mason had lived together in Dallas, she had known he was dealing drugs but insisted she had never suspected him of committing robbery until he was arrested in Houston.

In December 1983, on the night the *60 Minutes* report on Lenell Geter aired, Mason had called her from the Harris County jail to ask if she was watching the program. "She told me that they stayed on the phone during the entire Geter segment," Fowler recalled, "and Mason told her, 'That's me they're talking about, not Geter.'"

He admitted to her that he was the one who had robbed the Balch Springs restaurant and had even recognized two of the women who had been interviewed on the CBS show. She went on to tell Fowler of Mason's stealing her car and taking it to Beaumont, of joining him in Louisiana following his accident, and of his ultimate arrest while they were living in Houston. She again insisted that she'd had no idea he was a robber until police came to their apartment and placed him under arrest. Though she had known of her boyfriend's involvement in the Balch Springs robbery since December, she had not placed a call for advice to her Lufkin relative until March when Mason's attorney had approached her about serving as an alibi witness.

She began to cry as she continued telling Fowler her story. "I love Curtis," she said, "but I'm afraid of him. When that lawyer came to me and I realized that he wanted me to get on the witness stand and lie for him, I got really scared. I just didn't want to be a part of it."

"I'm glad you made the decision you did," Fowler replied.

And so, after a whirlwind blur, it was over. Though never tried for the Balch Springs robbery, Mason was sentenced to thirty-five years for seven other aggravated robberies with a deadly weapon, for firearm possession, and for possession of cocaine; he is incarcerated at the Clements Unit in Amarillo.

In the months that followed the dismissal of charges against Geter, the case was seldom out of Fowler's thoughts. Even after Geter's release from prison, people in the courthouse would stop him, unaware of his involvement, and ask if he really thought justice had been served. More than one person suggested that the entire episode had been nothing more than a case of Henry Wade's putting a troublesome and controversial matter to rest in the best way he could. Many still felt Geter was guilty. But since Wade had offered no public detailing of his office's investigation into the case, Fowler didn't feel it his place to do so.

"I never felt the district attorney's office was at fault in the case," he would later confide. "It just took the information brought to it, went to court, and got a conviction. What a lot of people were never aware of was that Norm Kinne worked just as hard to right that wrong as he ever did to get a conviction. You can't ask more of a man than that."

"I did my job," Kinne says, "and Billy Fowler certainly did his."

Why, then, in the years that followed did he never tell the media details of the investigation that freed Geter? "Because," Kinne says, "nobody ever asked me." For years after, a hint was in full view of anyone who en-

tered his office. In a bookcase lay Mason's gun, which Fowler had res-
cued from Beaumont, a constant reminder of the investigation.

After leaving the district attorney's office, Fowler decided to try to
contact Geter. "I just felt he had a right to know how he had been
cleared," he said. "That way, if he ever wanted to he would be able to explain it to his friends and family.

"I had read a number of articles in which his mother, in particular,
had expressed dismay at the fact her son had been convicted of a crime.
I thought maybe he would like to be able to tell the story to her."

For several weeks, Fowler left messages for Geter with a supervisor
at E-Systems. His calls were never returned.

At forty-three years old, Lenell Geter has distanced himself, mentally and
physically, from the nightmare he was swept into back when an all-white
jury found him guilty of a crime he hadn't committed. If there is anger,
he hides it expertly.

Having lost his enthusiasm for work as an engineer after regaining
his freedom, he left E-Systems and Texas and returned to South Carolina.
Now married and the father of three daughters, his attention is focused
on Lenell Geter Enterprises, an organization that conducts inspirational
and motivational workshops at churches, schools, and businesses. Today,
he says, he no longer dwells on his days behind bars.

He was sitting in the meeting room of the *Dallas Post Tribune*, taking a break from greeting old friends and signing copies of his new book,
when he finally heard the details of the investigation Fowler and Kinne
had long-ago conducted. And what was his reaction? Shaking his head,
he first said he'd have to think about it. Then, after a while, he ticked off
three words: "Surprising," he said, "and shocking . . . and belated."

With that he smiled and volunteered a point many who followed
his judicial travails might find surprising. "I do believe in the system," he
said. "I was exonerated. And I'm free."

Billy Fowler would have liked hearing that.

DALLAS
Observer

JOHN MULLEN IS A MODERN-DAY ACTION HERO STRAIGHT OUT OF TELEVISION, A FULL-TIME EMERGENCY ROOM PHYSICIAN WHO FIGHTS CRIME AND SOLVES MURDERS ON THE SIDE

DR. COP
BY CARLTON STOWERS

10

DR. COP

At first blush they sound like scenes from a newborn television series, one in which the network brain trust has combined the two most time-honored story lines available to them: life-saving doctors and crime-busting cops. For instance . . .

In the predawn hours of a quiet East Texas morning, the tall, lanky emergency-room doctor, still dressed in his blue surgical scrubs after a twelve-hour shift at nearby Mount Pleasant's Titus Regional Medical Center, is en route home when a two-way radio anchored on the dashboard of his '94 Capri crackles. A sheriff's department dispatcher announces that there has been a hit-and-run accident nearby and the suspect has fled the scene.

The doctor, feeling a welcome rush of adrenalin, jumps into action and is soon in pursuit of the suspect, following him right to the driveway of his home. As the man steps from his car, Dr. John B. Mullen, fifty-four, is out of his unmarked Chevrolet, gun and Franklin County deputy sheriff's badge in hand, preparing to make an arrest.

Or . . .

A young couple, having recently left the urban rat race behind, is in the process of remodeling a home that had stood vacant for years. The wife, busily taking inventory of things that needed to be done, suddenly screams and immediately places a call to the sheriff's department. Breathlessly, she explains that she has discovered what appears to be a body lodged in her chimney. Deputy Mullen, the department's designated crime-scene investigator, is quickly dispatched. Indeed, what he finds are the mummified remains of a twenty-something male who, records would later show, had been reported missing eight years earlier.

And, how about this one?

Mullen, enjoying a rare evening off, is returning from Dallas after attending a book-signing party for friend and mentor Roy Hazelwood, the famed FBI profiler. Before he reaches the turnoff that will take him to his lakeside home near Mt. Vernon, Mullen's attention is drawn to a car that passes him at a high rate of speed. The off-duty deputy follows the car until it enters his Franklin County jurisdiction then pulls it over.

Not only does the young driver receive citations for speeding and driving without a license but gets a visit to the county jail where he is asked to explain what he was doing with ten pounds of marijuana in his car. A computer check later revealed that he was also wanted on an aggravated assault warrant that had earlier been issued in Dallas County. The bust, Mullen says, was almost as satisfying as the one that resulted after he'd stopped to question a hitchhiker during a routine patrol of the eleven miles of Interstate 30 that runs through Franklin County. The man, it turned out, was wanted in Oregon for seven sexual assaults.

Sometimes the "war stories" are less dramatic, but entertaining all the same. Like the night he stopped a carload of local teenagers for speeding. While talking with the youngsters, the deputy heard muffled sounds coming from the trunk and requested it be opened. Inside was yet another teen, surrounded by dozens of cartons of cigarettes. In short order the frightened boys admitted to breaking into a grocery store in a nearby town. Mullen radioed the neighboring police chief to whom the burglary had not yet been reported. "I've got the kids who did it in custody if you want to come get them," the deputy added.

When another teenager, bleeding profusely and weakly explaining that he had "fallen on a knife," was brought into the emergency room, Dr. Mullen quickly examined the young man and detected four stab wounds to the chest and stomach. "Son," he told the patient, "nobody falls on a knife four times. Who did this to you?" By the time the patient was wheeled from the operating room, his wounds tended, the doctor had switched hats and, as a deputy sheriff, begun his search for the assailant whose name and address he'd coaxed from the victim.

Proving once again that fact mightily trumps fiction, the life story of former Dallas neurosurgeon John Mullen—whether or not it ever makes its way to Hollywood—would make Walter Mitty proud and much of the world's adult male population green with envy. Not only is he living dual boyhood dreams, he's succeeding at both.

Along the way he's established a resume that sounds like a publicity department's fantasy. Born in the small upstate New York mining town of Port Henry, the son of a father who was a banker and a mother who was a telephone operator, he did his collegiate undergraduate work at the University of Vermont, earning a degree in chemistry; he then attended medical school at Southern Illinois' College of Medicine and served his residency at Duke. Along the way he funded his education tending bar, working as a bouncer, and finally, assisting a forensic pathologist.

His own medical career began in Dallas, where he would develop into a highly regarded neurosurgeon, gaining nationwide attention for a procedure designed to control epilepsy. Add that as a reserve officer with the rank of lieutenant colonel in the army's elite First Special Operations Command, he took a break from private practice to participate in Desert Storm, there to stand ready to tend wounded U.S. soldiers. Consider also that he is certified as a master scuba diver, a licensed pilot, and trophy-winning skeet shooter, and you quickly get the idea that Dr. John Mullen isn't Everyman. The guy's even been featured in *Ripley's Believe It or Not.*

Yet all he ever really wanted to be was a cop.

"I've always had a tremendous respect for people in law enforcement," he says as he looks out a rain-splashed window toward the lake that forms the far boundary of his rambling backyard. "I guess it goes back to my high school days when I'd be hitchhiking home from school in the winters and officers from the New York State Police would stop and give me a ride."

In truth, as a young man Mullen considered a variety of vocations. One, of course, was the medical profession, which his parents and several teachers back at Ticonderoga High (New York) encouraged him to pursue; a possible career in the military; or maybe an application to the FBI academy. Ultimately, he would opt to become a doctor, but only after a series of unexpected events.

While participating in ROTC drills during his third year as an undergraduate, he suffered a knee injury so severe that it was necessary for him to drop out of school for a year. During his academic sabbatical, he began working as an assistant chemist in the state medical examiner's office in Burlington, Virginia. In time, Mullen estimates, he assisted in at least a thousand autopsies and developed a fascination for the forensic science.

"After I graduated [in 1970]," he recalls, "I went to work full-time in the M.E.'s [medical examiner's] office. I did that for three years before my boss finally talked me into going to medical school. He told me about a new program at Southern Illinois University, where you were offered a board exam, which, if passed, amounted to completion of the first couple of years of med school. The bottom line was that if you could pass the exam and were accepted, you could be in and out of medical school in only two years."

Mullen drove all night from Burlington to Springfield, Illinois, stopped for a quick shower at a truck stop, reported for the exam, and was one of four candidates selected. By 1975, he was beginning his internship at Duke University Medical Center. In 1981, Dr. John Mullen made the move to Dallas.

First he served as an instructor at the University of Texas Health Sciences Center of Dallas Southwestern Medical School, then as codirector of Parkland Hospital's Epilepsy Center, and finally as a practitioner in private neurological surgery. During this time, he enjoyed a steadily growing reputation and all the financial trappings his profession made possible. He worked long hours to afford such lifestyle amenities as his own plane.

In time, however, came what he describes as "the burnout." "Cutting on nerve tissue is extremely stressful," he admits. "It was exacting and demanding, the kind of thing that appealed to the perfectionist in me. But, unfortunately, there was also a lot of routine work. Frankly, I became more than a little weary of treating people with back pains. Hearing the constant complaints of patients became monotonous." His bedside manner, he admits, was deteriorating swiftly.

"I'm not sure," he adds, "that I fully realized it at the time, but working around the clock, doing the same thing over and over, had begun to wear on me." In truth, he says, the fame and fortune of the medical profession had never been the driving force in his career choice. It was the challenge that motivated him. He had begun to feel that motivation slipping away.

Even in the early days of his medical career, Mullen would enjoy the occasional brush with another world that had long fascinated him. In 1985, a man named Abdelkrim Belachheb burst into a fashionable Dallas restaurant called Ianni's and opened fire, killing six people and wounding another. When his defense attorney made it known he would suggest the tragic event had been triggered by an epileptic seizure, assistant Dallas County district attorney Norm Kinne went looking for an expert witness. The man he found to testify that the accused killer had *not* suffered a seizure was Dr. Mullen. "My role was very small," he says, "but being involved in the case was fascinating." Though he does not boast of it, it was, in fact, that case that would ultimately make judicial history. Shortly after the Ianni's bloodbath, lawmakers ruled that the murder of three or more victims would qualify as a capital case, subject to the possibility of the death penalty.

In January 1991, Dr. Mullin exchanged his scrubs for a military uniform as he and fellow reservists were mobilized to Saudi Arabia for Desert Storm. "I had a lot of down time while I was over there," he recalls, "and did a lot of thinking about my life." There, in a foreign desert, he pondered an unsatisfactory life that had, during a twenty-year career, become far too work consumed and a marriage that was fast heading toward divorce, and he arrived at a decision that would send him in a new direction.

"I decided that when I got home I would enroll in the police academy and see if I could get into law enforcement," he says. His plan also included leaving the relentless pressures of the Dallas medical community behind. Several years earlier, after purchasing a "getaway" home on picturesque Lake Cypress Springs, he'd opened a second office in nearby Mount Vernon. The clinic, which soon demanded all the rest-and-relaxation time he'd planned for his trips into the piney woods, would, he decided, have to be closed. The lakeside home, however, would eventually serve as his year-round residence.

Lest one think his dramatic career change was spur-of-the-moment, understand that John Mullen has never been one to proceed through life without plan. Because of his responsibilities to patients, he realized that completing the demanding requirements of the Northeast Texas Police Academy would likely take as much as a year. Only when that step was nearing completion did he pay a visit to the Titus County Regional Medical Center and apply for a job as an emergency room surgeon. He was hired immediately. Then he stopped in on longtime Franklin County sheriff Charles (Chuck) White and offered his services as an unpaid deputy. "When he didn't immediately show interest," Dr. Mullen says, "I told him I'd even furnish my own car."

"At first," says Sheriff White, "I was more than a little surprised to see him sitting in my office, making the proposal he was making. I can't honestly say that I immediately took him seriously. But, the more he talked, the more I realized he wanted to give it a try. I figured, why not?"

That the doctor was an honor graduate of the police academy spoke to the seriousness with which he approached his task. Texas Peace Officers Association certificate in hand, he went looking for a car. It was, in fact, Sheriff White who tipped him to the fact that an almost-new Caprice with a souped-up Corvette engine was available at a modest price. Purchased originally by the Plano police department, it had been in use only three days when it was rear-ended and insurance adjusters ruled it a total loss. It had been sold to a mechanic in Oklahoma who specialized in the restoration of wrecked police cars for resale.

"The car, which all the kids around here call the Batmobile, had less than seven hundred miles on it," Mullen says, "and I bought it for twelve thousand dollars." It is that same car, now with 130,000 miles on the odometer, which he continues to drive when on patrol. "The fastest I've ever had it," he admits, "is 145 during a chase."

His dual-job juggling act works like this: At the beginning of each month, his twelve-hour emergency room shifts, which begin at 7 P.M. and end at 7 A.M. (or vice versa), are scheduled. Once aware of what his hospital routine will be, he then reports to the sheriff's department to schedule the forty hours per month he averages as a deputy. While Sheriff White has routinely offered him a salaried position on his eight-man force each time an opening has occurred, Mullen insists he is content with the current arrangement.

"We're fortunate to have someone with his expertise," the sheriff says. "For instance, having a medical doctor working a violent crime scene is a big plus in this business. John is excellent with virtually all aspects of forensics. More important, though, he is good with people. He's well liked because he's a very compassionate person. When you're working a domestic situation or dealing with victims or the family of a victim, that's one of the most important parts of the job.

"I'd say the majority of the people he meets on the street or while on patrol have no idea he's a doctor as well as a deputy. It isn't something he flaunts. When he's on duty he just another law enforcement officer, doing his job, whether it is working a homicide, patrolling, or helping a farmer get a stray cow back in the pasture."

Among those inspired by Dr. Mullen's career choice is Sheriff White's father, a general practice physician in Mount Vernon. Dr. Robert White, sixty-six, recently followed Mullen's path and now serves as a reserve deputy on his son's staff. "He'd never have considered it had it not been for what John has done," the sheriff says.

"Having grown up in a doctor's home," White adds, "I naturally questioned why someone would give up the kind of salary a neurosurgeon makes to do the kind of work I do. But, the more I've gotten to know John, the better I understand. Law enforcement is a passion for him."

Still, to make the switch from full-time medical practice to the life he now leads, Mullen admits, demanded a major scale back. "I'm probably making about a third of what I earned in private practice in Dallas," he admits. The first thing to go was his plane. Yet he insists he's enjoying life like never before. Even the routine work of a rural sheriff's department—stopping speeders along the interstate, calming domestic waters—hasn't dulled his enthusiasm for the job.

Dallas neurosurgeon Dr. Richard Jackson has known Mullen since the early eighties, when the two worked together. "John," he says, "has walked to a different drummer for as long as I've known him."

Still, he admits he was stunned when his friend announced his decision to leave his Dallas practice for the unique lifestyle he now leads in East Texas. "He walked away from a sizable investment of time and work— medical school, internship, building a reputation. Not many people are willing to take that kind of step. He was very skilled, and his patients loved him. But there came a point where he became more and more frustrated by people who came to him with imagined pains. He had a low tolerance for that sort of thing."

"Intense," Dr. Jackson says, is a good description of the Mullen he worked alongside. "He was never one to sit around and chitchat. He didn't play golf or go to the symphony. He didn't seem to have any outside interests. He didn't laugh a lot. In fact, I always felt he was a little too serious."

Recalling Dr. Mullen's call to Desert Storm, Jackson says he occasionally sent him "care packages" and notes. "I recall one letter I received from him in which he expressed his frustration at being there only in the role of a doctor, with so much time on his hands. John wanted to be a soldier, to be in on the action."

Mullen, it seems, has constantly searched for new ways to be certain that neither boredom nor apathy visits. Fascinated by the forensic phase of criminal investigation since his days as a medical examiner's assistant, he began taking law enforcement courses even while still a full-time neurosurgeon. Since 1989, when he attended a seminar on ritualistic-cult investigation, he has studied everything from the analysis of bloodstain patterns to forensic hypnosis, child abuse to forensic entomology.

Today Mullen is the one who is called on to investigate all major crimes scenes in his jurisdiction as well as many in neighboring counties. Within a year after earning his Texas peace officer's certification at the Northeast Texas Police Academy, he was asked to serve as one of its instructors. Among the courses he has taught are classes on sex offenders, serial killers, and a unique course in forensic nursing, in which he instructs emergency room personnel on techniques for detecting child abuse and sexual assault, and the collection and preservation of evidence.

Then there is the Texas Major Crimes Committee on which he now serves alongside eleven other law enforcement officers from throughout the state. "It is," Mullen explains, "a group which includes sheriffs, Texas Rangers, and police department homicide detectives. We meet quarterly at the Texas Department of Safety academy for a week and just brainstorm about unsolved cases, developing profiles, things of that nature. Most importantly, it gives everyone the opportunity to take a fresh look at a case that has been worked by others."

Indeed, there is evidence that a different set of eyes does see things that have been overlooked. For instance, in a recent murder case, the investigator had several suspects but nothing that would single out the actual killer. A technique that Mullen has long followed in the course of his own crime-scene investigations was to check date books and calendars found at the scene or residence of a suspect. "We were going through all the evidence that had been collected on the case," he remembers, "and among the material was a calendar belonging to one of the suspects. He was obviously a compulsive type who logged everything on his calendar, from a trip to the grocery store to movies he'd seen. The only date with no entry at all was the one on which the crime had occurred."

Mullen suggested to the frustrated detective that he'd found his man. The officer looked at the calendar and began to shake his head. He'd been over every scrap of evidence in the case hundreds of times, he said, but had never noticed that one blank spot on the calendar. In time, it was Mullen's observation that led to the arrest and conviction of the killer.

Former FBI behavioral science unit expert Hazelwood recalls first meeting the doctor at a law enforcement seminar in New Orleans in the late eighties. "When he came up and introduced himself and told me he was a neurosurgeon, I didn't believe him. Even after he convinced me, my reaction was much the same as everyone else: Why would a person consider leaving a profession where he was earning a tremendous amount of money to get into one like ours?

"Over the years, as we've become friends, he's explained his decision to me. First, it was something he badly wanted to do. Second, he'd reached a point financially and psychologically where he felt comfortable making the move.

"I have tremendous respect for him. As a law enforcement officer with a medical background, he brings an insight to criminal investigation that others of us simply don't have. His understanding of the human body, how it reacts to various degrees of assault and trauma is invaluable. And he's a very open-minded individual, something vital to any crime investigation. Add the fact that he has a great deal of common sense and you have all the ingredients for an outstanding law enforcement officer."

While the police work has added new energy to his life, Mullen makes it clear that his enthusiasm level does not drop when he reports to the emergency room where, over the course of any shift, he finds himself dealing with everything from heart attacks and strokes to accident injuries and broken bones. "Life in any emergency room," he says, "seldom offers a dull moment."

It isn't unusual for him to be in a position of treating patients he'd first met while writing them a speeding ticket or escorting them to jail for being drunk and disorderly. Also, more than one criminal investigation has begun while he was on the clock at the hospital. For instance, an out-of-towner was brought into the emergency room by ambulance, complaining that he was suffering the kind of chest pains associated with a heart attack. Upon examination, the doctor judged the man to be in perfect health. In truth, his trip to the hospital was a scam the inventive "patient" was using to skip out on a sizable motel bill he had no intention of paying. "After I had thoroughly examined him," Mullen recalls, "I phoned the sheriff's department and asked them to run him on the computer. Up popped a felony warrant, so they came and got him."

On a more serious note, there was the time a distraught mother brought her child in, saying that it had recently stopped breathing. The badly bruised infant, Dr. Mullen quickly surmised, had been dead for over an hour. "It was pretty obvious that the child had been beaten to death," he says, "so I had photographs taken and we measured the progress of lividity in order to help determine the actual time of death."

Ultimately a murder case was made against the mother and her boyfriend.

Of course, in the small county in which he works, there is always going to be some overlap of professions. Once, he remembers, he arrested one of his former surgical patients. "He was drunk and passed out in his car on a service road just outside town," Mullen says. "When I tried to help him out of his car, he became belligerent and wanted to fight. He didn't recognize me as his doctor until after I got him to jail and he'd sobered up a little. Once he realized who I was, he was surprised and apologetic."

Today it is not unusual for fellow lawmen—local police, Texas Rangers, or fellow deputies—to stop by the emergency room while Mullen is on duty, hoping to find him not busy so they can discuss a particular case they're working on.

"He's one of those rare people," says Titus Regional Medical Center CEO Steve Jacobson, "who has found the best of both worlds. We're just as happy to have him working for us as the sheriff's department is. Dr. Mullen earned a great deal of respect during his career as a neurosurgeon and now has that same kind of respect as an emergency room doctor.

"I used to kid him about all of this being some kind of midlife crisis thing, but the truth is that had nothing to do with the decision he made. He's obviously had a long and burning desire to work in law enforcement, and now that he's realized that dream, he takes it very seriously. Just as he does his work here at the hospital."

Only Mullen, it seems, fails to see anything unusual about his dual careers. "My whole life has been spent in some kind of public service," he says, "and I get a strong sense of reward from that. Just as I've done as a doctor, my work as a deputy sheriff has provided me an opportunity to help people. I enjoy what I do and I'm comfortable with who I am, whether I'm in scrubs, a uniform, or jeans."

Always motivated by a challenge, he insists he now finds it in both jobs. "In many ways," he says, "they are similar. I've always felt that the medical procession and law enforcement are both a matter of detective work. As a doctor, you're trying to solve the mystery of whatever illness or injury a patient is suffering from. In law enforcement, you're trying to figure out who committed a crime."

He's not one who leaves the work at the office. His wife, Martha, who was working as a nurse at Titus Regional when they met, shares John's interest in crime detection. Long before they married in 1998, the forty-four-year-old mother of two sons was an avid reader of true-crime books. "Late one night he came up on the floor where I was working and found me reading (former FBI agent) John Douglas' new book, and we immediately struck up a conversation." Soon she was enrolled in his seminar on forensic nursing.

Now retired from nursing after seventeen years, she looks forward to the day when she can work alongside her husband at crime scenes. Currently taking correspondence courses in pediatric and childhood violence, her goal is to catch up with her husband's knowledge of forensic science. They talk of one day forming a husband-and-wife consulting team to assist law enforcement in criminal investigations.

"When he first told me he was a deputy sheriff," she admits, "I couldn't believe it. I'd known a lot of doctors and couldn't imagine one giving up a lucrative practice like he'd done. By the same token, I'd also seen a lot of people in the medical profession reach that 'burnout' stage he talked of. The more I got to know him, the more I understood that he was a person who liked helping people, whether they had medical problems or needed protection from the criminal element."

Leave it to Deputy Mullen to leaven the praise. After almost a decade on the job, he says, he is still learning—and making the occasional wrong call. Two days after the bludgeoned body of eighty-seven-year-old Leafie Mason was discovered in her home in nearby Hughes Springs, local police chief Randy Kennedy phoned to ask that Mullen make a trip over to evaluate the crime scene. On the basis of what he was told by the chief, what he saw at Mason's home, and in the crime scene photographs, Mullen's initial reaction was that whoever killed the elderly woman by beating her with an antique iron had, in all likelihood, been someone she knew.

Months later, following the celebrated capture of Rafael Resendez Ramirez, the nationally infamous "Railroad Killer," a palm print found on Mason's windowsill was matched to his. Ramirez, a total stranger to Mason and all of his other victims across the country, later pled guilty to the murder.

"I certainly didn't get that one right," Mullen volunteers. "But, hey, I'm glad the case was finally solved. In police work, that's the bottom line."

Such admission is yet another example of the comfort level he's reached. "When I was in Dallas," he says, "all I did was work and think about work. Today my lifestyle is so much better. This place and the people here are wonderful. I've never felt so relaxed."

So, okay, get me the Coast. This guy's story beats that sappy lawyer-goes-to-small-town-and-runs-a-bowling-alley hit all to hell. Pitching it will be a snap: You've got *ER* meets *NYPD Blue* with a touch of *Mayberry RFD* tossed in to give it a little down home flavor. How can it miss?

DALLAS Observer

February 1-7, 2001
Volume 535
dallasobserver.com

The PHANTOM MENACE

IN 1946, A SERIAL KILLER HAUNTED SLEEPY TEXARKANA, STALKING HIS VICTIMS UNDER THE COVER OF NIGHT. INVESTIGATORS WONDER IF HE DIED DECADES LATER IN A DALLAS REST HOME—OR SIMPLY DISAPPEARED.

BY CARLTON STOWERS

11

THE PHANTOM MENACE

The enduring legend began not with death, but with a frightening and vicious attack on two young lovers who managed to survive.

On a February night in 1946, twenty-four-year-old Jimmy Hollis and his girlfriend Mary Jeanne Larey, nineteen, had attended a downtown Texarkana movie then decided to prolong the evening with a romantic visit to a secluded lane on the edge of town. They had, according to the story the young woman would later tell authorities, been parked no more than ten minutes when a man, his face hidden beneath a white hood, approached the car, pointing a flashlight and pistol at them.

She would recall the assailant telling her boyfriend, "I don't want to kill you, fella, so do what I say." He then ordered both of them out of the car, angrily demanding that Hollis remove his trousers. Then, with the young man clad only in his boxer shorts, the attacker hit him twice in the head, knocking him unconscious. When Larey tearfully tried to convince the gunman that they had no money, even pulling a billfold from her date's discarded pants to show him, she, too, was struck in the head. As she lay bleeding and dazed, the man sexually assaulted her with the barrel of his gun.

When Hollis began to regain consciousness, her attacker's attention was diverted long enough for the young woman to get to her feet and run. The intruder, however, quickly caught up to her and hit her in the head again. "I remember looking up at him and saying, 'Go ahead and kill me,'" she later said. Then, for reasons she would never know, the masked man suddenly turned away and disappeared into the darkness.

Though badly injured, Hollis managed to make his way to a main road and flag down a passing car. Larey, meanwhile, had run to a nearby house where she pounded on the door until a farmer woke, let her inside, and telephoned the sheriff. After receiving medical attention—Larey needed stitches to close her wounds; Hollis was hospitalized for several weeks with two severe skull fractures—the victims could only describe their attacker as "thin and approximately six feet tall." Neither had recognized his voice or seen the face hidden behind the makeshift mask.

Today, over a half-century later, that event is looked back on as the precursor of a nightmare that would long terrorize this quiet East Texas railroad center. In the weeks following the attack on Hollis and Larey, five murders would occur in its rural shadows, prompting one of the most intense manhunts in the state's history. Twice on moonlit nights, an unknown assailant interrupted young lovers, leaving them brutalized and dead. On another evening, a farmer sitting in his living room, reading the newspaper before retiring, was shot through a nearby window.

The city became paralyzed by rampant fear, its citizens wondering if yet another attack would come before an arrest was made and calm restored. In other parts of the world, a safe-distance fascination quickly grew as law enforcement frantically searched for the person the colorful media of the time had begun referring to as the "Phantom Killer."

Yet the story that long screamed from newspaper headlines and the pages of such magazines as *Life* and *Time*, even ultimately earning the attention of Hollywood, never reached a satisfactory ending. While the lone surviving law enforcement officer involved in the investigation believes he knows the identity of the man responsible for the crimes, they officially remain unsolved. In fact, cable television's TLC (The Learning Channel) has a series tentatively titled *Famous Unsolved Serial Murders in History*. Among those on the list are the Green River killings in the Seattle area, London's historic Jack the Ripper murders, the still-controversial Boston Strangler case . . . and the infamous terror reign of the Texarkana Phantom Killer.

For the residents of this geographically strange city, half of which sits on the Texas side of the border, the other on the Arkansas side, it was a time of bright new hope and better days to come. The war had finally ended, and its victorious sons were proudly marching home to heroes' welcomes. The rationings of things like gasoline and tires had come to an end; jobs were still plentiful at the local munitions plants despite the fact peace settled over the nation; and never had the scent of the region's tall, cool pines and its tangled ropes of honeysuckle and lantana been more fragrant. In Washington, President Harry Truman was promising the country, including their own Bowie County, a swift return to prosperity. It was a simpler, more gentle time when people sat on their front porches in the evenings, sipping iced tea and visiting with neighbors who stopped by; a more trusting time when few even thought of locking their doors. On warm nights, people slept with their windows raised, letting the breezes do the job that would one day fall to air conditioning.

If not idyllic, it was about as close as a city of forty thousand could hope to get. At least that's how Dallas forensic psychologist Dr. James Grigson remembers it. Now sixty-nine, there is a nostalgic lilt to his voice as he recalls a Texarkana boyhood that included weekend visits to the double features being shown at the downtown Paramount or Strand; a quarter was all that was needed for bus fare, admission, and a large box of popcorn. He can still remember the sound of summer rains on the tin roof on the family house on Hazel Street, of the days working at Adam's Grocery, participating in whatever sport was in season, and the regular trips into the woods for campouts with Boy Scout Troop 25. Two of his childhood buddies, Bobby McClure and Mitchell Young, were even featured on the cover of *Life* magazine after it was determined they had, at the time, earned more merit badges than any other Scouts in the United States.

It was a great time in his life, Grigson says. Until the killings started.

In a nightmarish period spanning the end of March through early May, the five brutal homicides that invaded the innocence of the community gave rise to unprecedented fear and suspicions. Hard-earned money, generally reserved for household needs, was suddenly being spent on guns. Doors were locked and lights left on through the long nights. Wives of men who worked evening shifts out at the Lone Star Arsenal assembled their children and took up nightly residence in the downtown Grim Hotel. The local Western Union office suspended after-dark delivery of telegrams when shots were fired at an employee as he approached a residence. Suggestion of a curfew met with little argument.

Law enforcement officials from throughout the state came running. Heading the investigation was legendary Texas Ranger captain M. T. (Lone Wolf) Gonzaullas. Close behind was the nation's fascinated media. Wrote Kenneth Dixon, a columnist assigned to chronicle the case for the New York–based International News Service, "I have arrived in Texarkana, the home of the Phantom Slayer, and the hair is rising on my neck."

"There was a kind of mass fear that I've not seen since," says Grigson, who was fourteen at the time. "The murders were all the adults talked about. And while the kids didn't read the paper much or listen to the news on the radio, we heard what our parents were saying and quickly came to share their concern."

In the wake of the traumatic February attack, Mary Jeanne Larey's attempts to sleep were routinely interrupted by bad dreams of the horror she and her boyfriend had experienced. Fearful that her assailant might again seek her out, she soon began talking about leaving Texarkana to live with relatives in Oklahoma. It was, in fact, a second "lover's lane" attack, even more horrifying than her own, that convinced her to make the move.

On March 24, just a month after she and Hollis were assaulted, the legend of the Phantom Killer began to take its ugly form. A heavy rain was falling on that early Sunday morning when a motorist nearing the Texarkana city limits noticed an Oldsmobile sedan parked on a dirt lane near U.S. Highway 67. Thinking that someone might have become stuck in the muddy ruts the rains had created, he slowed and drove close enough to see that two people were in the car. At first it looked as if they might be asleep.

What he would soon learn was that Richard Griffin, twenty-nine and recently discharged from the navy, and Polly Ann Moore, a seventeen-year-old employee at the Red River Arsenal, were dead. Griffin's body lay awkwardly in the front seat, his hands still over his face. The pockets of his trousers were turned inside out, indicating a robbery had taken place. He had been shot twice in the head. Moore's body lay face down on a blanket in the backseat, her opened purse beside her, a ring signifying that she had recently graduated from nearby Atlanta (Texas) High School still on her finger. Noting a pool of blood in the damp sandy loam twenty feet from the car, investigators concluded that she had likely been killed there, her body then placed back inside the car. Yet, aside from several shell casings from a .32 pistol located near the murder scene, investigators found little evidence. The rains, which had continued throughout the day the bodies were found, had washed away footprints and made it all but impossible to locate any fingerprints on the exterior of the car.

"It was not until the first murders occurred," says Texarkana's seventy-one-year-old Dr. James Presley, a lifelong student of the dark episode in his hometown's history, "that people in law enforcement began to put the attack on Mary Jeanne Larey and Jimmy Hollis and the deaths of Griffin and Moore together." Sixteen at the time of the homicides, Presley, author of six nonfiction books, notes that his uncle, Bill Presley, was the Bowie County sheriff at the time. "He was involved in the investigation from the start. But he rarely spoke about it in his later years. What I was able to determine was that neither he nor anyone else initially thought the first attack was that extraordinary. While Texarkana in the forties was a great place to live, it did have its share of violent crime—Saturday night shootings, bar stabbings, those sorts of things. So, what happened early on wasn't something that turned the local law enforcement world upside down. "That came after the first double murder. And it got much worse in the weeks that followed."

Fifteen-year-old Betty Jo Booker was among Texarkana's best and brightest, a high school junior with a straight A average, a gift for music, and aspirations to one day be a hospital technician. Additionally, she played alto saxophone in a local dance band called the Rhythmaires.

On Saturday night, April 13, the band made its regular appearance at the local VFW hall, playing its final number just before 1 A.M. Normally, an adult band member would escort Booker home; but on that night she had been invited to an all-night slumber party, and a former classmate named Paul Martin, sixteen, had agreed to pick her up and drive her across town to the party. First, however, they stopped off at Spring Lake Park, then a popular "parking" spot of teenagers. They would become the third and fourth murder victims of the Phantom Killer. Though the term had not yet entered the American vernacular, a serial killer was apparently on the loose.

The following morning Martin was found by a family taking a shortcut through the park en route to Prescott, Arkansas. Seeing the young man's body lying beside the road, the travelers sped to a nearby house and alerted those living there to phone the authorities. When Sheriff Presley and several deputies arrived, they saw that Martin had been shot four times—in the back of the neck, the face, the chest, and shoulder—apparently by a .32 caliber pistol.

A search party was immediately organized to locate Betty Jo Booker. Shortly before noon, her body was found in a grove of trees, a mile away from where Martin had been killed. Fully clothed and wearing an overcoat that was still buttoned, she had been shot in the chest and face. Martin's car was found another mile away, parked near a railroad crossing, the keys still in the ignition. Miss Booker's saxophone had disappeared. Even before the funerals for the popular teenagers were conducted, a reward fund that would eventually grow to over five thousand dollars had been established and a half-dozen Texas Rangers, led by the flamboyant Gonzaullas, were in town to join in the investigation.

In the lobby of the downtown Grim Hotel, the nattily dressed Ranger regularly met with the growing number of reporters in town to chronicle the investigation, regularly vowing it would soon successfully end. His display of confidence was apparently overshadowed only by the colorful—and by today's measure, outrageous—quotes given to members of the media. According to a *Texarkana Gazette* article written years later, former editor J. Q. Mahaffey recalled a radio interviewer asking what advice Gonzaullas would give to the city's apprehensive citizens. His response: "I'd tell them to check the locks and bolts on their doors and get a double-barreled shotgun to take care of any intruders who tried to get in," he said. He reportedly ended each interview with a vow that he would not leave Texarkana until the murders were solved. "I remember him telling me that one time," ex-deputy Tillman Johnson recalls, "and I asked him if he'd thought about checking out the real estate market for a house to buy. He didn't think I was very funny."

Very little was at the time. Townspeople, remembers Dr. Presley, were keenly aware of the fact the murders of the two parked couples had occurred exactly three weeks apart. Then, shortly before nine o'clock on a Friday night, twenty days after the last murders, thirty-six-year-old

Miller County farmer Virgil Starks sat in the living room, a heating pad pressed against an aching back, reading the newspaper. His wife, Katy, already in her nightgown, was in the bedroom listening to the radio when two quick shots from a .22 rifle interrupted the rural quiet.

Fired through a window, both shots struck the back of Starks' head. Mrs. Starks entered the living room to find her husband slumped in his chair and ran for the phone. Before she could dial the number of the sheriff's department, two more shots rang out. One bullet struck her in the cheek, exiting behind her ear; another hit her in the lower jaw, splintering several teeth on impact and lodging beneath her tongue. In shock and bleeding badly, she became aware of the assailant's breaking a kitchen window in the back of the house.

Fleeing through the front door, she ran to the safety of a neighbor's house less than a hundred yards away. Even before she had been taken to the hospital for treatment, state, county, and city officers had made the ten-mile trip to the Starks' farmhouse. Though the details of the crime were far different from the murders of the local youths, the death of Virgil Starks was immediately assigned to the notorious Phantom Killer.

For the first time, clues had been left behind. Bloody footprints had been left in the living room where Starks' body had fallen from the chair onto the floor. Apparently, the assailant had even stopped to rub a hand across the pool of blood that had collected near Starks' head before leaving through the front door. Bloodhounds, brought to the scene from Arkansas state police headquarters in Hope, Arkansas, followed the killer's scent to the nearby highway then lost it a half-mile from the Starks' house. Crime-scene investigators, meanwhile, located spent .22 cartridges and bullet holes in the window glass near where Starks had died. The shots, they determined, had been fired from only a few feet away.

Additionally, the killer had apparently dropped a red-handled flashlight while making his retreat. A few days later, the *Texarkana Gazette*, eager to help with the investigation, would mark its place in newspaper history when it published a color photograph of the flashlight. Journalism historians would later point to it as the first time color had ever appeared in a daily newspaper. While there had been no evidence that anyone other than Mary Jeanne Larey had been sexually assaulted during the crime spree, the *Gazette*'s headline read, "Sex Maniac Hunted in Murders."

Despite the public outcry, weary investigators soon found them-selves back at square one. "My uncle had known Virgil Starks well, had gone to school with him," Dr. Presley says, "and because of that he took his death very personally. And like everyone else involved in the investi-gation, he became very frustrated. He was quoted in the paper at the time, saying 'This killer is the luckiest person I've ever known about. No one sees him, hears him in time, or can identify him in any way.'"

The only good news was that the killings abruptly ended after Starks' death.

Questions bred questions. Would the Phantom strike again? What kind of man could commit such crimes?

Dr. Grigson, who has interviewed and studied hundreds of murder-ers during his lengthy career, recently reviewed the facts of the crimes that occurred in his boyhood backyard and offered his thoughts: "The first three attacks," he says, "were obviously committed by someone with a psychopathic personality.

"The attacker was not only cold-blooded but obviously very angry. I suspect a great deal of that anger had to do with rejection he felt from women and, very likely, hostility toward males who had accomplished more with their lives than he had.

"And while there was apparently a degree of sexual abuse in at least one of the cases, these were not the traditional sex crimes. The killer wasn't in search of sexual gratification. He was venting an incredible de-gree of anger."

He says that it is highly unlikely that the murder of Virgil Starks was committed by the same person. "That one," Grigson surmises, "was ei-ther a copy-cat killing or done by someone with some kind of personal grudge against Starks or his wife."

The greatest difficulty faced by investigators in 1946, he suggests, was that they lacked much of the sophisticated crime-detecting equip-ment and forensic knowledge now routinely applied to investigations. "I seriously doubt crimes of this nature would go unsolved in today's law enforcement atmosphere," he says.

Back then, however, lawmen had no expert-produced "profiles" to sug-gest who they might look for. Still, rumors of suspects ran rampant. The son of a prominent Texarkana family was abruptly sent off to boarding school, causing whispered speculation that he was being hidden from law enforcement. That the murders ceased after he left only fueled gossip that he was responsible for the crimes. Calls even came in suggesting that a local policeman might have committed the crimes. Same with a downtown feed store owner and a gas station attendant who had been previously accused of rape. A German prisoner of war was briefly questioned. Virtually anyone walking the streets after dark was stopped by police and interrogated. For a couple of days, it was rumored that a local minister had quietly turned in his son. In Corpus Christi, a man attempted to pawn a saxophone and was soon being questioned by a Texas Ranger assigned to see if the musical instrument had belonged to Betty Jo Booker.

Of the hundreds of leads followed up on, all proved fruitless.

In what would eventually rank among the most absurd tips provided investigators was one in which an anonymous and apparently disgruntled taxpayer phoned to suggest that the murders had been committed by a local agent for the Internal Revenue Service. Several women in town contacted police to say they had experienced visions of the killer in their dreams and wished to provide descriptions.

And, of course, there was a steady stream of "confessions." Among them was a Missouri Pacific section hand who wrote to the governor, admitting the killings. The writer was obviously unstable since in the same letter he challenged FBI director J. Edgar Hoover and President Harry Truman to duels. An eighteen-year-old University of Arkansas student took his own life, leaving a note confessing to the Texarkana murders. Investigators were never able to link the teenager, who had suffered from mental problems for some time, to the crimes.

Late one spring evening, Tillman Johnson remembers, he received an urgent call from the police chief in Shreveport, urging that he get there as quickly as possible. An out-of-town patron of one of the city's bars, the deputy was told, had just admitted to the Phantom murders. The man had been talking about the crimes throughout a boozy evening, unaware that among his drinking companions was a reporter from the local newspaper. Seeing the possibility of the story of a lifetime, the journalist had begun buying the man drinks. Finally, in response to the generosity, the stranger had told in detail how he had committed the crimes. The reporter then telephoned the police and the man was soon arrested.

Excited over the prospect of getting his first glimpse of the killer who had so terrorized his community, Johnson drove immediately to Shreveport and raced into the jail. Behind bars, smiling at him, was a man he had known since childhood. Reeking of whiskey, the prisoner called out the deputy's name as he approached. Clearly angered, Johnson demanded an explanation. His old friend only shrugged. "I was in this bar and my money ran out," he said. "There was this young fella there . . . really interested in all this Phantom Killer stuff . . . so, what the hell, I figured if I told him a good story, he'd keep buying the drinks."

The deputy did not share in the laughter that erupted from inside the cell. Turning to the police chief, Johnson said, "Let him sober up, then turn him loose. He's not our man."

"Who the hell is he?" the bewildered Shreveport officer asked.

"He's our town drunk," Johnson replied as he turned to walk away.

Dead-end leads and false hope continued to plague the investigation for weeks. "One evening," Johnson recalls, "we got this call that there was someone prowling around out at the Starks' house. Thinking maybe the killer had decided to return to the scene of the crime, we took off out there."

What they found upon their arrival was the publicity-loving Ranger, Gonzaullas, inside the house, posing at the crime scene for a *Time* magazine photographer. Finally, as weeks passed with no apparent progress in the cases, the media began checking out of the Grim Hotel, off to other stories in other places. Lone Wolf Gonzaullas and the other Rangers left after spending three unsuccessful months working on the case. While local authorities continued to assign manpower to the investigation, the Phantom Killer quietly disappeared from the local headlines. Slowly, life in Texarkana returned to normal. In time, the fear of the darkness began to wane.

"One of the things we kept doing, long after the killings ended," says Johnson, "was to patrol the country roads where youngsters continued to go parking, despite all the warnings we'd been giving. One night, around midnight, I was driving down this dirt road and came up on a couple. I walked up to their car and tapped on the window and said, 'Don't you kids know that you could get yourselves killed being out here this time of night?'

"This young girl just smiled at me and replied, 'Don't you know *you* could have gotten yourself killed?' And with that she raised this big ol' pistol to the car window."

In the half-century that has passed, the Phantom Killings have taken on an urban legend quality. In the retelling, the story has become a mixture of myth and fact. For instance, there are those in Texarkana who are now wrongly convinced that each of the murders occurred on a night of the full moon. Despite little proof at the time, the attacks are today generally remembered as a series of perverted sex crimes. It's not difficult to find someone who still believes a mysterious, unnamed hobo jumped into the path of a passing train, taking the secrets of the Phantom to his gruesome death; the truth, however, is that the man, Earl McSpadden, had actually been stabbed to death and his body thrown onto the tracks. Theories are now cheap in Texarkana if you're in the market. Mostly, though, it is forgotten history, or at least blurred. Today, in neither the police nor sheriff's departments on either side of the border are there even files on the cases.

A brief renewal of national interest in the Phantom Killer occurred in 1976 with the release of a movie titled *The Town That Dreaded Sundown*. Starring Academy Award–winner Ben Johnson, playing the role of Gonzaullas, and directed by former Texarkana ad-man-turned-movie-maker Charles B. Pierce, it opened with a narrator darkly advising the audience, "The incredible story you are about to see is true. Only the names have been changed to protect the innocent. . . ."

Dr. Presley says that far more than names were changed. "Not many people around here thought much of it," he says before ticking off a lengthy list of fictional ingredients inserted into a badly overdramatized story line. Still, for those who had never before heard of the sensational crimes, it spawned a new fascination. "After the movie," says Texarkana public librarian Alice Coleman, "we began to get a lot of requests for information from people working on some article or a masters' thesis." Today, she notes, there are several websites devoted to the Phantom murders.

Tillman Johnson, now ninety, is the lone surviving member of the massive investigative team that worked on the 1946 cases. Though he'd not been released from the army to return to his deputy's position until shortly before the Starks murder, it was the death of Betty Jo Booker and her boyfriend that has always troubled him. He and Booker's mother had grown up together in Stamps, Arkansas, and had remained friends, regularly seeing each other in the courthouse where she had worked prior to his going into the service.

"That," he says, "was all a long time ago. Yet sometimes it seems like only yesterday."

Spread across the dining room table of his Texarkana home are files on the case—everything from crime-scene photos and field notes made by dozens of fellow officers, yellowed newspaper clippings, and his own handwritten reports from the time. Someday, he says, the material he's kept might help to finally prove something he's certain he's known for over a half century: the identity of the Phantom Killer.

Johnson, along with then-rookie Arkansas state trooper Max Tackett, was most likely the one who arrested the man who committed the "lovers lane" murders. Like Dr. Grigson, Johnson remains convinced the death of Virgil Starks was the responsibility of someone else.

"Max Tackett," Johnson recalls, "picked up on the fact that every time the Phantom struck, a car had been stolen then later abandoned. In fact, on the night Betty Jo Booker was killed, a car was stolen from a friend of her parents, and a witness had come forward with the name of the man who drove it away."

In late June 1946, Tackett had staked out a downtown Texarkana parking lot where another stolen car had been abandoned. He ultimately arrested a twenty-one-year-old woman recently married to the man he was looking for—a local ex-convict with a lengthy record for burglary, counterfeiting, and car theft.

"She told us that he was over in Atlanta [Texas], trying to sell another car he'd stolen, so we notified the police there to keep an eye on him," Johnson says. "It wasn't long before they contacted us to say he was headed back to Texarkana."

On a sweltering Saturday afternoon in July, Tackett arrested the man in the downtown bus station. "When we got him into the car," Johnson recalls, "he looked at me and asked if he was going to the electric chair. I laughed and told him we didn't execute people for stealing cars. That's when he said, 'Hell, I know what you guys want me for. You want me for more than stealing a car.'"

Reasonably certain the rail-thin twenty-nine-year-old was alluding to the Phantom murders, they took him to the Miller County (Arkansas) jail in hopes that he might soon confess to the crimes. Night after night, Johnson, Tackett, and Sheriff Presley took turns grilling the high school dropout without success.

Frustrated, the officers turned their attention to the wife, who told them a frightening story of how Martin and Booker had been murdered in Spring Lake Park: She and the man in custody had just returned to Texarkana from a visit to Dallas and had stopped in town to see a movie and purchase beer. Then they had driven out to the park to "get drunk and rob somebody." She told of watching as the terrified young couple was forced from their car at gunpoint and taken into the nearby woods. Later, she admitted, she heard a quick series of gunshots.

"Sheriff Presley wanted to take her out to the park and see if she could show us where the murders had taken place, and she agreed," Johnson remembers. "She couldn't locate the exact spot but got pretty close. Once we got her back in the car, the sheriff asked her if her husband had robbed Martin. She acknowledged that she remembered him taking some things out of the boy's pocket and then tossing them away in a nearby ditch.

"What very few people knew at the time," notes Johnson, "was that a small date book belonging to Martin had been found in a washed-out area not too far from his body." The woman also recalled her husband tossing Booker's still-missing saxophone from the car as they'd driven back toward town. It was later recovered in the area she had described.

Though polygraph exams had only recently become an investigative tool and were still viewed with considerable skepticism, the woman was taken to Austin, where she was administered a test. Results indicated she had been truthful in her description of the events in Spring Lake Park.

What authorities had, then, was an interesting circumstantial evidence case but, since law prohibited a wife from testifying against a husband if she did not wish to, very little that would attract the genuine interest of a prosecutor. "The only way we were going to close the case," Johnson says, "was with a confession."

Even when told what his wife had said, the suspect refused to talk. "Then, one night, out of the blue, he says, 'Okay, I'll tell you all about it.' But by the time we got everything ready to take his confession, he'd changed his mind."

Johnson remembers that the decision was then made to take the suspect to Little Rock, where he would be injected with sodium pentothal and questioned. "That was the biggest mistake we ever made," he says. "We got him there and the doctor injected him with too much of the stuff, knocking him out cold."

Thereafter, the suspect never spoke of the murders again. Ultimately he was tried for the car theft and, since he'd had two previous convictions, was sentenced to life in prison as a habitual criminal. Then, in 1973, the Texas Court of Criminal Appeals ruled that he'd not received adequate representation by his attorney during an arraignment on a 1941 auto theft charge, and he was paroled. A year later, however, he was back behind bars, this time convicted in Dallas of counterfeiting quarters and half-dollars, which he was passing off as collector's items. Sentenced to a two-year prison term, there was a twist of irony attached to the fact that he was assigned to serve his time in the Texarkana Federal Correction facility. His sentence served, he was again released and returned to Dallas.

"Max was always sure he was the man we were looking for," Johnson says. "And I've always been convinced that he killed the Booker girl and her boyfriend. What we did back then was everything we could think of to prove that he *wasn't* guilty and were never able to."

Quietly looking at the old files that have been a part of his life for so long, Johnson shakes his head as the memories rush back. "I guess," he says, "that since he's dead now there's no reason you can't say who he was." With that he acknowledges the name of the man he believes created such terror over a half century ago.

The man he talks of was Youell Lee Swinney, son of a local lay minister, who had been in trouble with the law since a teenager. In the years immediately prior to his arrest, Swinney had earned his living stealing cars then driving people to destinations throughout the United

States. (In wartime it had become common for people to share rationing stamps for gas and pay the driver a modest fee for providing transportation.)

Texarkana realtor Mark Bledsoe, a thirty-seven-year-old former probation officer who began researching the case in the early nineties with thoughts of writing a book, agrees with Johnson. "I am at least 99 percent convinced that he [Swinney] did the majority of the murders credited to the Phantom," he says. On the other hand, he notes that he has good reason to believe that the man who killed Virgil Starks was a local serviceman who had just returned to Texarkana in 1946. "The last I heard of him was that he was residing in a mental institution in Milwaukee," Bledsoe says.

After hearing from several retired law enforcement officers, including Johnson, that the prime suspect in the historic case had been Swinney, Bledsoe took advantage of his contacts in the Department of Pardons and Parole and began his own search for the Phantom. In 1992, he discovered that Swinney was still in Dallas, living at a Lemmon Avenue halfway house. "I was up there on business one day, and before heading home, I went by the address," he remembers. "As I approached the house there was this old man, frail and bent over, standing in the yard, wearing a big cowboy hat. We nodded at each other as I passed.

"Inside, when I asked for Youell Swinney, the lady in charge said he wasn't in but could usually be found walking around outside. She told me he wouldn't be hard to find since he always wore a cowboy hat."

Racing outside in search of the man he'd seen only minutes earlier, Bledsoe couldn't find him. "I looked for him for quite a while, and it was like he'd just disappeared." The alleged Phantom, it seemed, was still eluding his trackers. "Since I was pressed for time that day, I decided I'd just come back on my next trip to Dallas."

By the time Bledsoe returned later that year, Swinney had suffered a stroke and was wheelchair-bound, residing in a rest home. "I did talk to him for a while," Bledsoe says, "and he spent some time bragging about his counterfeiting days and talking about being in and out of prison. But when I asked him about the Phantom murders he became

angry and denied that he'd had anything to do with them. He even refused to admit that he'd ever been married."

A year later, at age seventy-six, Youell Swinney died.

For the aging Johnson, the case is rarely far from mind. "Over the years,"
he says, "people have gotten in touch with me about things they thought
might be of interest." The most recent contact came in February 1999
when he learned that the brother of Phantom victim Paul Martin had received a strange phone call at his Kilgore home. "Actually it was his wife
who took the call," Johnson says as he looks over his notes. "She said a
soft-voiced woman who sounded like she was in her late forties or early
fifties asked if her husband had a brother murdered in Texarkana back in
the forties. When she said he had, the caller said, 'Please tell your husband that I want to apologize for what my father did.'" The caller then
hung up.

At Johnson's request, a retired Texas Ranger living in Kilgore was
contacted, and he attempted to determine the origin of the call but
was unsuccessful. "It was almost a year later that I heard virtually the
same story again," Johnson says. "I was in church one morning and
someone came up to me after the service and mentioned something
about my having been involved in the investigation of the Phantom
Killer cases. A nephew of Virgil Starks was a member of our congregation and obviously overheard the conversation. He came over and
began telling me how his mother had received virtually the same call.
He said she'd not paid much attention to it, figuring it was just some
sick prankster."

Perhaps she was right. Nowhere in Johnson's faded records or the
research conducted by Bledsoe or Dr. Presley is there indication that
Youell Swinney, so long pointed to as the prime suspect, ever had a
daughter. Thus those strange and belated calls are legitimate cause to
wonder if, in fact, Swinney's lifelong insistence that he had not committed the murders might have been the truth after all.

Those who wish to argue his innocence often point to a night in
October 1946—while Swinney was in jail, being questioned about the
Texarkana murders that had occurred months earlier—when a young
couple was slain while parked on a secluded oceanside road near Fort
Lauderdale, Florida. Like the lovers lane victims in Texas, they, too, had

been shot with a .32 caliber pistol. Like the Phantom, the killer simply vanished; the case was never solved.

Maybe, it is suggested, the long-ago terror that visited Texarkana, sparking fear and frustration, dark secrets and discomforting memories, abruptly ended only because the person responsible for it had simply decided to move to new hunting grounds.

It is just such speculation, no doubt, that continues to fuel the legend.

12

CASE CLOSED

Everything points to insane cunning. Many things point to the cold-blooded, merciless and supernatural strength and madness of a morphal lunatic. . . . The murderer of Miss Florence Brown may be caught within the next five minutes, he may be arrested during the next six months; he may never be deprived of his liberty. . . .

—Daily Times Herald, 1913

The cemetery caretaker was at first reluctant, concerned about the disturbance he feared the curious intruders might bring. Members of the Dallas Genealogy Society had decided to make his longtime workplace a project, recording each of its thirty thousand burial sites. Only after considerable urging did Harold Williams begrudgingly resign himself to their presence and agree to serve as guide through the second-oldest graveyard in Dallas.

Here, he pointed out, is where the brother of John Wilkes Booth, the man who assassinated President Abraham Lincoln, is buried. Over there are relatives of reclusive billionaire Howard Hughes. Impatiently he directed them to the final resting places of former Dallas mayors and the socially prominent, the Confederate officers, the vaudeville luminaries, and even a few high-ranking members of the Ku Klux Klan. He pointed out that just beyond the eastern fence line, in an area now known as Opportunity Park, was the final resting place of slaves. Back in a far corner is the pet cemetery where once-beloved dogs and cats, even a horse and a chimpanzee, are buried.

Oakland Cemetery, established in 1891 and hidden away off Malcolm X Boulevard in east Dallas, is fertile ground for those in search of the city's history. Yet it was only when Williams learned that among the women visitors was a Dallas police officer that his own interest bloomed. He bided his time, waiting until she had distanced herself from the others, then he approached her. "There is a gravesite I think you might find of interest," he finally whispered. And then, without another word, he led the way to an overgrown spot in the center of the historic cemetery.

At first blush, Detective Shari Degan would seem an unlikely candidate to explore Dallas's history. Raised in Detroit, she aspired to join the police force there, but after learning they weren't hiring and Dallas was, she packed her bags and headed south. Clearly, it was Detroit's loss. In 1985 Degan was a nominee for Rookie of the Year. Two years later she moved into the department's evidence division and in 1997 became the first female winner of the Dallas police department's Officer of the Year award.

With three children finally grown and away from home, she found time for a new hobby. "A friend of mine introduced me to genealogy about five years ago," she says. Soon, she joined the Dallas Genealogy Society, never dreaming that soon her vocation and avocation would dovetail into a murder investigation.

Stopping in the shade of an ancient oak, the caretaker pointed to a small blue granite headstone and remained silent while the officer read its inscription:

FLORENCE
DAUGHTER OF J. R. & R. A. BROWN
BORN JULY 5, 1881
DIED JULY 28, 1913
"FAITHFUL TO HER TRUTH EVEN UNTO DEATH"

"She was murdered," the caretaker said. "From what I've heard, it was an awful crime. Her throat was slashed. It happened in downtown Dallas in broad daylight." Then, as though pausing for effect, he waited a few beats before delivering a tantalizing punch line: "The case has never been solved."

Thus begins the mythlike story of two women, separated by over three-quarters of a century; a story of a crime, bizarre and brutal, that occurred eighty-eight years ago. And it is a tale of a cop's fascination that quickly evolved into a determined obsession. Now, a year after being led to the modest grave of Florence Brown, once a thirty-two-year-old stenographer and daughter of a Dallas police officer, Detective Degan, thirty-eight, is convinced that she knows who killed her.

When not tending her responsibilities as a latent print examiner, the seventeen-year Dallas police department veteran and current president of the Dallas Genealogy Society researched the long-forgotten homicide that once stunned the burgeoning city to such a degree that local newspapers published "extras" on the day of the crime—DALLAS WOMAN IS MURDERED, screamed the *Daily Times Herald* headline—and lynch mobs gathered in hopes that the killer was quickly found. Eventually, then–Texas governor O. B. Colquitt even offered a reward.

Detective Degan's first order of business was to learn as much as she could about the victim and what occurred on that late July Monday in 1913. But where does one go to launch an investigation into a crime that occurred when Woodrow Wilson was president, when the just-opened viaduct connecting Dallas and Oak Cliff was being hailed as the longest concrete structure in the world, and when World War I was still several years in the future?

The "cold case" files of the police department provided only the first of numerous dead ends. Whatever records that might have been filed away by either the police or the Dallas County sheriff's office had long ago been lost or discarded. The funeral home where the victim's body was taken no longer existed. For that matter, the scene of the crime was gone, swallowed up by the restaurants and parking lots of the city's West End. Those involved in the original investigation had died years ago.

Only when she made a trip to the Dallas Public Library and began viewing microfilm of the three newspapers of the day—the *Morning News*, the *Daily Times Herald*, and the *Dallas Dispatch*—did she begin to make encouraging headway. "One of the things I learned," she says, "is that there was apparently a great willingness on the part of law enforcement to share information with the press back then." Witness statements, details from the crime scene, and daily updates on the case were printed. In fact, the reporting of the time was often quite colorful: "The throat of the victim was cut from ear to ear by the fiend," wrote one newsman. "Rumors of the wildest nature circulate about the city," reported another.

And it was then that Degan finally found her starting place.

On Sunday, the last full day of her life, Florence Brown had, as usual, sung in the choir of the McKinney Avenue Baptist Church; in the afternoon, she joined her brother and his wife on a drive to nearby Cleburne. Arriving home before dark, she spent the evening talking with her parents with whom she still lived in the 2700 block of Cedar Springs. Then, with the promise of a busy day ahead in the real estate office of her uncle, she went to bed early.

Normally, Jeff Robinson, senior partner of the Robinson-Styron Realty Company, stopped by the Brown home each morning to give his niece a ride to his downtown office. But since he was vacationing with his family at a northern Colorado resort, he had left instructions for S. B. Cuthbertson, a member of his sales staff for the past seven months, to take his niece to work during his absence.

On Monday morning Cuthbertson arrived to find Florence Brown's father, already in uniform, sitting on the front porch, smoking his pipe and reading the paper. Florence's mother stepped outside to say that Florence would be ready shortly. As he waited, Cuthbertson offered patrolman J. Randolph Brown a ride, but he declined, saying he wanted to finish reading his paper then would take the trolley into town.

He would later remember that his daughter and Cuthbertson drove away from his house at 8:05 A.M. En route to work, Brown seemed in good spirits, talking of the trip to Cleburne and plans for a vacation she was scheduled to begin in just a few days. Arriving at the Field Street office in what was then in the heart of Dallas's business district, the salesman unlocked the front door. Inside, he said, Miss Brown removed the hat she was wearing and began turning on lights and ceiling fans while he gathered papers from his desk for a quick trip to the nearby courthouse and city hall. He would later tell police that it was approximately 8:20 when he left the office. Minutes afterward, three employees in an adjacent office saw Brown standing in the doorway as her uncle's salesman left.

Cuthbertson recalled to investigators that he returned at approximately 9 A.M. and was seated at his desk when Robinson's partner, W. R. Styron, and G. W. Swor, the company's tax manager, arrived. Swor made the grisly discovery. Walking into the rear of the storefront office, he found Florence Brown lying in a pool of blood on the floor of the restroom, her hair disheveled, her clothing torn. "We heard him scream," Cuthbertson told the police. "Mr. Styron and I rushed back to where he was and found him supporting her head on his arm, wiping blood from her face with a towel. He was yelling for us to get a doctor."

The salesman ran to the nearby Southland Hotel Drug Store, where he located Dr. Wilford Hardin. In retrospect, there was no need for the men to rush. Dr. Hardin estimated that Florence Brown had been dead for at least fifteen minutes prior to their arrival. Her throat had been cut so deeply that she was almost decapitated, her jugular vein completely severed. She suffered trauma marks to her head, indicating that she had been struck several times above her right eye and temple by a blunt object, and deep scratches to her face, neck, and upper portions of her chest. She had defensive wounds that suggested Miss Brown had struggled with her assailant. On her right hand, two fingers were cut to the bone, indicating she had attempted to grab the blade of the weapon used to kill her.

As the doctor examined the body, it fell to Cuthbertson to locate Brown's father and alert him to what had occurred. Aware of the officer's assigned beat, the salesman quickly located him directing traffic at the corner of Main and Lamar. "I hesitated, thinking how I would break the news to him," Cuthbertson recalled to the police. "He was talking to a man at the time, and I called him aside. I thought it best to tell him right away, so I just said, 'Florence is dead. She has been killed.' I remember him looking at me as if he didn't believe it, then grabbing my arm for support."

By the time Cuthbertson and the woman's father arrived at the office, Miss Brown's body had already been taken to the Weiland Funeral Home. In a time before securing a crime scene was standard procedure, police chief John Ryan and chief of detectives Henry Tanner were summoned to the realty office only after the victim had been removed. By the time they arrived it was obvious that a number of employees and curious passersby had made their way into the office. Even bloody footprints remained at the scene, which investigators assumed were left by one of the firm's two other women employees. "There is no way," Chief Ryan told the press, "that the footprints can be established as those of Miss Brown's slayer."

All that remained was a grotesque amount of blood on the bathroom floor and a small gold ring belonging to Florence Brown that had been stepped on and crushed during the struggle. In an adjacent office was a blood-soaked button, apparently torn from a man's shirt.

No murder weapon was found.

Most odd, however, was indication that someone had used a nearby sink to clean up following the murder. Speculation soon grew that the killer might even have taken time to change clothes before walking out into the busy morning foot traffic on Field Street. Or—and this seemed even more bizarre—the murderer had stolen a page from the infamous Lizzie Borden case, committing the crime in the nude in a premeditated effort to keep blood from being transferred to any clothing.

Whatever the scenario, it was clear that the killer had somehow eventually managed to walk unnoticed from the crime scene into the morning bustle of unaware people hurrying to get to work. A neighboring businessman did come forward to say that only minutes before Brown's body was discovered, he had been walking along Field and saw a man he did not know inside the Robinson and Styron office. "He was standing by a little telephone table in the main office," the witness said. The man he described to police was clean-shaven, wearing light-colored trousers, a dark coat, and a straw hat. Authorities discovered that the "sighting" he described had occurred some time after Brown's body had been found. The man he described, however, was in fact Detective Tanner.

Even before Brown's body was taken away by a funeral home wagon, word of the horrific crime had spread through the business district and a large crowd gathered outside the Robinson and Styron office, chanting for vengeance. With great difficulty, police finally managed to disperse it and seal off the entire block.

"The whole affair," wrote the *Daily Times Herald* in the two-cents-a-copy extra edition it quickly published, "is as deep a mystery as [Edgar Allan] Poe's murders of the Rue Morgue."

During a later examination of the body at the funeral home, coroner J. T. Watson found deep bite wounds on Miss Brown's right wrist and elbow and made wax impressions of the teeth marks. "They can," he told reporters, "be used to make a comparison to the teeth of the killer once he is apprehended." What was significant, the doctor added, was that the person leaving the mark on Brown's wrist was missing a tooth in the front of the upper jaw.

The wound to the neck, Dr. Watson ruled, was clearly the cause of death. "It must have been inflicted by a very powerful man," he added.

For weeks that summer, Detective Degan's free time—lunch hours, after work, and weekends—was spent in the library, lost in the fascinating accounts she had discovered. Reading, rereading, making notes, she searched for the most minute detail that might point to an overlooked suspect, sharing information from her quest only with husband John, a Dallas police sergeant.

"I had no idea where I was going with it," she confides, "but it was a great murder mystery. The more I read, the more hooked I became."

In the days following Brown's death, a number of local vagrants and "suspicious-looking individuals" were arrested, questioned, and quickly released. The alibi of Cuthbertson, the last man to see the victim alive, was checked and several workers at the courthouse and city hall assured the authorities that he had been there at the time of the murder.

As the investigation proceeded, it was learned that Miss Brown dated occasionally but had no steady boyfriend who might be viewed as a suspect. Her most serious relationship, in fact, seemed to be with a young man who lived out of state. Searching her room, police found a dozen or more letters she'd received from him over a period of several months. However, he had not been in Dallas in months, and certainly not at the time of the crime. Old friends from her high school days in Garland were questioned, and none could think of an enemy she might have made.

Investigators, meanwhile, lacked the most essential indicator of why such a crime had occurred—motive. Nothing had been taken from the realty office, ruling out robbery. A check of Brown's bank account revealed only a modest balance. A check of records to see if a disgruntled client might have scheduled an early morning appointment that Monday was fruitless.

In time, the kooks came out of the woodwork. Several letters arrived at the police department, their authors claiming responsibility for the crime. "I am still in Dallas," one wrote. "Yesterday, I rubbed elbows with your chief. You had better be careful." Others wrote to offer wild theories and suggest suspects.

One of the most puzzling reports came from a doctor working in the emergency room of a Dallas hospital on the morning of the murder. He told police he had received a telephone call at approximately 8:30 A.M. on the day of the crime from someone wanting to know if "you've got a woman there whose throat has been cut." The call had come before Brown's body was discovered.

Soon calls began arriving from law enforcement agencies throughout the state—San Antonio, Waco, Brownwood, Mount Pleasant, McKinney—advising that they had suspects in custody and expressing their willingness to join into the investigation.

- In Montague County, the sheriff arrested a young man who had done nothing more sinister than purchase a new suit of clothing, assuming he was doing so to replace bloodstained pants and shirt.
- An east Dallas barber called to say a man entered his shop wearing bloodstained clothes and had used his restroom to change.
- A woman phoned police from Oak Lawn to say that a black man appeared at her door, offering to mow her yard. What she reported as blood on his pants turned out to be red paint.
- A farmer called in to say a "suspicious-looking" man was seen walking along a country road. Soon, he was arrested and the buttons on the tattered shirt he was wearing were compared to the one found at the crime scene. They didn't match. Nothing did as every new tip proved worthless.

Predictably, the unfounded rumors soon followed: The bloody knife had been found. Police had made an arrest, and the man in custody had provided a full confession before being taken to a jail in another county for protection against vigilantes.

The hysteria was nearing the boiling point even before a block letter headline asked, IS A MANIAC AT LARGE?

Among the few calm voices was that of Miss Brown's mother, who was asked by a reporter if she hoped to see her daughter's murderer put to death once apprehended. Demonstrating that the death penalty was a volatile issue even then, she surprised many when she said no. "I don't want more killing. I just want him put away in the penitentiary where he will not bother anyone else."

By the time Florence Brown's funeral was conducted (McKinney Avenue Baptist was filled to its six-hundred-person capacity and an estimated two hundred stood outside), the reward fund had grown to over eleven hundred dollars. Private detectives from all over the state were arriving in hopes of claiming it. Investigators from the legendary Burns Detective Agency were hired to assist the Dallas police and sheriff's department on the case.

"We are absolutely up in the air as to who committed the murder of Miss Brown," Dallas County sheriff B. F. Brandenburg finally admitted to the press. "All clues we have been working have played out." At a similar press conference, police chief Ryan echoed the sheriff's frustration: "We have done everything that could be done. We've run down the most absurd rumors and supposed clues. We have established no motive, found no weapon, suspect nobody, and are utterly at sea. We are trying hard not to be discouraged and we will not give up."

Detective Degan found that in time, however, they apparently did, as the news reports abruptly ended. It was as if the tragedy of Florence Brown had been played for all it might be worth and then abandoned. She, too, had come to a dead end. But with a suspicion she could not shake. Finally, she went to coworker Detective Dennis Williams, a veteran crime scene analyst, for help.

"I'd never heard of the case," he says, "but as she outlined it to me, I found it fascinating." Degan asked if he might review the material she had collected and suggest a profile of the murderer.

"Back when this crime occurred," Williams says, "there was very little forensic expertise. As far as I know, fingerprinting hadn't even made its way to Texas. From the reports, the crime scene was an investigator's nightmare. I found it hard to believe that the body had been removed even before the police arrived. It was pretty clear that, aside from the button they found, there was no real evidence."

Certainly, there was no such technique as "profiling" at the time. Detective Williams points to one of the brief news reports as an example of the archaic nature of crime investigation in the early teens of the twentieth century: "Chief of Detectives Henry Tanner," it read, "in company with a Dallas photographer, visited the Weiland Undertaking establishment shortly before noon Wednesday. According to reports, he was planning to secure a picture of the eyes of Florence Brown.

"In some instance, it is said, a likeness of the slayer has been found reflected in the eyes of murdered people. The officer and the photographer examined the eyes of the corpse but determined the experiment was impractical."

For several days Williams reviewed Degan's findings and ultimately came to the same conclusion she had secretly kept. "This was one of those over-the-top kinds of homicides," Degan says. "It was a classic case of overkill. Obviously, one heck of a struggle took place in that bathroom. The biting, the scratches, the brutality suggested a highly emotional exchange."

Williams agreed. "The motive for this type murder is usually very personal," he says. "The killer was obviously extremely angry at the victim." From the descriptions of Brown's wounds, he speculated that they were inflicted by a left-handed person. The blows to the head, he felt, might well have been from the handle of the knife that was used on the victim. In fact, Brown was probably already unconscious when her throat was cut.

"So," Degan finally asked, "who killed Florence Brown?"

"A woman," Williams replied. "A very angry, left-handed woman."

Degan nodded. "That's what I think, too," she said.

But why? And who?

Detective Degan, the weekend genealogist, had one long-shot avenue of research left to pursue. Florence Brown's obituary had listed surviving members of her family. It was time to put the hobby she'd been pursuing for five years to work. She began tracing the victim's family history on the off chance that someone with information about the crime might still be alive. In time, her research led her to the name of a distant cousin for which she found no death record.

One day in the fall of 2001, she placed a long-distance call and heard the frail voice of a woman named Lucille Samcaster. In her nineties and in bad health, she agreed to talk about the crime that had haunted her family for generations. What she had to say in a conversation that lasted no more than fifteen minutes caused the detective's heart to pound.

"She told me that Florence Brown had been going out occasionally with a young man in the weeks before her death," the detective recalls. "Previously, he had been seeing another woman but had broken off the relationship. She didn't know the ex-girlfriend's name, but she had been led to believe she was from a wealthy Dallas family. She said the story she'd been told years ago was that this woman had hired someone to kill Florence."

Jealousy, then, was the elusive motive. In a socially fragile time when such matters as romantic involvement were carefully guarded, the family had never spoken publicly of the matter. The issue, Samcaster told the detective, was soon resolved when the woman moved to Denver and committed suicide. Her memory failing, Samcaster could not recall the woman's name.

Soon after their brief conversation, Samcaster, the last surviving member of the Brown–Robinson family, died. "Some day," Degan says, "I'd like to go to Denver and research the old newspaper files there to see if there are reports of any suicides at the time. If I could find a name then trace it back to Dallas, I'd be satisfied that we've solved the case."

Would it finally show that it was not a "large, very strong" male killer, not a hired hit man, but, rather, an enraged, jealous woman who committed the crime? "We'll never know for sure," Degan admits, "but I think this is what happened: The woman, knowing when Florence Brown went to work, was probably watching the realty office from some nearby location. When Cuthbertson left, she saw her opportunity and went inside. Since she obviously had a weapon with her, the crime had to be premeditated.

"In all likelihood, the struggle began in the room where the button was found then continued into the bathroom where the murder took place. I think it is very likely that Miss Brown had already been knocked unconscious when her throat was cut.

"And, I believe, the ring probably had some significance. The killer could have assumed that it had been a gift from the boyfriend. She removed it from the dead woman's finger then stomped on it.

"That done, she took time to wash up and even change clothes. Then she placed her bloody clothing and the murder weapon into some kind of bag she was carrying, walked out the front door, down to Commerce, and caught a trolley."

Those women's footprints, found eighty-eight years ago on the bathroom floor of the realty office, were not those of some curious onlooker, Degan suggests. They were, in fact, left by the person who killed Florence Brown.

June 28, 1990

Dallas Observer

The Weekly Newspaper of Dallas   Now 88,000 copies every Thursday

Mother and Child by Chuka Akoye, from Kinfolks: A Collection of African-American Art.

KINFOLKS
A GALLERY OF THEIR OWN — 30

ARTSWEEK

STREET CULTURE IN A CAN — 22

New graffiti artists Tripzy Thompson, Mezqulto, and Q: Coming to a wall near you

WITHOUT A TRACE
Six months ago, Ashley Reed disappeared.
So did 45,000 other Texans last year — 12

★ **Free tickets to *The Jetsons* — 25**

13

WITHOUT A TRACE

Karen Reed still replays the conversation in her mind, as if it were on a nonerasable tape made only yesterday. It was on a Sunday afternoon in January 1990, just before 6 P.M., and she had telephoned the North Dallas apartment she shared with her nineteen-year-old daughter, Ashley. Although the teenager had just wakened from a nap (she had earlier completed a busy shift waiting tables at a nearby JoJo's restaurant) her mother remembers the sound of youthful excitement in Ashley's voice as she discussed an upcoming date for a concert being held in nearby Corsicana.

It was the last time Karen Reed spoke with her child.

Now the name of Ashley Reed is among the almost forty-five thousand entered annually into the Texas Department of Safety's missing-persons clearing-house files. In Dallas alone, there are an average of six to eight thousand missing adults yearly. The number of missing juveniles and reported runaways triples that figure. Yet the numbers, blinking from a computer or printed in annual crime reports, do little to mirror the agonies shared by parents and loved ones of those who, for whatever reason, seem to have vanished into thin air.

For Karen, forty-two and divorced, the pain of her daughter's disappearance has not lessened with the passage of time. There are the nightmares, which continue to interrupt her fitful sleep; there are the long days when she tries to concentrate on her job; and there are the needs of her young son. There is all of this, while at the same time there is the taxing of her mind to determine if there is something—anything—she has not yet done to aid in the search for Ashley.

One recent morning she was overwhelmed by an anxiety attack while preparing for work. "I just sat down in the middle of the floor and cried," she recalls. She admits that in the days immediately following Ashley's

187

disappearance, the thought of suicide entered her mind. Now, she says, "The sense of urgency is still there, but I've finally come to realize that a logical approach to the situation is best. . . . I'm more in control."

For Karen Reed, like so many others struggling through the netherworld of uncertainty over a missing child, the negative thoughts are pushed aside. She refuses to refer to her daughter in the past tense and angrily scolds anyone who does so. No "worst case scenario" is acceptable to her, only hope. It is what sustains her.

"I'm grieving," she admits, "but I truly believe I'm going to get Ashley back. I'm optimistic. I have to be." Karen battles to maintain such an attitude despite the fact there has, as yet, been little to give cause for such optimism.

According to Dallas police detective John Easton, who has worked the case, he is no closer to finding Ashley Reed than he was when he started the investigation. "As with all cases like this, initially you have a lot to do," he says. "You get all the information you can on the missing person, you do the posters and the composite drawings of suspects, you get leads because the press has made the public aware of the situation. But the time eventually comes when you don't have anything else to go looking for." Reed's disappearance, he acknowledges, has evolved into a game of hurry up and wait.

Also, other missing persons are demanding his attention.

Still, daily, Easton would pull out the two thick files on the case and reread the reports, which he had all but memorized, searching for something overlooked, something that might trigger another avenue of investigation. "When it gets to this point," he says, "you feel worthless, like you're not doing your job, like you're letting people down."

Despite being recently transferred from the youth division to property crimes, Easton makes it clear that he will continue to aid in the investigation of Ashley's disappearance. "Of all the cases I worked," he says, "hers was the one I most hated to give up." In truth, he has not given up. "I still keep my hand in," he says, "though the case now officially belongs to Detective John Westphalen. He and I have had several meetings about it since he took it over. I've gone over the files with him, and we've retraced everything I did."

Detective Easton also continues to stay in touch with Karen Reed. "We talk at least once a week," he says. "I just want to let her know I haven't forgotten about her daughter." To Karen, Detective Easton has been a lifeline. "I have a great deal of respect for him," she says. "He's become my counselor and my friend. He's my only real link to Ashley. He's patiently listened to me when I've cried and in those times when I let my anger boil over when I doubted he was doing everything he could."

For Ashley Reed, a loving, brown-eyed brunette with an engaging personality, life in Dallas had been a drastic change. Prior to graduating from Harding High School in Saint Cloud, Minnesota, she had been a cheerleader, homecoming queen, president of the student council, and had been offered a prelaw scholarship to the University of Minnesota, Saint Cloud. A superachiever, her teachers called her; the all-American girl, said her friends.

"When I got notice that I was being transferred to Dallas," says Karen Reed, a business-forms designer for Standard Register, "we talked at length about whether she should stay in Minnesota and go to college there. I left the decision to her and was delighted when she said she wanted to come to Dallas with Josh [her two-year-old brother] and me. "Ashley had everything planned. She would work for a few months, helping me get settled, then she would enroll at the University of North Texas for the spring semester."

Thus, for the four months they had called Dallas home, Ashley's life had been a routine of work, occasional trips to a nearby mall for shopping or a movie, and solitary visits to a nearby Denny's restaurant, where she would sit in a back booth and write long letters to friends back in Minnesota. It was there she smoked an occasional cigarette, a secret, newfound habit of which she was certain her mother would disapprove.

On the Sunday when they last spoke, Ashley told her mother she had met the man she was going out with at the restaurant. He'd invited her to the concert, and they had agreed to meet in the parking lot of an International House of Pancakes (IHOP) in Mesquite; they were then to drive on to Corsicana. As was her cautious practice on any first date, Ashley had planned to drive her own car. Things had worked out nicely, she explained to her mother, since her date had told her his car was not running well.

For several minutes during their phone conversation, Ashley discussed the outfit she had decided to wear—her denim skirt, black pullover shirt, and the brown leather bomber jacket her mother had given her for Christmas—and she promised to phone once she arrived in Corsicana. She would give her the location of the concert and some idea of when to expect her home. The cheerful conversation ended as had so many others. "I told her that I loved her, and she said that she loved me," Karen remembers.

But when Ashley failed to call by 9:30 P.M., Karen phoned her mother, Eileen Hogstad, who lived nearby, to ask if Ashley might have phoned there. Aware that her granddaughter was a responsible person, Hogstad suggested that maybe Ashley had just been unable to locate a phone or, in her excitement over the concert, simply forgot to call. "Just go to bed," she told Karen. "I'm sure she's just having fun."

Karen, however, knew something was terribly amiss when she woke at 2 A.M. and realized her daughter had not returned. By four she had begun calling police in Dallas, Corsicana, and Mesquite. Eileen Hogstad phoned area hospitals, fearing there might have been some kind of accident. Long before dawn, Karen Reed was gripped by a panic that seemed to squeeze the breath from her.

The following day her brother Robert located Ashley's 1984 Citation parked at the side of an Interstate 635 exit ramp near the IHOP where she was to have met her date. The battery was dead (the result, police determined, from hazard lights being left on for hours), and the keys were missing. There were no signs of a struggle, and the driver's seat was still in the position that the five-foot-two, 115-pound Ashley generally kept it.

In those frantic days following Ashley's disappearance, bits of information filtered in that led to concerns that she had likely been the victim of an abduction. For two days, Karen, joined at times by her mother and brother, stood on the shoulder of the intersection of 635 and Military Parkway near where her daughter's car had been found, holding signs asking help of any passersby who might have seen something.

Attendants at a nearby Mobil station said they had driven by at 11 P.M. and noticed the parked car, its hazard lights blinking. Meanwhile, volunteer members of the Rockwall search and rescue group and Fort Worth–based Children's Education Search and Rescue spent several hours walking the fields and a creek bed near the spot where the car was found. They had no luck.

After police interviewed the manager and waitresses of the nearby IHOP, a possible scenario began to develop: A man in his mid- to late twenties, wearing a tan corduroy jacket with brown sleeve patches, tan cowboy hat, and tan boots had been at the counter drinking coffee when the phone rang. The waitress who answered the call said a female explained that she was to meet her date there. She described him, said his name was Dave, and asked if he might be called to the phone. Another waitress recalls the cowboy briefly talking with the caller then mentioning that his girlfriend was picking him up but had gone to the wrong IHOP. She remembered his mentioning that the girl was "from up North and doesn't know her way around very well." He seemed friendly and well mannered.

Shortly thereafter, the manager told police, the man went to a pay phone near the entrance and made two calls before returning to pay for his coffee. Then the manager saw a brown Citation, driven by a woman, pull up in front of the restaurant. The customer had said, "That's her," and walked out to get into the car. It had been a few minutes after 7 P.M., the employees agreed, when he and the woman drove away. From the description the IHOP personnel provided, a computer-generated composite of "Dave" was prepared and immediately distributed.

Shortly, a waitress from the Preston Road Denny's that Ashley frequented contacted the police to say the composite resembled a "regular customer" who, weeks prior to Ashley's disappearance, had been seen "hitting on her" on several occasions. No one at the restaurant, however, knew the man's name or what kind of car he drove. Nor had they seen him in the restaurant recently.

The search was nine days old before what appeared to be a solid lead came via an anonymous 911 call. According to the caller, he and a fellow fisherman had happened on the young woman's purse on a roadside near a water-filled gravel pit in south Dallas County. He described the purse—a new, brown Liz Claiborne with a shoulder strap—and its contents: Karen Reed's gasoline credit card, her temporary Texas driver's license, a mirror, and an assortment of family photos. The caller, who said he and his friend had left the purse where they found it, suggested that police check the gravel pit for Ashley Reed's body. Search and rescue teams combed the waters with drag lines and found nothing. The purse, whose exact location had been provided by the caller, had also disappeared.

Detective Easton remembers the gravel pit search as the last time it appeared there might be a break in the case. After eventually locating and talking with the fishermen who found the purse, he ruled them out as possible suspects. The same applied to all members of the missing girl's family. Adding to his frustration was the fact no useful fingerprints were found on Ashley's car.

Easton has spent much of his career searching for missing people. The workdays, which often stretch to fourteen hours, and the ever increasing caseload offer both reward and frustration.

"If you let all these cases get to you, it can be a real problem," he says. "That's not to say you don't sympathize with everyone who has lost someone or that you don't do everything you can to find everyone who comes to your attention. That's the job. But you have to do everything possible to keep your emotions in check. If you don't, you put yourself in danger of losing the proper perspective necessary to investigate the case."

Still, Ashley Reed is one of those he can't put out of his mind. "Because of the kind of person she is and the circumstances of the case," he says, "I've got to find her. I'm going to find her. It has become a personal thing, a challenge, maybe even a vendetta.

"I feel like I know this girl," he continues. "I've spent a great deal of time talking with her family, her friends back in Minnesota, and people she knew and worked with here in Dallas. Ashley's a young woman with all the attributes that benefit our society; the type person we hope to put our trust for the future in."

To date, though, his search has been an endless maze of blind alleys. He has checked out reports that Ashley was seen at a truckstop near Fort Worth, hitchhiking; that she was working as a topless dancer in a Dallas nightclub; that she was in a bar near Oklahoma City with two men and a woman, high on drugs, her hair teased, and wearing a revealing miniskirt; that she had forsaken her family and friends and moved into a lesbian lifestyle in Dallas' gay community.

"Every time I get a call like that," Easton says, "I say to myself, 'This isn't the girl I'm looking for.' Still, I have to check it out." Easton admits he even spent most of one day in the company of a local psychic in a fruitless attempt to determine the missing girl's whereabouts.

The police are not alone in their quest: Ashley's father, now remarried and living in a Boston suburb, traveled to Dallas and joined in the searches. Karen's younger brother, Randy, came from Michigan immediately after learning his niece was missing.

During their recent spring break, several of Ashley's former Saint Cloud schoolmates traveled to Dallas to spend time with Karen and distribute posters. Old and new friends have contributed to a fund to assist in the search. Route drivers for Coca-Cola have distributed over one thousand posters. Employees of a JoJo's franchise in Arizona sent donations they collected. A steady stream of phone calls and letters from supportive friends have come in, asking ways they might help.

"I've been told by police at various missing persons agencies that it is relatively easy to keep a search like this going for a year," says Karen. "Then, they tell me, it gets more difficult. People begin to give up or forget. I just won't allow that to happen."

For now Karen Reed busies herself with the distribution of posters, soliciting help from a variety of national organizations whose purpose is to help find missing persons, and trying to restore some normalcy to her life and that of her young son. At some point in the future, she hopes to establish a nonprofit organization that would offer support to the families of missing persons. She has taught her son a prayer, which he says nightly before going to bed: "Dear God, please bring Ashley home soon."

"Josh and I talk about her every day," she says. "I don't want him to forget about her."

On Valentine's Day and Easter, she purchased greeting cards that she's kept to give her daughter when she returns. Lately she has been talking with her mother about plans to redecorate Ashley's room in anticipation of the day she comes home. Ashley's grandmother, sitting at her dining room table, sipping a cup of coffee, says it is important for all the family to share in Karen's hope. "We can't give up," she says. "Quite honestly, in a few moments of weakness, I've resigned myself to the fact that she's dead and we'll never see her again. Then I say to myself, no, she'll be back. I've asked God to place a wreath of angels around her, wherever she might be."

While he says there has been no dramatic advancement in the investigation, Detective Easton says plans are under way to get the witnesses who saw the man Ashley is believed to have met that night together with an artist who might provide a better sketch. "In cases like this, what you do is wait until after you've checked out any new lead and determined if it has merit before you talk to the parent about it," the detective explains. "That way, you don't get their hopes up and then disappoint them and add to the hurt they're already feeling when nothing comes from whatever you've checked into. The emotional roller-coaster effect is what you try to shield them from as best you can.

"I think Karen understands at this point that there aren't likely to be any monumental leaps of progress. If it comes, it will be in little bits and pieces. About all I'm able to do now is reassure her that I'm doing everything I can.

"And that I do care."

POSTSCRIPT

In the thirteen years since this story was written, Ashley Reed has never been found.

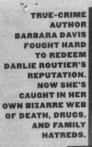

TRUE-CRIME AUTHOR BARBARA DAVIS FOUGHT HARD TO REDEEM DARLIE ROUTIER'S REPUTATION. NOW SHE'S CAUGHT IN HER OWN BIZARRE WEB OF DEATH, DRUGS, AND FAMILY HATREDS.

FALLEN ANGEL

BY CARLTON STOWERS

PHOTOS BY MARK GRAHAM

With Christmas just 10 days away, the petite blonde sat at her computer screen, engaged in her night-owl habit of checking e-mails and responding to chat-room questions posed by a growing collection of fans she'd never expected to have. True-crime author Barbara Davis, at 49 a latecomer to her profession, was still a stranger to the *New York Times* best-seller list. It had, in fact, taken a public admission that she had become convinced that Darlie Routier, a convicted murderer whom she had vilified in print, was actually *not guilty*, to turn her into a minor book-world celebrity.

Her epiphany had vaulted Davis from the role of chronicler to active participant in the controversial and ongoing saga of Routier, the Rowlett mother accused of killing her two children and convicted of the murder of 5-year-old Damon. And with her almost evangelical pleadings on TV talk shows, in newspaper articles, and in the new world of cyberspace, Davis had earned a public awareness that went well beyond the mid-list sales of the original paperback, *Precious Angels*, that she'd written on the case. The high praises solidly coming her way via the www.forburieroutier.org Web site, then, were not applaud-

ing her writing so much as her conversion and new-found conviction.

Such was the tenor of most of the e-mails she read and replied to that night, as December 14th passed into the wee hours of the 15th. Earlier she had responded to a question about her career with the explanation that time spent away from writing while spreading the word of Routier's innocence had created a financial hardship that had made taking a part-time job at a local hospital necessary.

And then, shortly after 1:30 a.m., she read a

Continued on page 24

14

FALLEN ANGEL

With Christmas just ten days away, the petite blonde sat at her computer screen, engaged in her night-owl habit of checking e-mails and responding to chat-room questions posed by a growing collection of fans she'd never expected to have. True-crime author Barbara Davis, at forty-nine a latecomer to her profession, was still a stranger to the *New York Times* best-seller list. In fact, what turned her into a minor book-world celebrity was a public admission that she had become convinced that Darlie Routier, a convicted murderer whom she had vilified in print, was actually not guilty.

Her epiphany had vaulted Davis from the role of chronicler to active participant in the controversial and ongoing saga of Routier, the Rowlett mother accused of killing her two children and convicted of the murder of five-year-old Damon. With her almost evangelical pleadings on television talk shows, in newspaper articles, and in the new world of cyberspace, Davis had earned a public awareness that went well beyond the midlist sales of the original paperback, *Precious Angels*, that she'd written on the case. The high praises suddenly coming her way via the website dedicated to Darlie Routier (www.fordarlieroutier.org), then, were not applauding her writing so much as her conversion and newfound conviction.

Such was the tenor of most of the e-mails she read and replied to that night, as December 14 passed into the wee hours of December 15. Earlier she had responded to a question about her career with the explanation that time spent away from writing while spreading the word of Routier's innocence had created a financial hardship that had made taking a part-time job at a local hospital necessary.

Then, shortly after 1:30 A.M., she read a message that caused her to bolt upright in her chair. "If you're so hard up for money," the unsigned e-mail questioned, "why don't you sell some of that marijuana you're growing in your house?"

A new true-crime story was about to unfold—one involving dark suggestions of conspiracy and retribution, family feuding on a grand scale, lawsuits, and accusations of overzealous actions on the part of a suburban police department and one of its officers.

Shortly after 10:30, later that morning, December 15, 1999, Davis's twenty-five-year-old son, Troy, clad only in drawstring pajama bottoms, peeked into his mother's bedroom and announced that he was preparing breakfast. Barbara, who had remained at her computer until well after 3 A.M., said she wanted to sleep a while longer.

Minutes later, all hell broke loose. A booming sound signaled that leaders of a seventeen-member police task force were shattering the front door of the one-story tan brick home in the 8200 block of Ulster Drive of North Richland Hills. The officers were armed with a "no-knock" warrant to search for "a substantial amount of marijuana," which an unnamed informant had assured them they would find.

Across the street, John and Rose Sanderson, longtime residents of the neighborhood, had seen the police's unmarked van pull up two doors down from the Davis house and watched the scene unfold through the window of their garage. After several officers disappeared into the alcove leading to the Davises' front door, John Sanderson heard the loud sound of the door being broken down, then "about two, maybe three seconds later," two rapid gun shots.

What neither he nor his wife could see was the tragic scene playing inside the Davis home. On the living-room floor, his head just a few feet from wrapped gifts beneath a gaily decorated Christmas tree, Troy Davis lay stretched on an Oriental rug. He was bleeding badly from gunshot wounds to the chest and upper thigh. Although he would be administered CPR by the same officer who fired the two .45-caliber shots, Davis was pronounced dead upon his arrival at Columbia North Hills Hospital. An autopsy revealed cannabis, trace amounts of alcohol, and the prescription drug Darvon in his system.

In the somber days that followed, what happened during those flash-bang seconds after the officers stormed into the Davis home would quickly develop into a bizarre controversy that has lost no steam in the four months since the event. In fact, the incident, which eventually led to Davis's being charged on three felony drug counts, has brought about a series of allegations from all corners of the controversy: allegations by police of a drug-dealing family that tried to shoot first; by the Davis family, which blames Barbara for killing her ex-husband—after she shot him; by Darlie-is-innocent supporters who say Barbara was set up because she now believes Darlie didn't do it; by a lawyer who accuses the cops of a cold-blooded killing; and by observers who say that no matter what went on behind Barbara Davis's closed door, the police should never have knocked it down and killed her son.

The police version was straightforward and dry, as police versions usually are. At a news conference three weeks after the raid, law enforcement officials described the possibility of great danger to the tactical team, a situation they say made the use of the increasingly controversial "no-knock" warrant essential. The confidential informant, police chief Tom Shockley noted, had told investigators that a paranoid and reclusive Troy Davis routinely met people at the door with a gun loaded with Teflon-coated bullets (known on the street as "cop killers" since they are capable of penetrating body armor).

Upon entry, Shockley stated, members of the raid team loudly identified themselves as police and were immediately confronted by Davis, armed with a SIG-Sauer nine-millimeter pistol. The young man took "an aggressive shooting stance," pointing the gun at the officers. He was then shot twice by thirty-seven-year-old North Richland Hills officer Allen Hill. Shockley says that Davis's pistol was loaded, with a bullet in the chamber, although it had not been fired during the confrontation. While Hill administered aid to the dying young man, other members of the tactical team found Barbara Davis still in her bedroom, a loaded Smith and Wesson .38-caliber revolver beneath her pillow. Only after considerable coaxing did the hysterical mother hand over the weapon.

During the subsequent search of the Davis residence, the "substantial amount" of marijuana addressed in the search warrant wasn't found, only a couple of pill bottles and film canisters containing a few marijuana-plant seeds, a glass bong, a "marijuana smoking pipe," a set of scales, and a book titled *Marijuana Grower's Insider's Guide*. A closet at the rear of the house had apparently been transformed into a "growing room," outfitted with lights, humidifiers, irrigation equipment, and an assortment of growing chemicals. But no plants. No marijuana, in fact, was found until investigators went into the backyard of the Davis home. There they located three plants growing in pots. Officials later determined that collectively they had a usable weight of only two to four ounces.

The evidence hardly pointed to the major pot-selling operation the arresting officers had expected to find. (In fact, the marijuana possession charge, a misdemeanor, was recently dismissed.) What they did stumble into, however, was something far more disturbing: enough weaponry to put a smile on the face of the Montana Freemen—sixteen firearms, ranging from handguns to shotguns to a loaded AR-15 assault rifle, and seven hundred rounds of ammunition—and 193.2 grams of GHB (gamma hydroxybutyrate), commonly known as the "date rape" drug. Enough, police chief Shockley would later say, to make as many as six hundred doses of the odorless, colorless, and potentially lethal designer drug. In Davis's bedroom, officers also found printed instructions for making GHB.

Davis, arrested and originally charged with four counts of possessing and manufacturing drugs, insisted that she had purchased the GHB over the Internet for use in her battle with insomnia. She said she knew nothing about the marijuana plants growing in her backyard. And the guns, most of which had belonged to her late husband, were all legally owned.

Davis, who insists she had recently been receiving threats over the Internet in the wake of her defense of Routier, says, "I think this was done to destroy my credibility. Troy was in the kitchen cooking and had just tapped on my bedroom door to ask if I wanted something to eat. He could not have been armed." She describes her son, who was planning to join the Haltom City First Baptist Church the following Sunday, as someone who "did not drink, smoke, or use illegal drugs."

In short order, Internet chat rooms hummed with new conspiracy theories, most based on the notion that Davis had been set up, targeted for reprisal for her new role as a Routier advocate. The truth is less Machiavellian, but just as strange. It leads not to a setup by police, but one by relatives. It's the first piece in a family-feud puzzle that had been building since a young woman named Barbara Jean McNabb married into the Davis family in 1970.

When Bob Davis, the fifty-five-year-old brother-in-law of Barbara Davis, arrives at the office of his Budget Casket Company ("Prices to Die

For"), he is dressed in a bright print sport shirt, his graying hair pulled back in a short ponytail. A self-described "old hippie," he smiles warmly from behind frameless glasses, settles behind his desk, and begins to talk of the stormy relationship between his late brother Jim and the woman he refers to as "Barbara Jean."

He quickly admits that it was the wife of his other brother, Dan, who sent the mystery e-mail to Davis. He acknowledges that it was Bob and his twenty-eight-year-old son, Chris, who alerted the North Richland Hills police to drug activity in the home of Barbara and Troy Davis. Yes, he says, it is Chris who is the "confidential informant" mentioned in the affidavit for the search warrant. Chris Davis, his father says, will not speak with reporters. "This has really upset him. He's lost a lot of weight; he's lost his job. He just got caught in the middle of all this."

But Bob Davis, even though he's been asked by the Tarrant County district attorney's office not to talk about the case, has a story to tell. He has, he says, long been suspicious that Barbara Davis was responsible for the late-night heart attack that claimed the life of his forty-seven-year-old brother in 1995.

"She [Barbara] met Jim when she was seventeen or eighteen, working in a dime store," he remembers. "She was a pretty little thing, and he fell in love right away." They soon married, purchased a trailer house, and moved it onto the northeast Tarrant County farm of Jim Davis's father. In time the couple made the move to the three-bedroom house on Ulster Drive, where they would live for the remainder of their twenty-five-year marriage.

The Davises had two children: daughter Lisa, born in 1971, and son Troy, born in 1975. Jim Davis worked as a title investigator for the Texas Department of Transportation and joined the Tarrant County sheriff's department as a reserve deputy. Barbara did secretarial work for several attorneys and in 1982 became a clerk in the Tarrant County district attorney's office. By 1984, she had been promoted to work with survivors of violent crimes. Four years later she became court coordinator for state district judge Everett Young.

The marriage was not without its storm clouds. In September 1982, Bob Davis, living in Houston at the time, received a phone call alerting him that his brother Jim had been shot and was in the hospital. The shooter, he was told, was Jim's wife, Barbara. At the hospital where his brother was recovering from wounds to the stomach and leg, Bob Davis learned what had transpired.

According to Bob Davis, his brother had been concerned that Barbara was cheating, and he had confronted her about it one evening. In response, she stormed out of the house and drove to a neighborhood 7-Eleven. Her husband followed Barbara and found her talking on a pay phone. "She saw him and ran to her car, got in, and crouched down in the seat," Bob Davis says. "Jim had bought her this little chrome .25 caliber pistol, and she just pointed it out the window and emptied the clip."

With Jim Davis writhing in pain in the parking lot, his wife sped away. "She drove straight to an osteopathic hospital over on [Highway] 183 and checked herself into their loony bin [psych ward]," Bob Davis says. "Now, Jim tells me all this, how he laid there until an ambulance came, and then asks me if I would go talk to Barbara for him, see if she's OK. I find her, and she wants me to go back and tell Jim that she was never unfaithful to him, how much she loved him, and all that."

Returning to his brother, Bob Davis passed along Barbara's message. "I could tell he was believing her story," Davis says. "A week later he got out of the hospital and went over and picked her up. Jim was a family man and felt whatever it took to make the marriage work, he'd do."

Barbara's account of the motive for the shooting and events that transpired afterward is quite different. Her husband, she says, had been diagnosed as manic-depressive and was taking lithium at the time. "I was getting ready to go to UT-Arlington, where I was taking a criminal justice course, and while I was getting dressed I sensed something was wrong with Jim," she recalls. "He was acting strange, and I asked if he was taking his medication. He gave me a hug and a kiss and assured me that he was.

"When I came home at around 8:30, I pulled into the driveway and saw that all the lights in the house were out, and I could hear the song 'War' playing loudly inside." Fearful of what she might find in the house, she decided to drive to a nearby convenience store and phone the house, she says. "I knew if I could hear his voice, I'd know everything was OK. I remember it ringing thirteen times with no answer. Then I saw him pulling into the parking lot in his pickup, getting out, and coming toward me with a rifle. He was yelling something like 'Viet Cong . . . Viet Cong . . .' over and over."

Her husband, she says, had long been conflicted over the fact that he had been exempted from the draft and thus had not served during the Vietnam conflict. "I had this little gun he'd gotten me, and I just started shooting. Then I ran into the store and told someone to call 911 because I'd shot my husband."

While she did check herself into Northeast Community Hospital, it was only after a visit to the Richland Hills police department in the company of officers investigating the shooting. "They never even cuffed me," she says. "In fact, one of the officers there told me that my husband had called from the hospital and asked that I be told he loved me and not to worry, that everything was OK."

Jim Davis, who his widow says was hospitalized only overnight, later filed an affidavit in which he swore the incident was his fault, and all relevant records were ultimately expunged. "Jim and I saw a counselor afterward," she says, "and he promised never to skip his medicine again."

Says Tom Carse, Barbara Davis's attorney, "It's not something that bears any relationship whatsoever to Troy being executed by the North Richland Hills police department. This is the Troy Davis case, not the family feud."

You couldn't tell it by listening to Bob Davis.

When Howard Davis died and the family farm was sold, each son—Bob, Jim, and Dan—received in excess of three hundred thousand dollars. "We were driving back from picking up the checks," Bob Davis remembers, "and Jim said, 'I've got to do something with this money so Barbara can't get her hands on it.' He kinda laughed and said, 'But if she can't get her hands on it, I'll be dead in two years.'"

Joking or not, Jim Davis's estimate of his life expectancy was accurate. His death only widened the gap between Barbara Davis and her suspicious in-laws. It led to extreme (and unsubstantiated) charges being leveled against her by Bob Davis.

"Leading up to his death," says Bob, "Jim had three heart seizures, all at around 2 A.M." He and other members of the Davis family began to wonder whether Barbara might have given him something that brought on the heart problems. Bob says that after his brother's death, he went to the Tarrant County sheriff's department and voiced his concerns. "I was told that since we had no proof I'd best forget about it," he says.

Prior to her husband's death, Barbara Davis says, he had been hospitalized with meningitis for a week but had never experienced heart problems. "He had only the one heart attack," she says. "That night, I was up writing until around three then went to bed. When the alarm went off the following morning, Jim didn't shut it off like he usually did. Then the dog began barking. That's when I knew something was wrong. I called 911 and gave him mouth-to-mouth, but he was already gone."

Davis says she feels betrayed by her brother-in-law and nephew. "None of it is true," she says. "Not a single word. I loved my husband very much."

The words "greedy" and "violent" in no way describe the Barbara Davis I had known casually since the publication of her first book. Shortly before the paperback version of *Stalked* was to be published, a chilling story she'd written with rape victim La Vonne Skalias, she had phoned asking whether I might read it and write a cover blurb. I did so and later attended a local book signing, where I met her for the first time. In the years that followed we appeared together on a panel discussion of crime writing and said our hellos at occasional book gatherings. For a time, we were represented by the same literary agent.

She was an attractive woman who struck me as a bit shy. Only when she talked of making a career for herself as a writer of true crime did real passion enter her voice. She brought no journalism background to her task, but she had experience working in the legal world and was regularly attending meetings of the Dallas–Fort Worth Writers group to improve her skills.

Davis, by all accounts, worked hard at her newfound craft. When a piece of evidence in the Routier case troubled her, she went in search of her own answers. When she learned that a bloodstained sock had been found in an alley some distance from the Routier house, supposedly left by a nameless intruder who defense attorneys alleged did the crime, Davis, stopwatch in hand, timed herself as she raced from the Routier house to the location of the sock. She concluded (for the time being, at least) that Darlie Routier had ample time to plant the evidence before the police arrived.

In her book on the Routier case, published in January 1999, Davis pulled no punches. After attending the Kerrville trial, conducting numerous interviews, and poring over police reports, she concluded that the twenty-eight-year-old Darlie Routier had simply reached the melt-down point in a young mother's life and savagely murdered her five- and six-year-old sons on an early June morning in 1996. That done, she self-inflicted a wound to her neck, staged an elaborate crime scene to match a concocted story she planned to tell, summoned crocodile tears, and dialed 911. To readers of *Precious Angels*, the author, without question, strongly believed not only that Routier was guilty but that she defined evil.

Then, shortly after publication, Davis reversed her field, citing evidence that neither she nor the jury had been privy to, testimony that she was convinced was perjured, and a less than stellar performance from Routier's defense team, as well as questionable practices by the prosecutors. What gave Davis pause was a self-published book by an amateur Lewisville sleuth named Christopher Brown, *Media Tried, Justice Denied*, which contained photos taken at the crime scene and the hospital where Routier was taken for treatment. In short order she was a believer in Routier's innocence, had visited her in jail to ask her forgiveness, and emerged as the most celebrated voice in the Darlie-didn't-do-it chorus. Virtually everyone Davis had once praised, thanked, or written positively of in her book became a target in her postpublication turnaround.

A statement Davis posted on the busy Darlie Routier website offers ample proof of her new posture. In part, it reads: "Now is the time for us to rise up and exert so much relentless and tremendous pressure on officials that they will have no other choice but to set Darlie Routier free. I'll probably never get this out of my system but I was WRONG! WRONG! WRONG!"

Such, apparently, was her mind-set when things began to unravel, beginning a month before the raid on her house—beginning, in fact, on Thanksgiving Day.

The Bob Davis family had gathered for its traditional Thanksgiving meal and was just preparing to sit down at the table when Chris Davis received a phone call. The caller was Troy Davis, asking Chris to come to the North Richland Hills home immediately. "Chris told us," Bob Davis says, "that Troy was talking about committing suicide, and he left immediately."

It would be several days before Bob Davis really learned what had transpired among his son Chris and Troy and Barbara Davis.

"He came around to the office, and I gave him a hard time about not coming back that day. He seemed really upset and said that Barbara Jean and Troy had been calling him at all hours, wanting him to get them some marijuana. He told me that Troy had been very upset, talking about how depressed he still was over his father's death," Bob Davis says. "Chris said he finally told his cousin that what he needed to do was get out of the house, get himself a job, and quit using drugs."

Bob Davis, who claims that years earlier he had regularly purchased marijuana for Barbara Davis ("I quit because my brother didn't know anything about it, and I didn't like the idea of doing things behind his back," he says), told his son the best way to put an end to the harassment was to call the police. With that, the father picked up the phone in his East Lancaster Avenue office and dialed the number of the North Richland Hills police department. After relaying the story his son had told him, Davis handed the phone to Chris, who described to an officer what he had seen and heard on his visit. Police urged young Davis to return to the Ulster Drive address and make certain the items he was describing were still there. A few days later he did so then placed another call to the police.

Again Barbara Davis has a different version: Chris, she says, was not in her home on Thanksgiving Day. He had, however, visited the day after. She says that the reason he abruptly left was a conversation during which Troy had begun questioning him about his faith, asking whether he was a Christian and had been saved.

As to Chris Davis's accusation that there was marijuana in the house, she says, "That's a lie. All you would have found was water, Diet Pepsi, and my GHB." She insists that neither Bob nor Chris Davis ever provided drugs for her or her son. Still, the information provided by Chris Davis would serve as the foundation of the affidavit for a search and arrest warrant prepared by Sergeant J. A. Wallace of the North Richland Hills police department and signed by state district judge Sharen Wilson.

In the affidavit, Sergeant Wallace states that his "confidential informant" (CI) had, within the last seventy-two hours, been inside the Davis residence and observed both suspects in possession of and concealing substantial quantities of marijuana. Additionally, Wallace wrote that "the CI has observed Troy Davis in possession of several handguns kept inside the residence." A criminal-history check on Troy Davis revealed that he had been arrested on a weapons offense. The police believed the next step was obvious. In retrospect, it was nothing of the sort.

From the outset, it seems, the case was fraught with problems in preparation and execution. Of course, besides the standard lawyerly issues with technicalities, the entire case raised other concerns as well, including problems with the police's crime-scene scenario, the background of the officer who shot Troy Davis, and the "no-knock" warrant itself.

Dallas attorney Tom Carse, who is representing the estate of Troy Davis, says the affidavit that led to the "no-knock" warrant is flawed on several counts. Among his concerns is the glaring fact that the wrong name and driver's license number appear in the document. It states that a white female named Barbara Lynn Davis was a suspect residing in the Ulster Drive home. That name, and the accompanying driver's license number, actually belongs to a Fort Worth businesswoman with no knowledge of Barbara Jean Davis or her activities.

"If this defective warrant hadn't been issued," says Carse, "we wouldn't have a dead twenty-five-year-old."

Carse also questions the credibility of the police's confidential informant, pointing out that even in the affidavit it is noted that Chris Davis had previously been arrested on drug charges. The earlier weapons charge assigned to Troy Davis, the civil attorney says, could easily have been explained. According to Carse, the young man was stopped for a traffic violation in 1998. While talking with the officer, Davis volunteered that the car belonged to his mother and that a handgun registered to her was under the driver's seat. Though he was arrested on suspicion of unlawfully carrying a weapon, the case was eventually dropped.

Carse has filed a lawsuit against the city of North Richland Hills, asking that a judge order depositions from officers involved in the fatal raid. Carse says he is also considering filing a suit seeking damages. Because of the pending litigation, says North Richland Hills police spokesman Captain Sid Johnson, "the department has been advised by legal counsel not to discuss the case."

Though it is not unusual for cases to be thrown out should a judge rule an affidavit or warrant seriously flawed, few in the law enforcement community whom the *Observer* spoke with believed the case would be dismissed. "So long as they had the right address," said one lawyer who wished to remain anonymous, "everything's probably OK."

But it's not the technicalities that are most troubling. What transpired inside the Davis home begs the important questions. According to the press release issued by the North Richland Hills police, officers were "immediately confronted by an armed twenty-five-year-old male suspect [Troy Davis] who pointed a handgun at officers in the front foyer of the residence."

Evidence collected at the scene of the shooting suggests a different scenario. Upon entering the Davis house, one looks down a fourteen-foot-long hallway/foyer with floor-to-ceiling walls. At the far end of the foyer, where plants and an antique Victrola sit, is an open doorway where a left turn leads into the sunken den where the dying Troy Davis lay before being transported to the hospital. One spent shell casing from Hill's gun was found in the corner of the den, the other at the end of the foyer near the doorway. Assuming the casings from the officer's gun were discharged to the right as is the normal case, their location would strongly suggest that the shots were fired not as the raiders entered the house, but only after Hill had reached the end of the foyer and turned left to face the den.

"I do not believe Troy Davis was armed, not for a minute," Carse says.

The discovery of an empty canvas pistol holster lying on Troy Davis's bed on the opposite side of the house fuels at least three possible scenarios: It suggests that upon becoming aware the house was being broken into, Davis would have had to run from the kitchen, where he was allegedly preparing breakfast, past the foyer, into his room, to get the gun, then to return to the den in those few seconds that neighbors describe between the sounds of the door being knocked down and hearing two gunshots.

Meanwhile, those willing to play devil's advocate are quick to suggest that from the kitchen window, which faces the front of the house, Troy might have had a bird's-eye view of the approaching SWAT team before their entry and thus had ample time to arm himself before officers actually burst into the house. Or, is it possible that officers did first see Davis in the foyer before he had begun a retreat through the doorway and into the den? That there was no blood trail leading from the foyer to where Davis's body lay and that the fatal wounds were to the front of his body make it seem unlikely. The case, then, offers the kind of mystery that writer Barbara Davis might well have been drawn to, were she not the story's central figure.

Also prominent in the tragedy's cast of characters is North Richland Hills officer Allen Hill, the member of the entry team who fired the fatal shots. Though cleared of any criminal wrongdoing by a grand jury investigating the shooting, he has, during his law enforcement career, been the focus of controversy. In November 1998, while on a tactical-team training exercise at Fort Hood, the officer exposed his penis as a group photograph was being taken and was later suspended without pay for two weeks. The lone female member of the SWAT team at the time of the incident has since left the department and is no longer involved in police work. She has a sexual-harassment complaint pending against Hill.

In a statement written by Hill in response to the internal affairs investigation of his behavior and obtained by the *Observer*, the officer provides a convoluted explanation of his strange actions at Fort Hood. "I realize," he writes, "that there have been comments, usually humorous in nature, about what appears to be my desire to show my genitalia at any opportunity. This is not true, nor do I have a fetish concerning my penis or anyone elses [*sic*] body for that matter. The truth is, via the medium of humor, I have tried to break down the barriers that I am sure we all have concerning the various sensitivities about our bodies."

Two months prior to the photo incident, Hill was investigated by internal affairs following allegations that he had physically abused a thirty-eight-year-old Hurst woman. According to police documents, Hill was accused of striking the woman with his nightstick and shoving her over a couch. Later the woman assured officials that she had had no problems with Hill, saying that the allegations were the result of a false report made by "an acquaintance with an overactive imagination." After Hill passed a polygraph test, the investigation was dropped.

It did, however, fit a pattern that seems to have followed the officer through much of his career. While a member of the White Settlement city water department in July 1984, he was fired following a physical altercation with his supervisor. Employment records of his dismissal, however, eventually acknowledged that it had been the supervisor who initiated the fight. A city report on the matter noted that "Mr. Hill was wrongly fired for his action."

Later Hill worked briefly in Blue Mound and with the Tarrant County sheriff's department before joining the Watauga Department of Public Service, first as a fireman, then as a police officer. Despite being characterized by several fellow workers as "confrontational," Hill's work earned him a number of commendations, one for his investigation of drugs being delivered to the Tarrant County jail.

At North Richland Hills, he became the designated paramedic for the department's SWAT team. Hill's responsibility to be ready to administer treatment to any member of the SWAT team injured during a raid begs a question that Davis's attorneys are likely to raise: Why would the person who would be called on to provide medical aid to fellow officers be in the lead when the house was entered, thus placing himself in maximum risk of injury?

After being no-billed by the grand jury, Hill returned to work and has been assigned to desk duty. According to Richland Hills police officials, he will not return to enforcement work until the legalities of the Davis case have been cleared up.

Meanwhile, the controversy of the "no-knock" warrant hangs over the case like a shroud. While legal experts nationwide criticize use of the tactic, for which there are few clear-cut guidelines, law enforcement continues to request it and judges continue to sign off on it.

The number of lawsuits resulting from military-style police raids continues to grow. In Los Angeles, a jury awarded the family of suspected drug dealer Donald Scott $5 million after sheriff's deputies shot him as he emerged from his ranch house bedroom carrying a pistol.

While North Richland Hills police chief Shockley insists that the threat of an armed Troy Davis placed his officers in potential danger, thus making the "no-knock" warrant essential, it is a law enforcement procedure that is clearly under fire. Recently, the Illinois Supreme Court struck down the provision allowing police to search a house without knocking if they believe guns might be inside.

"The use of the 'no-knock' warrant," says Fort Worth criminal defense attorney Jack Strickland, "clearly heightens the potential danger to everyone concerned. In recent years, it seems that the smaller [law enforcement] agencies have been more prone to use the Rambo-type tactics."

And so it is a mystery of many levels, best and most simply described by North Richland Hills police chief Shockley, who refers to it as "a tragic event."

Today Barbara Davis, free on a sixteen-thousand-dollar bail, leaves her home only to visit her son's grave, attend church and grief counseling sessions, or occasionally say hello to supportive friends in the neighborhood. Word is that many of the Darlie Routier supporters who once warmly embraced her have now distanced themselves. While Davis has not changed her mind about Routier's innocence, she admits she's lost the burning desire she once had to campaign for her freedom.

She says she now suffers from short-term memory loss that developed the week after Troy's funeral and has lost almost twenty-five pounds. Everything, she says, is an effort: "I have to talk myself into getting out of bed, getting dressed, doing anything. And I cry a lot. I'm just trying to make it through one day at a time."

Her home, she says, is a constant reminder of the darkest moments of her life. Unable to enter the den where her son died, she restricts herself to her bedroom and the kitchen. Her mother and daughter Lisa visit occasionally but won't come to the house. "We meet somewhere," Davis says.

As Easter approached, she was back to her late-night routine, staying up until six in the morning coloring eggs for the children at her church and to place on her son's grave. "I go there and talk to him," she admits. "Sometimes I leave little notes."

Meanwhile, her lawyers tell her it may be months before her case goes to trial. If convicted, she could face a prison term ranging from two to twenty years or as much as ten to ninety-nine years.

Only recently has she returned to writing. Wearied of true crime, she's working on a novel.

POSTSCRIPT

In April 2002, Barbara Davis was sentenced to two years probation for possession of GHB. Her federal lawsuit against the North Richland Hills police department for the death of her son is still pending. Allen Hill has resigned from the police department.

DALLAS

Observer

www.dallasobserver.com

Little yellow Balls:
Let's give Jimmy Connors more
than a backhanded compliment

Volume 566   FREE

IN THE LINE OF FIRE

WHEN A GUNMAN TERRORIZED WORSHIPERS AT WEDGWOOD BAPTIST CHURCH, ONE UNLIKELY HERO SUMMONED THE COURAGE AND FAITH TO CHALLENGE A KILLER

BY CARLTON STOWERS

Scarring the body:
Some say it's
painful, others
say it's art

News: Forbidden Books
learns from vice cops that
some things really
are forbidden

Vonnegut milk?
*Breakfast of
Champions* will
fill you up.

15

IN THE LINE OF FIRE

When the time comes for historians to reflect on the decade of the nineties, one of the troubling issues they will face is the headline-grabbing litany of violence that all too regularly has visited unlikely places. Misguided outcasts sprayed lethal gunfire into schools in Pearl, Mississippi; Littleton, Colorado; and West Paducah, Kentucky. The same horror found its way to a Jewish day-care center in Los Angeles and to business offices in Atlanta.

Then, on a hymn-filled Wednesday evening, Wedgwood Baptist Church on the southern edge of Fort Worth felt the terror.

On September 15, forty-seven-year-old Larry Gene Ashbrook became the nation's latest time bomb. Living alone since the death of his eighty-five-year-old father last July, Ashbrook was described by neighbors in the city's quiet Forest Hills section as strange and solitary—"Weird Larry," some called him. Discharged from the navy in 1983 for marijuana use, he was convinced that authorities conspired to brand him a serial killer and thus wrote rambling antigovernment tirades to local newspapers and in personal journals.

But his final fury was launched in private at his modest home, where he bashed holes in the walls with a shovel and crowbar, poured concrete into the toilets and motor oil onto the shower heads. He destroyed family photographs and ripped the family Bible apart, page-by-page. He poisoned fruit trees growing in the front yard.

Ashbrook then climbed into his beat-up old Pontiac sedan, armed with two handguns (purchased seven years earlier in Grand Prairie), ten clips of ammunition, and a homemade pipe bomb. The time had come to express his rage publicly.

As he wound his way through the quiet, middle-class neighborhood that surrounds Wedgwood Baptist, a youth rally was already under way in the church's sanctuary. Teenagers from numerous churches in the area had accepted invitations to extend the celebration of a nationally proclaimed "See You at the Pole" day, which had been set aside for school students to meet for morning prayers at flagpoles on campuses throughout the country. About 150 youngsters were already singing along to the music of a Christian rock band when Ashbrook, a dark-colored baseball cap pulled low over his brow, steered his car into a handicapped parking space near the entrance.

As Ashbrook approached the sanctuary, custodian Jeff Laster, thirty-six, asked that he put out his cigarette before entering the building. Ashbrook pulled a Ruger nine-millimeter semiautomatic from beneath his jacket and critically wounded Laster with a shot to the chest. He then turned to Sydney Browning, the thirty-six-year-old children's choir director who was seated on a couch in the foyer, killing her with a single shot. Stepping over the bleeding, unconscious Laster, the gunman walked down the hall and killed Shawn Brown, twenty-three, who was staffing a booth set up to sell Christian music CDs. Then he fired a shot into a window separating the hallway and sanctuary. Finally arriving at the entrance to the main room, Ashbrook burst through the double doors and began methodically walking along the back row, shooting into a stunned and screaming crowd. In the next ten minutes, eight people, including Ashbrook, would die.

In the days to come, the media, clergy, parents, and survivors reviewed the nightmare in minute-by-minute detail. They attended memorial services and held prayer vigils for injured friends and family. Ashbrook's brother and two sisters issued a written statement of grief and donated his body to the University of Texas Southwestern Medical Center in Dallas, asking that it be used for research.

Somewhere, all but lost in the strained recollections and reams of reporting, was this story.

At some point during Ashbrook's murder spree, a young man stood and challenged the gunman face to face, urging him to stop the bloodshed, pointing out that he needed God in his life. Some of those who mentioned the brief incident ended the anecdote with the assumption that the unnamed teenager's courageous stand had cost him his life.

Wrote *Time* magazine: "That's a version being offered by someone who was there, but it's unconfirmed. Yet even if it is pious invention, it gives a glimpse of the way some evangelical Christians, children and adults alike, are thinking about the string of killings around the U.S."

The story—one of remarkable faith and courage, one that may well have prevented the carnage from being worse—is not pious invention. Rather, it is that of a six-foot, 190-pound former Boy Scout and high school football lineman named Jeremiah Neitz, a young man whose brief life is a mixture of winding turns, troubles, and triumphs.

A week had passed since the Wedgwood nightmare, and the outside darkness was doing little to mask the lingering summer heat. Inside a small, sparsely furnished upstairs apartment on the southern edge of Fort Worth, a young couple, unmarried but expecting their first child, sat in front of a fan that had been stirring the steamy late-summer air since the air conditioning went out. They had no idea when the landlord might get it repaired, only hoping it would be soon.

The nineteen-year-old father-to-be, a Crowley High School drop-out on probation for a misdemeanor theft, is simultaneously working toward his GED and being a breadwinner. The wages he earned first as a fast-food cook, then as an apprentice electrician, have made it impossible for the couple to afford a phone or an automobile. When he gets his IRS refund, he says, then maybe he can find a used car. Of course, they have plans for a marriage as soon as they save a little money.

His seventeen-year-old fiancée, excited about the daughter she will soon give birth to, nods her head in agreement to the optimistic plans and adds that she intends to return to her high school studies sometime after her baby arrives. She's not a "dropout," she insists with a heart-melting smile; she's only taking time off to have her child. Both, in fact, are smiling, as if hard times and an uncertain future had never visited their home. The positive attitude is unexpected. Just as the fact that theirs is the home of one of the bona fide heroes to emerge from the horror visited on the Fort Worth church.

Had it not been for the sudden, inexplicable act of Jeremiah Neitz, a young man who six months ago made the decision to turn his troubled life around and return to the church he had briefly deserted, Ashbrook's legacy might have a higher death count.

"What Jeremiah did that night," says Sheila Klopfer, a seminary student and Sunday-school teacher at the Southwayside Baptist Church, which Neitz and fiancée Shellie Rhinehart attend, "has been an inspiration to every member of our church. It has not only made people take notice of him, but it has caused each one of us to ask ourselves if we would have the same courage and conviction if put into a similar circumstance. What Jeremiah has done is issue a challenge to all of us."

As he sits in his apartment and as the tragic event that became headline news throughout the world grows distant, Neitz insists that he is making every effort to put it all behind him, to occupy his mind with other things—anything—that will erase the sights and sounds of that evening. He tries to forget, but the images still visit, even as he sleeps. "He won't admit it," Rhinehart says, "but he's having nightmares. He'll kick and moan and doesn't stop until I wake him." It is a memory that will be difficult to discard. As he retells the story, a somber look crosses his face. His hands fumble with a gimme cap in his lap; he stares at the floor and recalls:

"Adam Hammond, our [Southwayside Baptist] youth minister, had received a flier from the Wedgwood Baptist Church about the Wednesday-night youth rally they were planning and suggested it would be a fun evening," Neitz says. "There were about a dozen of us who planned to go, and we met at Southwayside and went together in the church van." The rally would offer a band, singing, and fellowship for 150 teenagers. Neitz was sorry that Rhinehart, feeling the effects of her final weeks of pregnancy, had decided at the last minute that she didn't feel up to joining the group and stayed at home.

At a few minutes past 7 P.M., Neitz was standing near the wall of the sanctuary, listening as the band Forty Days began its second number, a song titled "Alle, Alleluia." Suddenly, over the music, Neitz heard a loud "pop," and the window that separated the hallway from the sanctuary shattered at his feet. The stunned teenager immediately rushed to take a seat by Hammond near the rear of the sanctuary. Unlike some of those in the congregation who first thought the intruder was acting out a skit, Neitz knew otherwise. "I sat down by Adam and told him, 'This is real. Something bad's happening.'" Seconds later he saw Ashbrook, wearing jeans, a black jacket, and a black baseball cap, a cigarette dangling from his lips. In one hand he held a .380-caliber pistol; in the other he had the Ruger nine-millimeter, pointing, shooting, aiming, shooting. At one point he threw a handmade pipe bomb toward the pulpit where the band had been playing, cursing his disappointment when its explosion did no real damage. Neitz recalls screams of fear and pain as fellow worshipers were shot before they could duck beneath the cover of the pews.

By the time those attending the rally realized they were actually under siege, they had no time to run from the building. With Ashbrook spending most of his time at the back of the room near the main entrance, they were trapped.

For Neitz time froze. Though in reality the deadly rampage lasted no more than ten minutes, it seemed to go on eternally as Ashbrook fired, yelled obscenities, reloaded, and fired repeatedly. A video, taken by seventeen-year-old Justin Ray before he was fatally wounded, was later viewed by Fort Worth police and offered an eerie, almost surrealistic view of the early stages of the tragedy. Acting police chief Ralph Mendoza told the media after viewing the video: "He [Ashbrook] is just slowly pacing the aisle in the sanctuary, pointing a gun and firing at selected victims. On the film, he ejects the magazine, reloads, and continues firing. It wasn't rapid. It was slow and methodical, picking a target, aiming, and shooting. He didn't seem in a panic. He would stand in one place, shoot, and then move to another position and shoot again."

"I was sitting there, just praying it would end," Neitz recalls, "and then as he approached me, I turned and looked at him. I really couldn't see his face that well because of the dim lighting and the way he had the cap pulled down on his forehead, but he seemed very calm."

As the gunman neared Neitz, youth minister Hammond, having already taken cover on the floor, began to pull at the teen's pants leg, urging him to get down before he, too, was shot. Recalls Neitz: "I don't know why, but I just sat there, looking at him as he came toward me. When he got to within about five feet, he pointed one of his guns at me and just glared. I told him, 'Sir, you don't have to be doing this.' He told me to 'shut the hell up.' Then he asked me what my religion was, and I told him I was a Christian, a Baptist. He said 'that sucks' and that it was 'a stupid religion.'"

Still seated in the pew, hands folded in his lap, despite Hammond's urgings that he get down, young Neitz continued to look into the eyes of the killer. "No sir," he replied, "it doesn't suck. It's a wonderful thing. God put me on this earth for a reason. I'm certain of that."

Without a reply, Ashbrook sprayed several more rounds through the sanctuary, yelled, "This religion is bullshit," then returned his gaze to Neitz. "That's the only time I really noticed his face," he remembers. "What I saw was pure rage.

"That's when I stood up," he says. "I looked at him and told him, 'Sir, what you need is Jesus Christ in your life.' I told him that I knew where I was going when I died and asked, 'What about you?' He just looked at me for another second or two, then said, 'f-off,' sat down, and shot himself."

Nearby, another act of courage had just been played out. Seventeen-year-old Mary Beth Talley was handing out programs to latecomers when the shooting began and had raced toward the mother of longtime friend Heather MacDonald, eighteen, who is physically disabled. Seeing that Heather's mother was having difficulty getting her daughter onto the floor and out of the line of fire, Talley draped her body over her friend as she heard Neitz, whom she did not know, confronting Ashbrook.

"I heard him telling the man that he needed Jesus Christ," she says, "and I started praying that God would protect him." Seconds later a bullet ripped into her right shoulder.

Then there would be the final shot, one that youth minister Hammond was certain had been aimed at Neitz. In the confusion that followed, the story quickly circulated that the outspoken teen was among those whose lifeless bodies remained inside the church after the shooting had ended.

"What I did," Neitz says, "was get up and walk outside just as soon as he killed himself." There he did what he could to help those who had been wounded. "There was this one kid—I don't know his name—who I helped out of the church and onto the lawn out front. He had been shot in the back. All I can remember was that he was a short kid and was wearing a black shirt."

Nearly two hours passed after the last shot had been fired before Neitz was given a ride home by a woman who attends his church. Rhinehart, meanwhile, had been pacing, tearfully watching the event as it was being reported live by local television stations. "They weren't giving any names," she remembers, "only saying that there were a lot of people still inside the building and that they were dead. I kept praying that Jeremiah was OK, wishing I had gone as planned so I could be there and find him." Finally she borrowed a neighbor's phone and called the

Southwayside Church and learned that none of its members who had made the trip to the youth rally had been killed or injured.

Neitz says he doesn't recall what prompted him to confront Ashbrook.

"I've tried to think back about what was going through my mind at the time," he says, "and I come up with nothing. There just wasn't time to think. But I do know that I never thought I was going to die. I had this feeling that God was there for me, helping me to face up to the guy. All I was thinking was that I had to do whatever I could to make him stop shooting people. I'm no hero, but maybe I got to him. I don't know how, really, but I think that's why what happened [Ashbrook's suicide] happened. He had more [ammunition] clips in his jacket. He could have killed a lot more people. I just did what I felt I had to do."

Did Neitz's action persuade Ashbrook to end the shooting and, ultimately, his own life? "I can't say for sure," says Fort Worth Police Department homicide detective Mike Carroll, who later interviewed Neitz. "Maybe he did frustrate Ashbrook with what he was saying. There's no way we'll ever really know. All I can say is that I'm impressed by what he did that evening. It was a very brave thing. You have to admire that.

"What impressed me when I spoke with him was that he was in no way trying to take credit for doing anything special. He's a young man with a strong belief that he was willing to make a great sacrifice for."

Adds youth minister Hammond, "I don't even know if Jeremiah realized at the time what he'd done." He is, however, convinced the teenager's action saved lives.

"There's no doubt about it," Hammond says. "I think he was there for a reason. I don't know what it was. If he did make the man stop and think, I don't know how he did it. But something happened between them. He [Ashbrook] had six more clips in his pocket when he decided to stop the shooting and take his own life."

Hammond, married and the father of two, recalls crouching on the floor in front of the pew where he'd been sitting, listening to the steady stream of shots being fired off by Ashbrook. "From where I was, I could watch his feet as he moved around. I could hear the sounds—the screams, the shots, and each empty clip as it fell to the floor.

"I could hear him yelling out against religion, cursing, saying something about the Masons. And there would be more shooting. I was praying. I was sure I was going to die."

At some point as he lay on the floor of the sanctuary, Hammond became aware that a young girl who had been seated in a nearby pew had been shot. "I looked down on the floor and saw that her blood was all over my clothes.

"It was just a few seconds after that when I heard Jeremiah talking to the man," he says. "I kept pulling on his pants leg, telling him to get down. When I heard that last shot, I was certain that Jeremiah was going to die.

"The whole thing was just so unreal, from beginning to end."

Neitz says that Hammond has been a big help to him as he attempts to sort out the events at Wedgwood Baptist Church. "He's been like another father to me," Neitz says. "I talk to him every day. I can go to him with any problem I have. I thank God every day for Adam—and for my church. The church is my family.

"What happened last week has brought us [the church membership] even closer together. I love that."

Rhinehart, who has been with Neitz for a year and a half, has also noticed a change. "People are getting to know each other more," she says. "The adults and the young people are mingling and talking. There are people—a lot of the adults—who didn't even really know who Jeremiah was until all this happened. Now they look up to him. That makes me very proud.

"There was a time in his life," she adds, "that I know he wondered if God really had a purpose for his life. Now he knows He does."

Hammond sees the effect the shooting has had on the young man. "For the first few days," the youth minister says, "he was trying to act as if nothing had happened, that it was something he could put behind him and move on. Now, though, the magnitude of what he experienced—what we all experienced—seems to have set in, and he's been much more somber and reflective."

Not long ago Neitz's life was on a downward spiral. Moving to Fort Worth from Vallejo, California, four years ago, he was active in the church for a while and then strayed. "I let too many other things become important to me—a car, material things, me and my own needs," he admits.

Once an easygoing high school student who sang in the choir, started at tackle on the Crowley High football team, and enjoyed the teen life with his friends, Neitz suddenly found himself dealing with a number of frustrations as his junior year approached. Because of academic difficulties in grade school, he'd been held back, and he realized that he would be too old for future eligibility on the football team despite the fact that he was two years away from graduation. Then came the announcement from his mother and stepfather that they would soon be moving to nearby Burleson, away from friends and familiar surroundings.

Neitz chose to drop out—out of school and out of a family life he felt was too strict and governed by too many rules. Then reality set in. He soon found that cooking at a fast-food restaurant was a difficult way to make ends meet. For the first time in his life, he got in trouble with the law. "I stole something that didn't belong to me," he says only when pressed for an explanation. "I did something I shouldn't have, and I felt guilty about it. When I heard that a friend of mine was about to be arrested for what I'd done, I went to the police and told them it was me."

He will be on probation for the misdemeanor offense until August 2000. "Sometimes," he reflects, "you wind up learning things the hard way. If I had it to do all over again, I'd pay more attention to what my parents were trying to tell me."

While working the evening shift at a Whataburger, a group of youngsters he'd known at Southwayside Baptist came in and introduced him to the church's new youth minister. "That's when I met Adam [Hammond]," Neitz says. "I liked him immediately. We talked for a few minutes, and he told me if I ever needed anything to give him a call."

The need arose quickly. Evicted from the apartment where he and Rhinehart were living, he did something he'd never before done: Neitz reached out for help, telephoning Hammond. "At that point," the youth minister recalls, "his feeling of self-worth was pretty low. We had several long talks, and we found him and Shellie a new place to live."

While appreciative of the help, Neitz says the thing he is most grateful for is the fact that Hammond convinced him to return to the church. "Since I've gotten back to the church, returned Christ to my life, I'm a new person," he says.

Longtime friend Josh Waters, also nineteen, agrees with Neitz's self-assessment. "When we were in school together," Waters says, "about the most important thing in our lives was hanging out, partying, and drinking beer. It was just what high school kids in Crowley did. I can remember a couple of times when Jeremiah's parents were out of town and he threw some pretty good parties at their house. He just liked to have fun, do silly things, and didn't worry about much else. He was really immature."

Recently returned from a stint in the marines, Waters was surprised at the transformation in his friend. "It was like night and day," Waters says. "He had grown up, was serious about things. With the baby coming and his involvement in the church, he seemed to have found a real purpose in his life."

Although Neitz urged him to attend the Wedgwood youth rally, Waters had to work late and thus didn't make the drive from Crowley into Fort Worth until that evening when he learned of the shooting. "I knew that my younger brother and Jeremiah were there," he recalls, "so I drove up there immediately after learning what had happened." He soon learned that his brother Daniel Waters had escaped uninjured but did not find out about Neitz's fate until the following day.

"Then," he says, "when I heard what he had done that night, I was blown away. I don't know many people with that kind of courage."

Neither does another friend, twenty-one-year-old Richard Manzano. "I've known him for four years now," Manzano says, "and I've seen him grow up so much. There was a time when he really had a temper. I don't go to church much myself, but I've got to believe that's where he got rid of a lot of anger he used to have. And, no, I wasn't surprised at all to hear that he stood up to the guy."

For Neitz, the attention he has received since that Wednesday evening in Wedgwood has in some ways been discomfiting; in others, it is the gateway to a new beginning. In recent days, he and his mother have had two lengthy conversations.

Jerri Gagne and her husband were out of town on the night of Ashbrook's assault on Wedgwood Baptist and didn't even learn that Neitz had been there until the following day, when he and youth minister Hammond visited her. When told what her son had done, her reaction was a mixture of emotions. "It scared me," she says. "On one hand, I felt anger over his having put himself in that kind of danger. On the other hand, what he did was incredibly heroic. At first I didn't know whether to slap him or hug him. What I did was hug him—very tightly."

In retrospect, she says, she is not surprised that her son would take such a stance. "He and his older brother [Michael, who lives in California] were always protective of smaller kids when they were growing up. They've always been there to stand up for the underdog.

"I'm very proud of him," she says. "But, then, I was even before this happened."

Neitz's father, who continued to live on the West Coast following his divorce from Neitz's mother seventeen years ago, has been in touch. A member of the Wedgwood Baptist congregation who had two teenage daughters at the youth rally recently helped Neitz secure a full-time job with a firm that manufactures floor-cleaning equipment. "Eight-fifty an hour and full benefits," he says elatedly.

The doctor tells him and Rhinehart that a healthy baby should be arriving any day now.

"I'm glad some good things are happening for him," says Manzano. "Jeremiah is a good person."

And, to many, a hero.

POSTSCRIPT

Recently Wedgwood Baptist marked the third anniversary of the tragedy without any special ceremony. Senior pastor Al Meredith, while mentioning the shooting in a sermon, decided it was time for his congregation to focus on the future. Still, the memories will never be erased. The church's assistant education director, Jeff Laster, is reminded every time he passes through airport security and the bullet, lodged in his back, sets off the security alarm.

Adam Hammond, who befriended Jeremiah Neitz back in those dark days, has moved to Bellview, Florida, where he is the youth minister at the First Baptist Church. He's stayed in touch with Jeremiah and Shellie, who now have two children: daughter Jessica who is three, and son Preston who is almost two.

DALLAS

Observer

November 20-26, 2001
FREE
Volume XXX
dallasobserver.com

WITH STATUES, CROSSES AND CHRISTMAS ORNAMENTS,
PARENTS MOURN AND CELEBRATE THE MEMORY
OF CHILDREN TAKEN BY VIOLENCE

THE *Garden* OF *Angels*

BY CARLTON STOWERS

16

THE GARDEN OF ANGELS

It is not known precisely where angels dwell—whether in
the air, the void, or the planets. It has not been God's pleasure that we should be informed of their abode. . . .

—Voltaire

Those who had come gathered near the Christmas tree to con-
tribute yet another ornament to its decoration, sharing carols and
warm holiday-season embraces. Made of glass and pewter, cloth and silver, each was in the form of an angel. On this December Sunday, when
an unseasonably warm breeze floated across the isolated hilltop in
southern Tarrant County, the mood was upbeat, the purpose clearly a
celebration.

The event is not easy to explain. Only the hundred or so on hand,
each bringing a toy to be placed beneath the tree and later donated to
charity, could fully understand the reason—the need—for the gathering. Forming a backdrop for the event were rows of neatly arranged
crosses, each representing a tragic loss suffered, each bearing the name
of someone, many of them children, who had been the victim of a by-
gone homicide.

Hidden at the end of rutted and potholed Mosier Valley Road, just
a few miles off FM 157, Our Garden of Angels is a unique memorial to
both life and death, a place that was never really planned but simply grew
out of the grief of a mourning grandmother and friends who helped her.
This is more than just a roadside memorial. Rather, it is a quiet, mani-
cured, softly lit half-acre with a brick walkway, concrete benches, and a
man-made waterfall spilling into a shallow pool. Newly planted live oaks
and pear trees will soon provide shade, and the crepe myrtle bushes that

border the area will burst into bloom. The white wooden crosses stand, all forty-four of them, erected in honor of those whose lives were claimed by society's misfits and psychopaths.

Some you've heard of or read about: one cross bears the name of Amber Hagerman, the nine-year-old Arlington girl who was abducted while riding her bike in her neighborhood and murdered in 1996; other ones are for seventeen-year-old Justin Ray and fourteen-year-old Joey Ennis, victims of the maniacal September 1999 Wedgwood Baptist Church shooting spree by a deranged Fort Worth man named Larry Gene Ashbrook; and one for Amy Robinson, the Grand Prairie nineteen-year-old who in 1998 was the torture–murder victim of two men who abducted her as she rode her bicycle to work. In a corner of the garden, near its entrance, is the small statue of an angel, placed there in memory of six-year-old Opal Jennings, the Saginaw child who was abducted from a vacant lot near her grandmother's home in March 1999, never to be found.

Families are not the only ones who requested the crosses. In the gruesome aftermath of the recent killing spree of Arlington mechanic Terry Lee Hankins—he murdered his estranged Mansfield wife and two children, then later confessed to killing his father and half sister Pearl (Sissy) Sevenstar almost a year earlier—the teachers of twenty-year-old Sissy were the ones who wished that their former student be remembered.

At least the man who bludgeoned Sevenstar to death, then hid her body in a car at his auto repair shop for months, is behind bars. In addition to Hagerman and Jennings, the abduction and murder of four-year-old Christy Ryno, also remembered in the garden, remains an unsolved case. A twin, she was taken from her Arlington apartment in 1999, her body discovered less than a mile away a week following her disappearance. Russell Yates, father of the five Houston children recently killed by his wife, has called to inquire about having crosses erected in their memory.

Most of those memorialized, however, are victims whose names never appeared in headlines, whose untimely loss was never felt by the masses. "Here," says Brenda O'Quinn, whose seventeen-year-old son Michael McEachern was slain in 1995, "everyone is important and not forgotten. That's the purpose of this place. We come here to remember them in life and make sure others do as well."

It is a feeling shared by fifty-year-old Grand Prairie police officer Gary Brooks, making his first visit to the garden to view the recently erected cross for his twenty-seven-year-old son Garry, who was murdered while the nation still mourned the World Trade Center tragedy in New York. "Because the world was so focused on the terrorist attack," the patrolman says, "Garry's death went virtually unnoticed. That didn't seem fair to me. Here, he will be remembered."

Donna Norris, the mother of Amber Hagerman, fully understands. "I feel honored to have a cross for my daughter here. I don't want her to ever be forgotten."

To those who visit it regularly, the garden has become something of a sanctuary. "On birthdays and holidays I go to the cemetery," says Carolyn Barker, the fifty-nine-year-old maternal grandmother who raised Amy Robinson, "and always feel an overwhelming sadness. But when I come out here, I can feel good again." She does not attempt to explain why.

The reasons for collectively memorializing those who died so violently are numerous. Some simply want a place to visit and remember. Some wish to make a statement, to feel assured that the world has not forgotten the nightmarish tragedy that ripped through their lives. For many, the garden has become a gathering place where they can draw strength and understanding available only from those who have suffered similar losses. Others hope that even in death their loved ones can make a difference.

Over the years, laws and ongoing legislation have resulted in the wake of the deaths the crosses represent. The Amber Plan, named in honor of Hagerman, is designed to quickly alert authorities and the public to the abduction of a child and is now used nationwide. To date, seven abducted children in the Dallas–Fort Worth area alone have been safely recovered because of it. U.S. representative Martin Frost is now promoting an Amy Robinson Memorial Act that would require that employers notify parents if their children are working alongside a person ever convicted of a violent crime. Robert Neville, one of those responsible for Amy's murder, had been a coworker and previously convicted as a sex offender, Barker points out.

Such are the myriad reasons that Our Garden of Angels has grown to a point where efforts are now under way to secure adjoining property for expansion. In truth, each cross in the garden echoes an ugly and heartbreaking story. Yet while those who visit do not pretend to have forgotten their nightmarish experiences, they have chosen to use the memorial as a place for remembering the good instead of the bad, for reflection on lives lived, however briefly, instead of the horrible way in which they were ended. For most, arriving at such a mind-set was no easy journey.

Ray Stewart remembers the morning he rose from another night of restless sleep and sat on the edge of his bed. Crippled mentally and physically for more than a year, he realized the time had come to make a decision. On that day in 1986, he would either end his life or find some new purpose for it. Debilitating back problems had made work impossible and had forced his wife to take a job. The physical pain and the vanishing feeling of self-worth, however, were secondary to another agony with which the sixty-five-year-old Stewart was wrestling.

On an October afternoon in 1984, he recalls, his plans were no more ambitious than watching a Cubs–Padres playoff game on television. Ignoring the pain generated by an unsuccessful disc fusion and a series of spinal injections, he was slowly making his way to the bedroom when the passage of a low-flying CareFlight helicopter caused the house to shutter. Then the telephone rang. It was his daughter's mother-in-law, and her voice sounded pinched and distressed. "Is anyone there with you?" she asked. No, Ray replied. His wife had gone shopping with her sister. "Are you sitting down?"

Moments later he received the news that would send him into an eighteen-month depression. A man had followed his twenty-five-year-old daughter Sheri home from a Watauga supermarket and, posing as a utility worker, managed to gain entry into her nearby home. Brandishing a knife, he had forced her five-year-old daughter into the bathroom, then, during an attempted rape, stabbed the young mother.

A sixteen-year-old next-door neighbor, hearing screams, placed a 911 call. When officers arrived, the intruder—a convicted felon named Jerome Lutterell—answered the door and at first tried to persuade the officers that a "family squabble" had occurred but had been resolved. When police insisted on entering the house, Lutterell shrugged, stepped back and said, "You might as well go ahead and arrest me. I think I've killed her."

Before Stewart's son could arrive and drive him to the hospital, his daughter had been pronounced dead. Days later he attended her funeral in a wheelchair, already thinking of suicide. Even the knowledge that his daughter's killer received a life sentence offered him little solace.

That day in 1986, then, he awoke and determined the cause that would make his life worth living. His physical condition improved, and he began making regular visits to the Tarrant County Courthouse, sitting in on trials, introducing himself to families enduring the same experience he'd barely survived, offering whatever comfort and understanding he might provide. In time, he started a support group called Families of Murder Victims. In 1989, he was offered the job of "victim assistance liaison" by the district attorney's office. It is a position he holds today.

"People have no idea how valuable the service he provides is," says Barbara Salter, whose son was murdered in 1986. "He not only understands what the family of a victim is going through, but is also able to explain the workings of the judicial system. There are a lot of good and caring people working in victims' assistance, but having someone who actually knows what you're going through is a rare bonus."

Carolyn Barker had begun attending the twice-monthly meetings of Stewart's support group shortly after her granddaughter's death. Determined to attend the trials of the men who had killed Amy Robinson, she reached out for Stewart's help. He sat with her through the proceedings as the grim and senseless death of her mentally challenged granddaughter was revisited.

Amy, who suffered from a genetic disorder known as Turner's syndrome, had been on her bicycle, en route to her job as a grocery sacker at an Arlington Kroger store on the February day in 1998 when self-proclaimed racists Robert Neville and Michael Hall decided to find a black person to kill. Unable to locate the particular youngster they had planned to murder, they were driving along Division Street in Arlington when they saw Robinson. Part Cherokee and dark-skinned, she became the target of the hate crime they were determined to commit. Promising her a ride to work, they put her bicycle in the back of their pickup, stopped to purchase wine coolers for themselves and a soft drink for Amy, then drove to the isolated area at the end of Mosier Valley Road on the far eastern edge of Tarrant County. They tortured their victim, shooting her with a pellet gun and a crossbow before Neville ended her suffering with a shot from a .22-caliber rifle. They left her body lying in a field of weeds beneath an electrical tower, laughing as they drove away. "I guess she'll be a little late for work," Hall later admitted saying.

The following day, realizing they had not checked to see if Robinson had any money they could have stolen, they returned. While there, Hall fired seven additional shots into the girl's body "to see what it felt like."

Seventeen days passed before Amy was found. Neville and Hall, arrested on the Texas border while attempting to flee into Mexico, quickly confessed to authorities and a stunned television reporter, laughing as they boasted, providing the gruesome details of Robinson's abduction and death. "She trusted us. It was easy," Hall bragged into the camera. Each would receive the death penalty. As she attended Hall's trial, Barker decided she wished to visit the place where her granddaughter had died. She was surprised to find that a small cross had been anonymously placed at the site. Handwritten on it were the words, "In God's Hands."

"Part of the American Indian philosophy," Barker explains, "is that one's spirit ascends into heaven from where the person dies. For that reason, locating the place where Amy was killed was important to me." In time she began to contemplate putting a more permanent memorial to her granddaughter at the site. During a support group meeting, Greg Price, a carpenter dealing with the murder of his Haltom City nephew, suggested she erect a larger, more permanent cross. If she liked, he volunteered, he would build it.

From that suggestion, Our Garden of Angels would eventually grow.

"Amy," Barker says, "had always enjoyed being around people, didn't like to be alone. The more I thought about it, the more I liked the idea of placing a cross where she died. The only thing that troubled me was the idea of her being out there by herself."

Friends in the support group understood. Vernon Price asked if she would mind if he placed a cross in memory of his son next to the one Greg Price (no relation) was building for Amy. In short order, others embraced the idea. Originally, then, Amy's cross was joined by four others: Vern Price, a stabbing victim; Bobbie Kafka, a victim of domestic violence; Marty Klozik, the victim of an argument over a debt; and Chad Houston, murdered during an altercation outside a neighborhood pool hall.

"It was nothing formal or fancy," Barker says, "just a place we could go and remember our kids." In time, twenty-seven crosses were placed among the weeds. Barbara Salter was the one who first suggested they call the spot Our Garden of Angels.

Then, in November 2000, construction began on the extension of Trinity Boulevard. Its planned course included the state-owned land where the crosses had been placed. Randy Miller, CEO of the Fort Worth–based A&A Construction company that had contracted to participate in the road-building, had long been aware of the memorial, passing it on the shortcut he took home from work each evening. "I'd watched as the number of crosses grew, and became curious," he says. Finally, a friend explained that they were erected on the site of Amy Robinson's murder. "So, it concerned me when I realized that the new road would cut through the memorial. I went to my partners and suggested that we donate a portion of a little pie-shaped piece of land we owned nearby." Soon after getting their go-ahead, Miller stopped at the small field of crosses one afternoon and introduced himself to a woman who was cutting away weeds. "It was Amy's grandmother," he remembers, "and I explained what we had in mind to do."

Receiving eager approval from the families who had erected crosses, Miller took his plan several steps further. He contacted an architect friend to ask if he would design a memorial park on the site where the crosses would be moved. Soon, companies such as GIO Garden Design, Aquatic Landscapes, and Acme Bricks volunteered material and manpower. "Everyone just came together to make it a reality," the thirty-eight-year-old Miller says. Today, he occasionally takes his wife and children out to view the memorial, which he insists is still not finished. He has plans to erect a donated flagpole, install an irrigation system, perhaps even pave a parking lot for visitors. "I'm not a particularly religious person," he says, "but I see this as a sacred place. I hope to be some small part of it for years to come."

"In truth," Stewart says, "Randy Miller became the driving force behind the garden."

On February 23, 2000, the new Our Garden of Angels, befriended by strangers and having taken on something of a life of its own, was formally dedicated. "I don't think anyone ever had the slightest idea that it would become what it has," Stewart says. "That it just happened, that it grew into something that has benefited so many just makes it that much more special."

For Arlington's Stacey Hassler, forty-one, it is the lone place she can go to escape the anger over her daughter's death and the ongoing frustration she feels for the slow-moving legal system. "Out here," she says, "you don't dwell on the negatives. This garden has changed me a great deal. When you go through the loss of your child, you suddenly find yourself in a world you don't understand. Everything looks the same, smells the same, tastes the same, but, really, everything is different. You feel crazy.

"I had a difficult time dealing with that until I met the people involved with this place." Now, she makes the trip to the end of Mosier Valley Road at least once a week.

On the first day of November 1999, Summer Ann Little was twenty and four-and-a-half-months pregnant with her third child when she was strangled and drowned in the bathtub of her East Arlington apartment. "For some time after my daughter's death, all I could feel was the anger. I was angry at the man who killed her, angry with the justice system that has kept postponing his trial, even angry at Summer for putting herself in a position where something like that could happen to her," Hassler says. "Friends kept telling me I needed to get some help," Hassler admits. "But I had no intention of spending time with some person who could never understand what I was feeling, what I was dealing with, because they'd never been through it. I was convinced there was no one else in the world who could relate to the pain I was dealing with."

After her husband, Ron, died in an automobile accident, she reluctantly attended one of the twice-monthly meetings of Stewart's support group. "That," Hassler says, "changed everything. Carolyn Barker told me about the garden and took me out to look at it. The minute I saw it, I knew I wanted a cross there for my daughter and Jacob, my unborn grandson."

Now, she says, she often brings Summer's daughters, four-year-old Kayleigh and two-year-old Sandra, along. "They bring little things they've made to place near 'Mommy's cross.' They talk with her and enjoy playing near the waterfall. They love it here."

The garden, then, has become a haven to young and old. Vernon and Linda Price are among those who delight in watching Hassler's grandchildren at play. When a close friend stabbed the Prices' son to death on Mother's Day in 1999, their distraught daughter-in-law, feeling the need of support from her own family in California, chose to move there after her husband's death. Thus, they were suddenly distanced from their newborn grandchild and dealt with yet another emotional void. The Prices understood and supported her decision but endured a new wave of sadness. "What happened," Vernon says, "not only took our son, but put us in a position of not being able to see our grandchild nearly as often as we would like."

For the Richland Hills couple, the garden became a welcome refuge. Living just a few miles from the site, they volunteered for the role of caretakers, seeing that wind-blown trash is collected and no weeds invade the area. In their garage, the lights for the Christmas tree and the wreaths that adorn the fence during the holiday season were carefully stored until recently put in place.

"There's a peaceful feeling here that I've experienced nowhere else," Vernon says as he walks along the brick trail that winds toward the cross that bears his son's name. "It is not a sad place, whether you're here alone or in the company of others who have lost loved ones. This is where our healing took place."

His wife agrees. "You can talk to people until you're blue in the face, trying to explain what the garden means to us, but unless you've shared a similar experience, it is an impossible task. That, I think, is why there is such a close kinship among those who have crosses here. You come here and you meet people who understand, who can share your feeling without so much as a single word being exchanged."

In October, when the man accused of their son's murder was acquitted during a trial that lasted only eleven hours over a two-day period, many of those who are regular visitors to Our Garden of Angels joined the Prices in the courtroom. "It was a difficult experience," Vernon Price says. "Sitting there, aware that three years after the crime occurred the prosecutor was unable to locate two important witnesses, listening to the judge repeatedly telling the lawyers to 'hurry things along' because he had other cases to try, and then hearing that 'not guilty' verdict, brought back all the ugly thoughts we'd dealt with after the murder."

Then they visited the garden. "There is no violence here," Linda Price says. "This is not a place for feeling anger or hatred or pointing fingers of blame. Here, we celebrate the lives of those whose names are on the crosses. We think and talk about the good times. We laugh and joke. And in doing so, gain the strength to look ahead to another day."

In his cluttered garage in Fort Worth, fifty-one-year-old Greg Price is working on three new crosses that will be dedicated this week. Like all others he's built—including the one for his nephew—the white crosses are four-feet tall and three-feet wide. (Those he makes for children are a foot shorter and only two-feet wide.) The crosses include the name, birth date, and date of death of those they honor. If a family is able, it reimburses Price the forty dollars that materials cost him; if they can't, he does the work gratis.

"Every time I do a cross," he says, "it reminds me just how fragile life is. Each one we've put out there is special to me because it has provided me an opportunity to help someone. That's what the garden's all about." With that he pauses for a moment. "Still," he continues, "it's been a bittersweet experience. I've met so many really wonderful people—but only because someone they loved died."

Several miles away, in a quiet residential area of Grand Prairie, patrolman Gary Brooks sits in his living room, watching as his grandson wrestles with the aging and docile family dog. A man who has encountered countless instances of death and violence during two decades as a law enforcement officer, he admits that dealing with a murder that visited his own family has been difficult.

"In my business," he says, "you never expect the chief and the department chaplain to come knocking at your door, notifying you that your own kid has been killed. You never think that you might be in a position of asking for time off to figure out what to do with the rest of your life. Or to have to place a long-distance call to an ex-wife and tell her that her child is dead. Suddenly, you find out that there are a lot of hard things in life to deal with, things we never anticipate or really understand."

Such were the feelings he was dealing with on that Sunday as he paid his first visit to Our Garden of Angels. As he mingled among those who had survived similar experiences, he felt the weight of his burden begin to ease. "What is happening here," he told his wife, "is a good thing."

DALLAS Observer

His wife murdered their five children, but
RUSTY YATES was the one labeled a villain.
He says don't believe everything you read.

TRACKS OF HIS TEARS

BY CARLTON STOWERS

January 23-29, 2003
FREE
Volume 23, Issue 4
dallasobserver.com

17

TRACKS OF HIS TEARS

The young girl, her face framed in a golden flow of ringlets, approached the man seated at a nearby table in the quiet restaurant and smiled, holding the Barbie doll she'd recently received for Christmas. When he asked her age, she proudly held up four fingers.

"You're even prettier than Barbie," he told her. Her smile grew larger, then she was off, happily skipping away in a crowd of parents and grandparents. Before reaching the door, however, she briefly stopped, turned, and waved goodbye to the stranger.

The child, innocent and unaware of the ills of the world she's growing into, was too far away to see the sadness that had suddenly spread across Russell (Rusty) Yates' face or the moist eyes that closely followed her leave-taking. She had not known who he was . . . or of the pain that he carries with him.

Until a mind-numbing occurrence on a June day in 2001, few had ever heard of the lanky thirty-eight-year-old whose adult life had revolved around his fast-growing family and his eighty-thousand-dollar-a-year job as a computer engineer in NASA's space program.

Maybe, he says, he'd had his name in the paper a time or two back when he was playing high school football in Tennessee. But never had he imagined that a time would come when he would become part of the national consciousness, his life's story suddenly important to total strangers. Nor was it conceivable that the day might arrive when, in the minds of many, he would be the target of bilious anger and ongoing criticism. Not until that morning when, shortly after he'd arrived at his Johnson Space Center office, his wife, more mentally ill than he realized, phoned to say that he needed to come home right away.

Just an hour earlier he'd watched her gently apply medication to the chapped lips of one of their five children, then begin preparing breakfast. He'd kissed her goodbye and reminded her that his mother, temporarily residing nearby, would soon be arriving to help her care for the kids. Shortly after he left, however, Andrea Pia Yates, thirty-six and dangerously psychotic, began methodically drowning each of their children, ages six months to seven years, in the bathtub of their home in the Houston suburb of Clear Lake. First to die in the cold water his mother had drawn was two-year-old Luke, then three-year-old Paul, and five-year-old John. Next was the baby, Mary. And, finally, seven-year-old Noah. Then, she telephoned the police and, moments later, her husband.

By the time Rusty arrived, investigators had already made the gruesome discovery: Four of the dead children had been carried to the master bedroom, their small, wet bodies placed on the bed and covered with a sheet. Noah, who had happened on his mother as she was drowning the infant, remained face down in the bathtub. Andrea, later described by law enforcement officials as being in a "zombie-like state" upon their arrival, readily admitted that she had murdered her children. Why? "Because," she said, "I'm a bad mother."

Quickly, the media swarmed. First the local reporters, then those from around the nation, the networks and news magazines, wire services and authors hurrying to the scene to determine if a book on the shocking aberration was merited. What, they all hoped to learn, had turned a former high school swim star and retired nurse, a once loving and friendly mom, into a mass murderer? What dark troubles had lurked in the Spanish-style home on the corner of Beachcomer and Sea Lark, triggering such an incomprehensibly evil act?

They began piecing together a disturbing profile of a woman who had given up her career to care for and home school her children; a mother who had suffered bouts of depression that had led to hospitalizations, medication, and two suicide attempts; a tired and overwhelmed caretaker whose spiritual inclination had steadily edged toward zealousness. Friends and neighbors told of watching her evolve from outgoing and cheerful to withdrawn and reclusive, healthy and vivacious to worn and unkempt. The Andrea Yates introduced to the American public was a submissive, Scripture-quoting wife on a razor's edge, a sad emotional time bomb just waiting to explode. In the Harris County district attorney's office, there was already talk of seeking the death penalty.

And what of her husband, the self-proclaimed adoring father and husband who, only a day after the bodies of his children were removed from his house, stood before members of the press to announce his love and support for the woman who had killed his children? He had shed tears that day, but the media focused on the generally controlled manner in which he had spoken of what he repeatedly referred to as "the tragedy." Whatever degree of shock and grief he was suffering clearly wasn't satisfactory.

Soon, Rusty Yates was also being vilified. Even before he attended the funeral services for his children and delivered a moving eulogy to each, one network talk show host blamed him for the children's deaths. A columnist suggested that it should be him being tried, not Andrea. A nationwide perception, fueled by the twenty-four-hour media and sound-bite psychologists, quickly formed: *He was a loner with few close friends, a self-absorbed man who involved himself little in such mundane chores as diaper changing and meal preparation; saw nothing wrong with his wife giving birth with no pain control measures; had, for a brief time, convinced her that the simple and untethered life of making their home in a cramped Greyhound travel bus was preferable to their four-bedroom house. It was reported that he babysat the kids one night a week only so Andrea could grocery shop alone and at her leisure; that he had dismissed the mental difficulties his wife was dealing with and continued to impregnate her, ignoring the building pressures while offering only marginal support.* By his own admission, he and his wife had always embraced the notion that "the man is the breadwinner; the woman, the caretaker of the home."

One published story, in fact, stated that Andrea had again been pregnant at the time she killed her children. Another said lice had been found in her hair when she was booked into jail. Still another described the interior of the Yates' home as "unkempt and filthy." All, Rusty Yates says, were untrue. Yet by the time his wife went on trial, a steadily growing number had reached the conclusion that he should also bear equal responsibility for the destruction of his family. Rumors spread that the district attorney was seriously looking at the possibility of charging him with child endangerment.

On a website he'd constructed in memory of his children (www. yateskids.org), electronic visitors often e-mailed scathing accusations and questions: Why had he left her alone with the children that day? How could he continue to support a woman who had committed such an evil deed? What was he thinking, having such a large family when his wife was so obviously ill?

Now, almost a year after a Harris County jury found his wife guilty of capital murder and she was sentenced to life in prison, after the cover stories in *Time* and *Newsweek*, the segments on *60 Minutes*, the harsh criticism of women's rights advocates, Rusty Yates endures. He reports to work daily, jogs three times a week, tinkers with a new website he's planning, visits his wife at the Seaview Psychiatric Unit in Rusk on alternate Saturdays, travels to participate in a Dallas support group once a month, and continues to ponder a question of his own: "I keep looking around," he says, "and asking myself: Where do I go now?"

"He's still struggling," says Debbie Wayne, who talks regularly with Yates as a member of the board of directors of the Dallas–Ft. Worth Families of Murder Victims. Wayne is one of several in the support group, which is best known for its Garden of Angels on the southern edge of Fort Worth, where crosses are erected in memory of young homicide victims (see chapter 16). "Quite honestly," she says, "there were those in our group who had reservations at first about contacting him. But what we've learned is that he's not at all like he's been portrayed by the media. Frankly, there are a lot of people who could benefit from knowing him."

But that, she adds, isn't likely to occur soon. "Since what happened to his family," Wayne says, "he is automatically defensive when he meets someone." Over the past year, Yates admits, he has adopted a low profile, wary of the media and of the prying questions of strangers. Still, little he does goes unreported—and, he says, what is reported is in many instances reported erroneously. "I've read that I'm planning to divorce Andrea. That's not something I've thought through," he says. When members of a singles group at the Clear Lake Church of Christ, which he now attends, invited him along for a night of bowling several months ago, a news report that he'd "joined a singles group" quickly appeared. "Our people know how lonely he is," says minister Byron Fike, "and did what any caring people would—they invited him to go with them. Nothing more, nothing less."

When, after living in the house where his children died for a year, he finally moved into a nearby apartment last August, reporters were quick to describe his new residence as "luxurious." Seated on a couch in his living room, unpacked boxes still stacked in the hallway and few photos or personal mementos adorning the walls or shelves, he briefly smiles and waves an arm at his surroundings. "Does this look like luxury to you?" Nice and comfortable, yes. But, no, the television program *Lives of the Rich and Famous* isn't likely to ever come visiting.

On this dreary day, with clouds hanging low and rain falling outside, the enigmatic Yates is, in a sense, striking back, not in an angry tone but in the measured, analytical way he's viewed things since his days as an honored science student at Auburn University. "The comments don't hurt as much anymore," he says, "because I think I've come to better understand what motivates them. People look at what happened to my family, and it frightens them to think such a tragedy could occur. They look for simple answers, something they can deal with. *He must not have been a caring father or a loving husband.*

"Behind all anger," he suggests, "there is fear."

With that he retreats to a time before the world knew his name, when he and the woman he's been married to for nine years were happy to watch their family grow; before the wife with "a good heart" fell victim to a "sick mind." He remembers those days when he coached his older sons' T-ball teams and when Andrea read to their children, of family trips to museums and the park, of the normal parental concerns over things like Paul's not beginning to talk as quickly as his older brothers had. "She was a great mother," he says, "and the children were healthy and happy."

There was never any form of abuse in their home, no money problems, no infidelity. "On the whole," he says, "we had an outstanding relationship. Someday, when Andrea is able to speak for herself, I'm sure she'll say the same thing.

"Even before we married, we talked a great deal about how many children we wanted to have. We agreed that we'd like to have a large family, as many kids as possible. On the other hand, if we had no children, we'd made up our minds to just enjoy life with each other." It was, they had agreed, up to God.

Religion played a major role in his family's life, but Yates insists they were not the "fanatics" the media would ultimately make them out to be. "We wanted to raise our children in a spiritual environment, so we had a simple little Bible study every third night of the week. We'd read stories to the children, say a prayer, and that was about it. Was it a positive influence on the kids? I'd say yes."

In time, however, Andrea's focus on her family's spiritual well-being consumed her. For that, Rusty now blames himself.

He was still in college, he recalls, when he first encountered a fire-and-brimstone preacher named Michael Peter Woroniecki. With his family in tow, the Florida-based, street-preaching fundamentalist traveled the country, visiting college campuses and distributing pamphlets that twisted Old Testament values into a jumble of doomsday prophecy. On several occasions, following shouting matches with disbelievers, he was arrested and charged with disorderly conduct and disturbing the peace. In Woroniecki's view, the world was wracked with evil, the curse of Satan in all to whom he spoke. The fate of women, he preached, was derived from the sin of Eve; they should therefore serve a subservient role to man. Any mother who worked outside the home was, according to the Woroniecki doctrine, wicked. One bad seed, he preached, led to generations of contamination; sinful parents could only spawn sinful and evil children.

Rusty says when he first met the evangelist on the Auburn campus in 1980, he viewed him as a "simple preacher who was doing nothing more than challenging the 'fat cat preachers' about their watered-down beliefs." Even as he and Andrea planned marriage, he told her of Woroniecki and his wife, Rachael, and urged her to join him on a trip to Florida to meet them.

It was one of several visits the Yateses would eventually make to counsel with the controversial couple. In time, they began making modest donations to the traveling ministry. In fact, Rusty purchased from Woroniecki the used Greyhound bus he and his family would, for a time, call home. Andrea regularly corresponded with Rachael Woroniecki.

"If I had it all to do over again," says Yates, "I would never have introduced Andrea to the Woronieckis." Even before his wife killed their children, he says, he had become concerned over her growing obsession with the Woroniecki style of religion. At one point she had even written the evangelist, asking that he help convert her Catholic parents to his thinking. Rusty says he had begun to distance himself from the zealous preacher whom he'd decided was far too judgmental, and he hoped to convince Andrea to do the same. "But it's hard," he says, "to criticize your wife for reading the Bible too much." Yet when Andrea Yates insisted to jail doctors that she was "possessed by the Devil and had the sign of Satan marked on her scalp," that her children had been "damaged," it was clear that her faith and psychosis had morphed into a dark and disastrous mixture.

Austin author Suzy Spencer, who wrote a book on the case (*Breaking Point*), suggests that because of Andrea's deteriorating mental condition, she began taking the Woroniecki message too literally; she viewed her increasing depression as a sign that she had been taken over by the Devil. "They bombarded her with talk of Satan and the idea that God can see people's wickedness," she says.

"For a mother to concern herself over whether she is doing the right things for her children, to worry about the influence of the devil, or if your kids are somehow damaged are, I think, the concerns of a lot of well-meaning people," Rusty suggests. "But when Andrea became delusional, living in her nightmare, hearing voices she never told me about, in her mind all these fears had already taken place."

Today, Rusty says, he is no longer in contact with the Woronieckis.

In retrospect, all had seemed well with the Yates until four months after the birth of Luke, the fourth of their children. Then Andrea began suffering from what doctors diagnosed only as postpartum depression, a condition suffered by 15 to 20 percent of new mothers. While the problem lingered, eventually making hospitalization necessary on several occasions, Rusty says that none of her physicians ever suggested that any form of psychosis might be involved. Finally, after experimenting with several antidepressant medications and dosages, Andrea began to improve.

"If I'd known she was psychotic, we'd never have even considered having more kids," her husband insists. "But all the doctors ever told us was that there was a 50 percent chance that she might become depressed again after having other baby, that she might even require some treatment. But by then we knew that the medicine—a drug called Haldol— had worked. Postpartum depression, we understood, was the worst-case scenario, and we thought we'd learned how to treat it if it occurred again. Andrea and I discussed it at length and felt everything would be okay if she got pregnant again. We loved kids."

Exactly four months after Mary's birth, her mother sank into a mental state from which she still has not recovered. Despite Rusty's insistence to doctors that she be given the same medication that had previously cured her, another antidepressant was prescribed. "If she'd been given what I asked them to give her," he says, "I don't think the tragedy would have happened."

If she had been diagnosed as psychotic, he would have known she was a danger to their children and he'd have handled the problems of her illness differently, would have better understood the danger. "That day," he says, "I didn't sense that leaving her alone with the kids until my mother arrived was a problem. In retrospect, was it wrong for me to have left that morning? Probably so. But was it reasonable at the time to think it was okay to go on to work? She seemed functional, and I saw no reason that day to think she might harm the children.

"Should I blame myself for what happened to my children?" For a moment he pauses before answering his own question, then says, "No."

Is, then, Rusty Yates a still-grieving father–husband locked in a monumental defense of denial or a man unfairly demonized by an unsympathetic society determined to find sinister motives in every corner of his life? That people must even ask such questions, he says, is hurtful. "They don't know me. They don't know how we lived our life," he argues. "All I ever wanted from life was a beautiful family. And in one day it was all lost and people began to point accusing fingers. " Finally weary of what he refers to as the media's misrepresentations and half-truths, he says he has belatedly decided to adopt a more defensive posture.

"I realize what a strong force the media can be," he points out, "and for that reason I've talked to reporters. Early on, I did so in hopes that they could provide a positive force in Andrea's defense; that they could help explain that it was her illness that caused the tragedy. I hoped by talking with them I could help them see the difference between Andrea, the mother with a good heart, and the Andrea with a sick mind." Rarely, he says, did it work. One reporter, he recalls, pored through his wife's medical records and ignored written proof that he and Andrea had carefully followed doctor's orders. "We'd done everything right," Yates insists, "yet the reporter picked out a phrase here and there to make the case we were irresponsible parents. I know for a fact that friends and neighbors were interviewed and said positive things about our lifestyle, but none of that ever appeared in print."

When a recent *Newsweek* article quoted him as saying "I've given all I want to give," Yates was certain that most readers would assume he was addressing his support of his imprisoned wife and angrily phoned the reporter. "I had made that comment," he says, "about payment for court documents to be used in her appeal, not about any personal feelings I have for Andrea."

Those feelings, he admits, remain tangled and unresolved.

A cursory glance at Rusty Yates' life today gives the impression that it is returning to some degree of normalcy. He works and attends church with people who are aware of his shattered past but are friendly and accepting. His in-laws, openly critical of him in several interviews immediately following Andrea's arrest, now stay in touch. Recently, he received a birthday card from his mother-in-law.

Still, he admits, the feelings directed toward him remain polarized. "One of the things that now seems to most bother people is my continued support of Andrea," he says. "They somehow equate it with my not caring about what happened to my children." He notes than an estimated 20 percent of those who send e-mails to the children's website continue to blame him for a laundry list of parental shortcomings. "I've reached a point where I pay less attention to what I call the 'go grab a rope' crowd and focus on those who are more inclined to take a constructive approach," he says.

Not long ago he made a weekend drive to Austin to join a couple of hundred others in a public demonstration for a moratorium on the death penalty, which he adamantly opposed even before threats that his wife might face it. While visiting family in Tennessee during the Christmas holidays, he received a late-night call alerting him that a Dallas family he'd met was having difficulties coping with a loss. Yates left immediately, driving straight through from Nashville to lend whatever moral support he could.

In addition to the acquaintances he's made during his visits to the support group, he has a few friends he occasionally meets for lunch and a buddy he plays a round of golf with now and then. "It's unfortunate that so many people have formed their opinion of Rusty without ever knowing him," says Carolyn Barker, whose granddaughter, Amy Robinson, was abducted and murdered in 1998. She recalls the day when the five wooden crosses, memorializing the slain Yates children, were erected in the Garden of Angels. "I've been out there hundreds of times," Barker says, "but that was the first time I ever cried. I watched as he sat by each of those crosses and saw a gentle man who dearly loved his children.

The Rusty Yates she's come to know, she says, is far different from what she expected. Despite a lengthy list of philosophical differences ("I'm a hundred percent for the death penalty and he's against it," Barker says) a mutual respect has developed. Outspoken, she continues to believe Yates is in denial. "I keep telling him he's not going to be able to really move ahead with his life until he accepts some responsibility for what happened," she explains. "But, we don't really argue; we debate."

Rusty grins when asked about his relationship with the sixty-year-old grandmother. "There's not much we agree on," he acknowledges, "but she's been a great friend." So, he adds, have many in the support group. Among them, miles removed from Houston, he first encountered the genuine kindness of strangers. Today, he says, when he makes his monthly visit to the Garden, it is rare not to find flowers and toys left by people he's never met at the base of his children's crosses.

Still, when all the talk and debate are over, the somber visits done, there remains that inevitable return home—first to the house where insanity and death forever changed his life, now to the apartment just a mile and a half away. "I stayed in the house for a year," he explains, "to better come to grips with the loss of my family." Methodically, he went through the children's possession—toys, clothing, drawings—sorting those he wished to keep and those he would eventually donate anonymously to charitable organizations. During long, solitary hours of poring over photographs, home videos, and notes scrawled in childlike penmanship, he also set aside those things that he believes Andrea might one day want. "Some of the things I've saved," he admits, "make no real sense to anyone but me. Why would I keep the big rubber ball that John loved to bounce on? Or some of Noah's electronic toys? Because they remind me of good times, of them."

Now, with the cleaning-out process almost completed, he plans to soon place the house on the market. That even the decision to do so made the local news causes him to shake his head. "First, I was the bad guy for staying in the house where my children died," he says. "Then there were those who questioned how I could move out and into this 'high-dollar' apartment." He shrugs. "Either way, I lose."

In a perfect world, how would the suddenly public figure like to be perceived? "I guess," he says, "that I'd like for the view of others to be the same perception I have of myself. I was a really good father to my kids. Anyone who says otherwise is wrong. And I was a very good husband."

He knows, however, that there are those unwilling to believe him, that there is much about the life of Rusty Yates that remains difficult to understand. Paramount among many is his continued support of the woman who murdered his children.

That, he says, is the primary purpose of the new website he currently spends much of his time working on. "What I hope to accomplish with it is to help people come to some understanding of her illness. First, I want to help others to detect the warning signs and seek proper treatment; second, I want to try and set the record about our life straight." It will, he says, also afford him an opportunity to speak out against a judical system that, he believes, chose to try his wife to appease a "lynch mob–minded constituency" rather than acknowledge the mental condition that led to her horrendous act.

Every other Saturday, as he makes the three-hour drive to visit his wife, Rusty Yates is never certain who he will see. "She's not stable yet," he admits. "They [prison physicans] are still in the process of adjusting her medication." Each visit, he says, is bittersweet.

As his two-hour stay begins, he is allowed to briefly hug and kiss his wife. Then they sit and talk, sometimes of their lost children, sometimes of the slow-moving process of preparing her appeal, at other times of nothing more personal than her occasional work in the prison laundry.

"She's sad," Rusty says, "and I'm sad for her."

At times, he says, Andrea was not very coherent and suffered from blurred vision brought on by high doses of medication. Occasionally, however, the Andrea who has greeted him in the visiting room is much like the woman he once knew. "She'll seem to be her old self." At such times she's confided things he was never aware of.

"Andrea was always one of those people who seemed happy to just go with the flow of things. I now know that wasn't always what she wanted to do, what would have really made her happy. Looking back, I should have recognized that and been more sensitive to it," he says.

In an ironic twist to their modern-day tragedy, the sensitivities seem to have reversed. "There have been visits, when I've cried—like one day when we were talking about Luke—but she didn't. She just couldn't. The medication she was on made it impossible for her to cry." Recently, the receipt of a rambling twenty-page letter concerned Rusty so that he phoned the prison physician to make certain she was taking her medication.

On the long, lonely drives home, he often finds himself pondering his uncertain future. What if Andrea should one day win her appeal and be released from the prison where she is now sentenced to stay until she is at least seventy-seven years old? What if she was, instead, removed to a mental hospital and one day judged well enough to return home?

"We've talked a little about that," he admits, but with no resolution. He ponders the matter for several silent seconds; then it is the "logical" Rusty Yates who continues: "It's impossible to conceive of a more horrible thing than what Andrea did. She's hurt me more than I thought it possible for anyone to," he says, "and that's a tough thing to deal with. It's like the old adage of putting your finger to the flame. If you do, you aren't likely ever to again. It's that instinct that causes me to feel that I never want to go through what's happened again."

It's apparently as far as he wants to go with the subject.

Then, in a voice suddenly quieted to little more than a whisper, he adds, "When you're dealing with your heart, there is rarely an easy answer."

DALLAS
Observer

September 12-18, 2002
FREE
Volume 22, Issue 37
dallasobserver.com

Inmates on Texas' Death Row leave behind immeasurable pain and countless victims—including their own families

Life without father

By Carlton Stowers

18

LIFE WITHOUT FATHER

On a recent August evening, sixteen-year-old T. J. Davis retreated to his room, stretched his six-foot frame across his bed, and for a time stared silently at the greeting card that lay on a nearby end table. Finally, he picked it up, propped it against one of his textbooks, and began to write. The A and B student from Richland High School wished his father "Happy birthday" and wrote of having run well in the previous weekend's cross-country meet, of the sophomore classes in which he was enrolled, and of his church activities. In a postscript, he recounted a recent fishing trip with his grandfather.

It was a card the youngster had not expected to send.

Just weeks earlier, his dad, a man he's never played pitch with, who's never taken him fishing or to a ball game, had been scheduled to make the short trip from the Texas prison system's death row to "The Walls" unit in Huntsville. There, he was to be executed as punishment for the brutal, fatal stabbing of a man from Humble, Texas, a crime committed eleven years ago.

The date, as fate would have it, coincided with the scheduled first day of the new school year his son had been eagerly anticipating. Yet young Davis, wishing to join other family members in a final goodbye visit, had already made arrangements for an excused absence. Just days before the grim event was scheduled, inmate Brian Edward Davis received a stay of execution. It was his second since being sentenced to die by lethal injection, and it happened when the Texas Court of Criminal Appeals ordered that his trial court conduct a hearing to determine whether he is, as his lawyers claim, mentally retarded. Earlier in the year, the U.S. Supreme Court had ruled that executing the mentally retarded violates the Eighth Amendment's ban on cruel and unusual punishment.

249

Just a week before Davis' scheduled execution date, Curtis Moore, convicted in Fort Worth of three 1995 homicides, had been granted a stay for the same reason. Thus, Davis would live to see his thirty-fourth birthday and receive the card sent by a son whose own life would, at least for the time being, return to a semblance of adolescent normalcy.

T.J., meanwhile, tries not to think about the possibility that the day will eventually come when there will be no more postponements, no more prison visits, no reason to mail a birthday card. "What I do," the polite teenager says, "is keep my mind occupied with other things." He studies hard in the evenings, reports to school at 6:45 every morning for preclass practice with his fellow cross-country runners, takes seriously his responsibilities as a youth group leader at church, and enjoys an active social life.

He talks of college and of one day becoming a lawyer. Or perhaps a fireman. But seldom of his incarcerated father. Friends and classmates don't know that his dad is a convicted murderer. Nor do his teachers. Recently, he sat mute and angry, as fellow classmates, asked to take a straw vote on the death penalty, voted overwhelmingly in favor of it. "I just laid my head down on my desk and didn't say anything," he recalls.

Though he has seen photographs of his dad holding him as an infant and though he has heard his mother tell stories of Brian's changing his diapers and feeding him his late-night bottles, T.J., only three when his father was first incarcerated, has no firsthand memory of a relationship that doesn't involve a prison environment. In the years since his first trip as an eleven-year-old elementary school student with no real understanding of the place or why his dad was there, T.J. has become increasingly comfortable with the routine. "I look forward to going down there," he says. "I always look forward to seeing him." They talk of the outside world T.J. is growing up in, the father always warning the son to avoid the pitfalls of his own youth; they talk of T.J.'s plans for the future; they share jokes, and, recently, the Bible.

One of the things the youngster notices as he looks around the visiting area is the absence of others teenagers. "I see older people—mothers and fathers and wives—and a lot of small children," he says, "but hardly ever is there anyone my age." Is it because of the discomfort so many, both young and old alike, feel inside a prison visiting room? Are peer-conscious teenagers embarrassed to make such trips? Or are they simply rebelling against a person they feel has shamed them? "I don't know," T.J. shrugs. "All I know is that I love my dad, and if the only way I can spend time with him is to go where he is, that's what I'll do."

He often makes the trip with his grandfather. "Sometimes the visits are really difficult," says fifty-four-year-old ex-marine Jim Davis, who lives in rural Tarrant County. "From the drive down to the return home you're riding an emotional roller coaster." Even before he arrives at the unit in Livingston, Texas, Davis knows he'll not shake his son's hand or be allowed to embrace him. They'll be separated by glass, talking on phones for a maximum of two hours. In eleven years of twice-a-month visits, the father and the inmate have never touched. "You try to make it as good a time as possible," Davis says, "but sometimes it's hard."

The pain he's seen on his grandson's face as they drive away from the prison haunts him. Almost without exception, Jim returns home from the visits mentally drained and physically exhausted. The worst, he says, came last May, on the day Brian had first been scheduled to die. There were tears and laughter, prayers and painful goodbyes. Brian talked at length with T.J., encouraging him to continue his education and make something of his life. "He was trying so hard to be strong for everyone," says Jim's wife, Pam. "He was doing his best to keep us upbeat. A scene like that is difficult to describe. Unless you've been through it—waiting for someone you love, a perfectly healthy person, to be taken away to die—you have no idea what it's like."

"No person," her husband angrily adds, "should be put through that kind of torture."

Watching as his son was shackled and escorted to the van that would transport him to the Death House, the elder Davis admits, was worse than any Vietnam combat situation he ever experienced.

Then, just two hours before the 6 P.M. execution was scheduled, the United States Supreme Court granted a stay, ordering that the mental retardation issue be reviewed. Greg Wiercicoch, an attorney with the Austin-based Texas Defender Service, which files pro bono death-sentence appeals, had successfully argued that Davis' IQ was within the clinically accepted retardation range.

"I never suffered any posttraumatic stress after 'Nam," Jim Davis says, "but in the weeks after that visit, I got a pretty good idea what it was all about." Even now he sleeps no more than a couple of hours at a time.

"I wake," he says, "and think about Brian, about where he is, about the possibility of what might eventually happen to him. It's all so barbaric." For a time he sought therapeutic help.

Tracy Tucker, Davis' ex-wife, says she completely lost her voice for a week following that tension-filled day. Her doctor told her it was a result of the stress; same with the severe chest pains that lingered for several days. Today, Jim Davis still searches his mind for something that might magically remedy the nightmarish situation, he says, but he always comes to the realization that there is really little he can do. He and Pam, whom he married in 1988, have paid out thousands in attorneys' fees, have written letters to high places, have sought help from anti–death penalty organizations. "In the end, though," he admits, "what you do is expect the worst and hope for the best."

T.J. and his grandfather are what some sociologists call the "other victims,"—innocent and unsuspecting family members whose lives have been indelibly scarred by a criminal act. Traditionally, society and the media focus sympathetically on family and friends of homicide victims while seldom addressing the ripple effect on those related to the person who committed the crime. "There is an unjust stigma attached to being related to someone who is in prison for committing a violent act," says Tina Church, a friend of the Davises and an Indiana private investigator who specializes in the reexamination of death penalty cases. "Society has adopted a guilt-by-association mind-set that is terribly unfair."

Houston's Dave Atwood, founder of the Texas Coalition to Abolish the Death Penalty, agrees. "Unfortunately, there's a long-standing tendency to assume that the family is somehow responsible for the criminal's actions," he says. "Certainly, there are a lot of people in prison who are the products of dysfunctional families, abuse, and neglect, but not always. I've met many families of death row inmates who are wonderful people, unjustly held responsible for something they had absolutely no part in. There's no question they've also been victimized."

For that reason, T.J.'s mother advises her son to keep his father's past a secret. "I know that just as soon as others know what his dad has been accused of, there will be some parents who no longer want their sons and daughters associating with him. I don't want him exposed to cruel teasing from his peers. It's a hard thing to explain and I'm not sure he fully understands it yet, but that's just how a lot of people are."

And so, for years, the alleged sins of the father have remained a family secret—despite the fact Brian Davis' father, his son, and his ex-wife are firmly convinced that he did not commit the crime that led him to death row. "My dad," T.J. says, "has always said he is innocent. He wouldn't lie to me about a thing like that." His mother, still a determined supporter of Brian Davis, despite the fact they've been divorced for years, holds to the same belief.

Their story is one that began eighteen years ago, filled with the warm excitement and adventure of teenage romance. During the Thanksgiving holidays of 1984, Davis, a handsome, green-eyed sixteen-year-old traveled with his parents from nearby Mineral Wells to the midcities community of Richland Hills and met a petite, freckled blonde named Tracy Clark. Also sixteen, she was immediately taken by Davis' good looks, sense of humor, and country-boy charm. Never mind that her worried parents expressed immediate concern over her spending time with a young man who already had a troubled history of alcohol and drug use, petty criminal behavior, an openly rebellious attitude toward school and authority, and a questionable IQ that had caused some who knew him to label him "slow."

Today, even Tracy acknowledges that Davis is not an intelligent person. "The truth is," she says, "he's not very bright." Still, back in those teen years, all parental warning fell on deaf ears. From the moment the infatuated young Davis promised they would "be together forever," the teenagers bonded and launched on a reckless journey. Sitting at her kitchen table, Tracy, now thirty-three, recalls the days and nights of her youth in stark, candid detail: how she evolved from being an occasional marijuana smoker to using "the white stuff" (cocaine) and then hash and acid; how she dropped out of school; how she lived with Davis on the streets of Fort Worth by day and how she slept in one seedy motel after another at night. She talks of a spur-of-the-moment cross-country trip to California in a car she learned had been stolen when the driver who had invited them was arrested, and she talks of the marriage proposal Davis made in a letter he mailed to her while in jail for a probation violation.

At a time when her high school friends were sending out graduation invitations, Tracy remembers sitting on the edge of her bed, crying

uncontrollably; at age seventeen, she was addressing birth announce-
ments. Their too-soon marriage would last just two years. When she became pregnant, Tracy had turned away from the rudderless lifestyle,
stopped using drugs, and urged her husband to do the same. He couldn't.
Her father, who had given him a job with his construction company,
soon wearied of his unreliable son-in-law's being a no-show and fired
him. Hired to work in a pizza restaurant, Brian returned home after only
a few hours on the job. When Tracy asked what had happened, her husband explained that he'd been fired when he'd been unable to properly
write down the phone-in orders and the addresses to which they were
to be delivered. Having dropped out of school after completing the
eighth grade, Brian could barely write and read at a third-grade level.

Though too young and feckless to realize it at the time, his life was
already spiraling in the wrong direction. Too much Budweiser and Jack
Daniels, too much time spent prowling the streets in a drugged haze, and
too many ill-conceived schemes not only to support his wife and newborn son but to finance his habits all took their toll.

In time, he was arrested again and sentenced to six years in prison
for distributing marijuana. Tracy felt it was time for her and her infant
son to move on. In the fall of 1988, she filed for divorce. "Back then,"
she says, "I can remember seeing Brian cry only two times. The first was
when T.J. was born. Those were tears of pure joy. The other was when I
told him I was filing for divorce."

Recently, however, she saw tears again. They came as she visited her
ex-husband as he awaited his fast-approaching execution date. Yet, while
their lives have now taken drastically different courses, that inexplicable
bond, forged as teenagers, remains. Though married to her third husband
and the mother of two, Tracy Tucker makes no secret of her ongoing
support of Davis. They've never lost touch, corresponding regularly, talking on the phone, and visiting through the Plexiglas at the Ellis Unit
more times than she can recall. "We've always had a relationship," she
says. "It's been that way since that first day we met as kids."

Her current husband, Paul, a heavy-equipment mechanic, tries hard
to understand, to not allow her feelings for her ex damage their four-year
marriage; but he struggles with it at times.

"He, like a lot of people, has told me I need to let go of Brian, to
move on and just focus on my life with him and the children" she ad-

mits. "I know he's right, but I just can't." She acknowledges that it is impossible for her to explain, but the passage of time and traumatic events have failed to dim her feelings—even despite the horrible crime for which Davis was convicted and sentenced to die.

The death of thirty-one-year-old Michael Foster had been ugly, violent, and senseless. According to a videotaped confession given by Brian Davis, he and Tina Louise McDonald, a woman he'd married just two months earlier, had met the mildly retarded Foster in a Houston night club at the end of an evening of drinking and listening to punk rock music.

Foster, who had suffered brain damage at birth and had no driver's license, routinely took a bus to the city's glittery Montrose area from nearby Humble to visit clubs on the weekends. In the early morning hours of August 10, 1991, he had been offered a ride home by Davis and his wife. According to his confession, Davis had accompanied the victim into his apartment, expecting him to pay gas money for the trip. When Foster said he had no cash, the drunken Davis allegedly stabbed him eleven times, then, with a ballpoint pen, drew a swastika and the letters "NSSH," the initial signature of the National Socialist Skin Heads, on his abdomen. Vulgar neo-Nazi messages were also written on the living room wall near where Foster, who was white, lay.

When the body was found three days later, investigators saw that Foster's nose had also been broken, as if someone had kicked him in the face. The pockets of his trousers were turned inside out. Several personal items, including a red leather jacket Foster had been wearing when last seen, were missing.

Even as the Humble police were still in the early stages of their investigation, Davis and his wife were already in the Harris County jail, charged with yet another offense—an aggravated robbery that had occurred just days after the Foster murder. Again, according to Houston police records, the bar-prowling couple had picked up another man, driven him to a nearby motel, then robbed and stabbed him. This time, however, their victim lived. A motel employee, hearing screams, had interrupted the attack. In short order, Davis and McDonald were arrested. Soon, members of a local skinhead group and the owner of the bar who had seen Davis and his wife leave with Foster on the night of his death provided authorities with enough information to also charge the couple with Foster's murder.

In November 1991, Brian finally reached an agreement with investigators who had repeatedly questioned him about Foster's death. He would confess, he said, but only if his wife, who he insisted had not participated in the crime, was not charged. Tina McDonald would ultimately receive immunity for any involvement she might have had in Foster's death. Davis, having no idea he would be the target of a death penalty prosecution, assumed he would most likely receive a life sentence that would require him to actually serve no more than fifteen years.

As he told his story, Davis—who once described himself to police as "a time bomb waiting to go off"—appeared at times to be confused about critical details, describing a two-edged dagger used to commit the murder when, in fact, the medical examiner's report indicated the fatal wounds had been made by a knife with only one sharp edge. His recollection of the date of the crime was almost two days later than it had actually occurred. A diagram he drew of the victim's apartment was generally accurate except for the fact he'd placed the rooms on the opposite side from where they actually were.

Still, in June 1992, after viewing his videotaped confession, a jury found Davis guilty of capital murder, and he was sentenced to die. Tina, meanwhile, pled guilty to aggravated robbery in the other crime and began serving a forty-year prison sentence in Gatesville. Per the agreement the prosecution had made with her husband, she was never charged in the Foster murder.

Last fall, however, McDonald, now divorced from Davis and no longer in touch with him, gave a detailed written confession in which she admitted that she, in fact, had killed Foster. Davis, she wrote, was not even present at the time of the murder. Before driving to Humble, she said, she had dropped her intoxicated husband off at the Houston motel where they were living at the time. Later, after they had reached his apartment, Foster began to make sexual advances toward her. That, she said, was what had prompted her to repeatedly stab him.

Though McDonald would later recant her confession, Davis' parents and Tracy Tucker feel there is ample evidence to support her original admission. "From the day I first visited him in the Harris County Jail soon after he was charged," says Jim Davis, "Brian has insisted that he didn't do it. His story has never changed." Strands of hair found clutched in the victim's hand matched the red-haired Tina. The victim's jacket and music tapes taken from his apartment were recovered from her car, along with a knife that had only her fingerprints on it. Additionally, her description of the crime scene more closely matched the one that police initially investigated.

McDonald has, for years, refused media requests for interviews.

In a time before DNA became an investigative tool, no physical evidence directly linked Davis to the crime. Fort Worth attorney Scott Brown has filed motions asking that the courts place Tina McDonald on the stand. "Have both sides question her," he suggests, "then let a judge decide if she's telling the truth or not." His requests have been routinely denied.

"There's no question," says investigator Church, "that Tina was a violent person, an avowed skinhead with a reputation for always carrying a knife. And, she was by far the smarter and more aggressive of the two."

Harris County assistant district attorney Kelly Siegler, who prosecuted Davis, does not dispute Couch's observation but dismisses McDonald's claim that she alone murdered Foster. "She's always flip-flopped," says Siegler, who is convinced both Davis and McDonald participated in the crime. "You couldn't imagine a worse couple hooking up," she adds.

But why, if he did not commit the crime as he now claims, would Brian Davis have confessed to it? "He's always told me that he did it to protect his wife," says Tucker. "He says he would have done the same for me."

The version of what occurred that late August night that Davis has told to his ex-wife closely parallels the one that McDonald described in her confession. He was, he told Tracy, too drunk to drive, so he got into the backseat of Tina's car after leaving the club. Since he woke the following morning, not even aware of how he got to the motel, he could only assume that she had dropped him off there before driving Foster on to Humble. Tina, who he describes as a "wild woman" who always dressed in fatigues and fervently embraced the skinhead philosophy, had never mentioned what occurred that night.

He had become briefly involved with the local skinheads at McDonald's urging. Only when she confessed, he has repeatedly said, was he aware that she had actually murdered Michael Foster. "At the time Brian confessed," Tracy says, "he had no idea they [prosecutors] would ask for the death penalty. He was willing to serve a long prison term for something he didn't do, just to protect his wife. But he never expected to be put to death for it."

But what of the second crime, the attempted robbery and stabbing of yet another victim? Davis again explained away his involvement. The real assailant, he tells his family, had barged into their motel room, stabbed the visitor, and safely fled into the night.

Again, those who continue to believe in him take him at his word.

Today, it appears that Tracy Tucker's life is far removed from her youthful involvement with Brian Davis. The home she keeps is immaculate and decorated with collectables and family pictures. Her husband, she assures, is a wonderful provider and a good father. She admits that she dotes on her children—T.J. and his nine-year-old half sister, Brooke—and brags unabashedly of their accomplishments. "Like any mother," she says, "I worry a lot about the choices they will make as they grow up." High on her list of goals is to do everything she can to see that they avoid the mistakes she made as a teenager.

Her other goal is to one day see her first husband set free. It is an obsession that has, over the years, made counseling and the use of antidepressant medication necessary at times. She stays in touch with Davis' attorneys, investigator Church, and Davis' parents. She looks forward to her ex-husband's rambling letters, filled with inaccurate spelling and poor punctuation, which always end with his promise to "love her for every."

"During his trial," she remembers, "he telephoned me from the courthouse every day." When Davis learned that a date of his execution had been set, he first shared the news with Tracy. At the time, she was married to her second husband and pregnant with her daughter.

In the years Davis has resided on death row, Tracy had visited him at least once a month, sometimes even more often. At times she's made the trip alone, sometimes in the company of her son and Davis' family. She has an album of smiling photographs taken, each with the white jumpsuit–clad Davis standing behind glass while his visitors pose in the cramped cubicle in front of him. In some you can see the swastikas tattooed on his chest and arm, a reminder of his early prison days when he was a member of a white-supremacy prison gang.

Occasionally her husband will drive her to the Ellis Unit, remaining in the parking lot during the two-hour visits. On Davis' first execution date, her parents took her to Huntsville. For a time she went weekly with the Arlington mother of another condemned inmate before he was executed. Recently, she made the trip with Dallas' Patricia Springer, the author of several true-crime books, who occasionally visits one of Davis' fellow prisoners.

"Tracy's an unusual woman," says Springer. "I think over the years she has convinced herself that if she'd not divorced Brian, if she'd stayed with him, none of this would have happened. She feels a lot of guilt, convinced that she's at least partially responsible for the situation he's now in."

Guilt, justified or imagined, is a common thread that binds Brian Davis' supporters. "He was never physically abused or anything like that as a child," Jim Davis assures, "but I regret that he had so little continuity in his life as he was growing up." The elder Davis points to his nomadic twenty-year career in the service—with stops in Alaska, Virginia, North Carolina, Washington, and Vietnam—and the fact that he and Brian's mother married and divorced each other four times.

Nor does he argue the claims that his son meets the legal definition of mental retardation. "He was loving and caring as a child, but he didn't always use good judgment and had great difficulty in school," Davis recalls. Brian, he says, was never able to read well; and when he did attend school, he fared poorly, even in the special-education classes to which he was assigned. When he was sixteen, his IQ was tested at seventy-four.

The Davises, Tracy, and her son, says Springer, are examples of the victimization that she's often seen during the research she's done over the years. "The public," she suggests, "has yet to understand that criminal acts create victims on both sides. The justice system and society rightfully show concern for those whose loved one was wronged while condemning the families and friends of the perpetrator. Lawyers generally ignore them, and no one seems to see it necessary to even explain to them how the system works. They're routinely given little consideration by prison officials when they go to visit. Over and over I've seen them treated shamelessly. It happens all the time."

Jim Davis puts it more bluntly: "You're treated like you're a criminal."

During the murder trials Springer has attended, it is commonplace to see families of victims turn their anger toward those there in support of the accused. "Rarely do people stop to consider that whatever event brought them there has been devastating to everyone," she says. "The accused's family has also suffered a crushing loss. Brian Davis' son had no choice in the matter which has affected his life; he didn't choose to have a father on death row." It is unfair, she says, for punishment, however subtle, to extend to the innocent.

Still, while the Davises and Mrs. Tucker and her son agonize over the state-ordered fate that awaits Brian, the family of victim Michael Foster sees things far differently. "I can't wait until this guy is fried," Foster's older sister, Pat Kupritz, told the *Houston Chronicle* shortly before Davis' execution was postponed last May.

Though she adamantly opposes the death penalty, Tracy can understand the lingering anger of Foster's loved ones. She's been there. Her older brother, a truck driver with three small children, was shot in the back of the head and killed by a man during a 1985 robbery in Carterville, Georgia. "I was fifteen at the time," she remembers, "and I had a difficult time accepting the fact that someone had done that to my brother, to me, to our family." The culprit later turned himself in, pled guilty, and served only a brief jail term before being released.

"I was angry about that for a long time," she admits. Today, however, she finds comfort in the fact that the family of her brother's killer was spared the death watch she has now lived with for a decade, the nightmares that still occasionally wake her.

Last spring, when Davis' family traveled to Huntsville they assumed it would be their final visit. "It was," Tracy recalls, "the most horrible day I've ever experienced. We were all convinced it was the last time we would see Brian." Funeral arrangements had already been made. Even before they arrived, Davis made it clear that he wanted none of them to remain and actually witness his being placed on the Death House gurney with the needles being inserted into his arm. "He told us," says his father, "that he didn't want that to be our last image of him."

The stay, however, only bought Brian Davis and his family a brief reprieve.

Three months later, as the second execution date approached, T.J. stood in the kitchen one evening as his mother prepared dinner. "Do you think it is really going to happen this time?" he asked. "I didn't know what to tell him," she recalls.

And so the ordeal continues. Too soon, Tracy Tucker fears, the day will come when her son will again ask the question.